TABLE OF CONTENTS

ZANE

DEREK

RENFRO

VIOLA

DARRION

DUKE

ANGELIQUE

DARRION

ZANE

RENFRO

DARRION

ZANE

ANGELIQUE

ZANE

ANGELIQUE

DEREK

ZANE

VIOLA

DARRION

ANGELIQUE

DUKE

VIOLA

DARRION

ZANE

DARRION

LINKS FOR A SNEAK PEEK AT CABRINI GREEN VOLUME II: THE KILLING FIELDS

CABRINI GREEN VOLUME I:

RETURN OF THE PRINCE

BY

CHAVOHN NAKIA

&

WARWICK SHACKLEFORD-MASTERS

Cabrini Green Volume I: Return of the Prince

For more information visit:
www.copyright.gov/

ISBN: 978-0-9890084-6-4

For a sneak peak at all things Cabrini Green:

www.chavohnnakia.com

or visit:

www.chavohnnakia.wordpress.com

For my beautiful Chi-Town.
For my mother Tommie Lynn.
For every Chicagoan who
loves the Windy City…

Chicago was a town where nobody could forget how the money was made. It was picked up from floors still slippery with blood.

--Norman Mailer, *Miami and the Siege of Chicago, 1968.*

PREFACE

During the Second World War, the CHA—Chicago Housing Authority—transformed the bleak, poverty stricken area, known as "Little Hell," to the Frances Cabrini Homes. These low rise houses were a racial mix consisting of poor Italians, Irish, Puerto Ricans, and African Americans.

During the 1940's, WWII—affecting virtually every part of the world—contributed primarily to the Cabrini Homes' population of war industry workers and their low-income families.

By 1950, the African American population soared from 20 percent to 79 percent. However, a significant populace of Caucasians still claimed residence in the area due to low crime, a reliable upholding of safety, and overall quietness among black residents.

With the CHA's development yielding positive results from their preparation to economize, the Cabrini Extension was erected in 1958, adding nearly 2,000 units totaling 15 buildings, the tallest of them rising to the height of 19 stories.

The Cabrini Extension tower units ranged from one to four bedrooms—each with their own heat radiators. In the interest of cutting costs on maintenance and repairs, brick comprised structural designs, elevators were exteriorly located and concrete took the place of grass landscaping. Most of the road-facing buildings sat a mere four feet from the street.

By the 1960's segregation all but drove out most Italian and Caucasian residents. This mass exodus was known as the White-Flight. In 1962, in an attempt to supply the ever increasing number of impoverished black families, what would be the last addition to the housing project was built and named the William Green Homes. Thus giving birth to a name that would soon go down in infamy: Cabrini Green.

This final extension added more than 1,000 three to five bedroom units to ease the mounting displacement of Chicago's poorest, comprising a total of over 15,000 registered residents.

Nearly a decade later, crime and unemployment swelled to an all time high and the 1970's all but epitomized the failure of the judicial system to resolve the desperation and scant conditions of the Near North's most impoverished.

Because of the project's close proximity to the Near North's most prosperous areas, many adolescent residents felt rejected and discarded by the upper echelons of society.

With the mass scarcity of employment and a steady decline of adequate health care, many gangs formed their own concrete underworld criminal economies: Cocaine, heroine, and marijuana. Territorial disunion splintered the housing project as three gangs in particular — the Gangster Disciples, Vice Lords, and P-Stones — controlled their own individual buildings.

One gang in particular swelled in numbers, rising above all others: The Gangster Disciples, or GDs. They successfully established their own criminal underworld and with GD drug dealers making thousands of dollars per day, the Disciples earned street profits in an excess of more than $100 million dollars annually.

Daily shootings, stabbings, multiple homicides, rape, dismemberment, and many other violent acts committed against inhabitants, police, and even paramedics became common practice as a brutal and ruthless means to protect their lawless empire.

By the 1980's, heroine was no longer the drug of choice. A new drug emerged and the crack epidemic swept the slums.

Warring gangs became gridlocked in an endless conflict for control of the drug trade, resulting in the brutal death of several innocent children. Unable to turn to authorities for help, Cabrini residents were often left powerless as hostages in their own homes. Parents were often afraid to allow their children out to play on the small lawns of what gangsters called the Killing Fields.

Laughably, the Mayor, Jane Byrne, moved into one of Cabrini's highrise apartments with her husband for three weeks in an effort to show authority and survey the living conditions there. Although police and bodyguards provided her with 24-hour security, the she also ordered the back doors to the building welded shut to ensure her safety.

At the end of her short stay, the Mayor moved back into her luxury condominium on the North Side, unwittingly leaving the welded doors in place.

Byrne's botched show of supremacy had an unforeseen consequence. Gangsters inhabiting the highrise used the welded doors to their advantage, keeping out police with impenetrable force. On the rare occasion when officers were able to infiltrate the buildings and search for any criminal activities, residents were forced to store the gang's weapons and other illicit possessions in their apartments to thwart authorities.

As a direct result of this ruthless control, over the years that followed well into the 1990's, Cabrini Green became a cash driven, venomous alcove where its gangsters blatantly walked the streets with AK-47s, Tech-9s, and pistols held in plain sight for all to see. Any efforts for police to near the buildings were met with a barrage of bullets. In response, Chicago police began closing off the streets during night hours. This only further emboldened Cabrini gang members, who carried their weapons from dusk until dawn.

Shot out windows and burned out units were often boarded up instead of replaced or remodeled. Daily, residents suffered rat and roach infestations as well as the incessant stench of rotting trash — which once piled up to the 15th floor in one building.

Old blood, urine, and insecticide stained the walls, doors, and stairwells. Constant structural problems, broken elevators, bursting pipes, knocked out lights and other failing utilities, created in-excusable surroundings of decline and decay. Incidents of intoxic-ated drug users falling from the upper tiers and beaten victims being thrown to their deaths, prompted the CHA to wall off the breezeways with steel enforced fencing. This gave Cabrini buildings the appalling appearance of animals in a cage.

Whenever authorities were called, they were shot at, threatened, and hit with rocks or other objects. Some were even killed by sniper fire before they neared the buildings.

For fear of their own lives, many Chicago police officers and medical response teams refused to go near the housing complex — despite orders from their superiors.

Many of the notorious incidents that took place inside Cabrini were nationally publicized, tainting the once picture perfect image Chicago held as the trendy city of class and upscale allure. Every effort to make the projects safer failed. As the city's crime rate gradually ascended, The Windy City became the murder capitol of the nation — with a death rate three times higher than New York City.

Spanning 70 acres over a 20 year period, Cabrini Green became known as the most ill-fated and notorious public housing project in U.S. history.

PROLOGUE

July 4th, 1991…

Jesus Christ," Renfro spat in disgust.

Bodies were strewn everywhere. Blood splattered every wall, every chair. Leaves of plants and flowers still dripped red. Sconces and framed paintings hadn't been missed either. Several door handles carried the smeared red prints of bloody hands that had turned, pulling frantically for escape. So many Mafiosi lay dead. So many jetted with bullet holes, the entire room faded into a sea of crimson. Some bodies were eagle-spread, face down on the floor.

Renfro knew by their fall pattern they had been gunned down trying to run. Most who laid dead were old, feeble Mafiosi, too slow to rise from their seats before they were killed.

This street war with the Italians was a long time in the making. For more than 20 years Samuel Renfro had worked the Robbery/Homicide division.

A case hardened vet — well numbed to most of the criminal savagery of the city he served. Wife beaters, drug addicts, con men, thieves, rapists, pimps, prostitutes, dope dealers. All the dregs of society detective Samuel Renfro had the privilege and curse of taking into custody. On a rare occasion he was graced with a suicide bomber.

Some of his cases involved the criminal — plagued with guilt — actually calling the police and specifically requesting him to cuff them.

Murder for a detached police officer was a trivial occurrence on the southside of Chicago. But never before had he seen death litter a five star conference room suite.

Carnage like this didn't happen inside the elegant Drake Hotel. Death never delivered this way on the upscale side of town near the Chicago River.

Chicago had a sordid history associated with her concrete jungle and the wars fought to claim her had a place in most of it.

Not since the notorious Valentine's Day massacre had Renfro known a mafia bloodbath this brutal.

To look on it all then, he felt a lifetime of hard earned bearings and wisdom suddenly weaken. It was a horrifying display of power and morbid aggression. This was the way business was done. Men avid for advancement. He suspected ties to the King Cobras or the King Disciples.

All of them were young men making a fortune from the drug trade and they had chose to cut out the D'Amico family as their main supplier of narcotics.

A course of attrition was expected after rumors spread that an ambitous capo from Little Italy's Sicilian Syndicate, Benzito Zosa, had orchestrated the mass killing of several high ranking Cobras with the promise of profit shares from King Disciples' drug revenues and revenge for his brother, Tommasino Zosa's, brutal murder. Thus ending the warring gangs' truce.

The slaughter made sense as retaliation from both gang leaders. Marcelus "Gipp" Givens — who headed the King Cobras — and Xavier Pope — boss of the King Disciples.

Even though their gangs took a loss of men from the killings, Gipp and Pope still had the muscle to come together to vanquish a common enemy and cripple the Chicago syndicate.

Or it could have been the worst sum of all of his fears. Duke DeGrate's darkest nature given full rein, backed by his eldest son, Darrion DeGrate.

Just one month after all out warfare had erupted in the Cabrini Green housing projects, the sovereign of the DeGrate Family proved clever in his father's absence. Renegotiating relocation for residents with the Mayor was credited to him in the media. Darrion proved well to owning his prime.

Now that Renfro thought on it more, Gipp and Pope were ruthless and bold, but they were common hoods. They didn't have the brains to pull off that kind of massacre.

Or the means.

He looked up at the sound of footsteps. His partner, detective Brian Bishop, appeared in the doorway. "Renfro, You got a phone call."

Renfro looked up from a body's rigor mortis. "Where?"

Bishop motioned to the blinking light of the multi-line phone in the center of the bloodied long table. "Line one."

Renfro crossed the room, pulled on a pair of latex gloves from his pocket, reached past another lifeless Mafioso keeled over in a chair and picked up the telephone. "Who is this?"

"Look to the plant in the room with no lighting to let you know it's there."

Renfro instantly recognized the voice. Though he sounded slightly different in person, Darrion DeGrate's still had a discernable one not easily forgotten on the phone.

Unmistakably assertive. That prominent enunciated tell always went straight to Renfro's blood stream. Setting up shop for dangerously high blood pressure long after their brief conversations ended. DeGrate kept well invested in his miseries.

Renfro looked around the room until his eyes hit a large earthenware pot made of ironstone.

Colossal leaves sprouted high, nearly blotting out a wall painting behind it. But if DeGrate had not pointed him to it he wouldn't have known it was there at all. A quick glance about the plant showed no lights in that particular corner.

Several other corners in the room revealed ceiling lights illuminating what would have otherwise been unlit angles.

Renfro crossed the room, carefully stepping over several more corpses, and stood over the large plant. He saw a pistol in the soil. A Glock 9.

His brow lifted. "And?"

"You're welcome," DeGrate said.

Renfro heard the telltale click and he just stood there.

Listening to a dial tone.

INTERVIEW

Zella Rice adjusted her posture and looked at her notes.

In the Stage Complex, on the hottest day of summer, every fan only blew warm air. She sat in the small filming studio trying not to sweat through her make-up.

In just moments she would be interviewing one of the city's most well-known gangsters, Dutch "The Dutchman" DeGrate, for HBO's new documentary: *Gangs of America.*

Quite handsome for a man in his 60's, Dutch DeGrate had graying short trimmed hair, even brown skin, and dark eyes. With the solid bulk of a man who took good care of hisself, came a serious glare that owned his eyes. It made Zella mentally aware she was bouncing a knee.

It was a nervous habit.

She stopped it.

The hangar-like sound stage sat quiet and still between them until the cameraman said he was ready.

"As a former King's Disciple yourself," Zella began, "As well as an O.G. from the 60's, 70's and 80's, what do you have to say about the streets today in the 90's? All of the escalated violence and killings? Just hours ago, news of the 4th of July massacre shocked the nation. Dozens of Mafiosi, brutally murdered in a mass shooting at the Drake Hotel. Things certainly seem to have gotten much worse over the past six months following Xavier Pope's incarceration in Federal. Wouldn't you say?"

"Honestly, you have Mayor Dailey to thank for that," Dutch DeGrate answered. "He thought indicting all of the upper echelons of the Kings was gonna stop the game. All it did was make it more ruthless than ever before. Now, with all of these young bloods out here, after what happened to the main chiefs of the Disciples, hell, you couldn't pay them to take a leadership position. '*Who? Me lead it? What? And get locked up for the next 30 to 50 years behind it? I don't think so.*' With them thinking like it's all about them now.

"It ain't about the Disciple Nation no more. When they locked up the Pope, the whole Nation thing just fell apart. There is no Nation. Now it's just I and me and mine. Fuck you. If you ain't from my set, you can get a wop. If you ain't from my block, you're nothing to me. You can get it. And this Mayor was stupid enough to think ending the Disciple Nation was going to stop all the violence and the stealing and the killing.

"Cutting the Pope off from all communication with his unders just took organized crime and left it so unorganized the streets are sheer chaos. There is no more righteousness amongst gangsters anymore. Now you got these little cliques everywhere. Because with all of the leaders gone, they don't have to answer to anybody. Back when the Pope ran the King's, the soldiers did what they were supposed to do and without rebellion. And if there was a mutiny, it got dealt with. Today...these young punks out here...you tell them to do something they'll just look at you and laugh. Then they'll go do whatever they want to do without a flinch because they know there's no repercussions. So, with the way the streets are today, I say again, you have the Mayor to thank for it."

"What do you think he should have done differently?"

"A smarter Mayor, who gave a damn, would have called for a truce. It happened once. We can come to peace again. If we try."

"You think so? Even after the first truce of 85' failed...leading to the most horrifying police stand off I can remember. After all of that do you really think another truce is the answer?"

"Just because something didn't work the first time don't mean you give up. You try harder."

"What about the opposition from gang members who may not want another truce?"

"Any elements that caused the first truce to fall apart are dead today. They're no longer any threat to a ceasefire. Their entire family has been wiped out. So why can't we try again? Whatever is hurting our young men and our women, let's heal it. Sending them to the penitentiary is not going to fix it. Like when Porter was our Mayor. A true Mayor would try to heal what's ailing before locking it up in prison. That's how you stop it. You have to give them a reason to put down their guns. Not a reason to buy more bullets. They're never going to put down the guns if they keep thinking this is the only way of life for them. Until they have a means of endurance that gives them hope of a better future, you're always going to have a gang problem."

"But doesn't that contradict even asking for peace again?," Rice asked. "During the first truce, there were no major job programs in place to help end the welfare and the poverty. Some Chicagoans believe that played a primary role in the truce falling apart."

"Regardless of why it fell apart, the consequences weren't in your neck of the woods. White people didn't have to worry about blood splattering the front door of their Gold Coast mansion. At least before, the evils were maintained by a strong hierarchy. The Pope kept the demons in the devil's mansion where they belonged...He kept the soldiers locked down to sanctioned territory. Back then, you could count on the violence being confined to the Near North. You could always count on the violence being on the Southside and no further than that. If you were wealthy, you knew the boundary streets and you didn't cross them. You stayed on your side of town where all was safe. Now, thanks to the Mayor, no neighborhood is safe. Be warned, Mrs. Rice, these young, blood-thirsty thugs out in Chicago are twice as brutal as they used to be out here. They're hungry with no respect for human life. And they're coming locked and loaded to a living room near you."

DARRION

Twelve years earlier, November 1984…

Alright, gentlemen," Vader said, "we know the layout."

His men nodded.

"The second we bust through those doors, our clock starts ticking. Remember, we're not in Chicago. A small town like Northbrook…a little suburban area like this means a faster response time 'cause the Sheriff doesn't have shit else to do but save a bunch of kittens in a tree. Especially on the week before Thanksgiving."

Vader laid the bank blueprint on the van floor and shined a flashlight for the Takers to see. He pointed to the layout as he assigned positions. "C3PO, you and Jabba go straight for the vault. Obi-Wan walks the doors. Anybody walks in you snatch 'em inside and put 'em on the ground. Chewbacca and Skywalker walk the floors but keep the tellers close. Pull them out from behind the glass and make sure everybody stays face down. I'll stay with the girl. Now, remember, our retainer said to be on the lookout for the security guards. One is a tall yellow complected bastard. He's not a threat. But watch for the one who's short, black, and scrawny. Long dreads that he usually keeps in a ponytail. Physically, he's not a threat, but he's got speed. Six months ago, he shot and killed the last man who tried to take this bank. So, if he doesn't toss his weapon, if he tries anything, he gets his halo."

"Who is this retainer anyway?" Skywalker asked. "We've never even seen his face."

"We don't have to. He gave us the score. He gave us the blueprints, the security system...the whole nine. Plus 80 percent of the take is ours. All we have to do is give him his cut. Now...no more than twenty seconds to get everybody's attention. No more than sixty seconds in the vault and we're out of there in ten seconds flat. Don't forget to torch what we can't take. That's a 90 second rumble, gentlemen. It's a tight window, but we can do it."

They nodded in agreement. Vader motioned to Han Solo and gave a nod in the girl's direction.

She sat trembling quietly in the rear of the van. Blind-folded and gagged. Her hands tied behind her back.

Mozart softly resonated from the headphones covering her ears. When Solo took them off she flinched and began to cry.

"Shhh, sweetheart," Solo soothed. "We're not going to hurt you. Not unless your daddy makes us. We're going to go for a little walk. You're going to do exactly what we say. Your daddy's gonna play nice too. And in 90 seconds or less, this will all be over, hmm?"

She didn't answer.

She just sat there. Bottom lip quivering.

"Nod your fucking head!" Solo spat.

She flinched at the bite of his tone and nodded.

"Good," Solo said. "And if your daddy tries anything, he's going to regret it for the rest of his life."

Vader checked his watch and looked at his men. "We're syncronized?"

They all nodded.

"It's time. Let's move."

♛

Bullets thundered from their AR-15s, spraying the lights and chandeliers as the Takers stormed the bank and spread out. Their assault rifles aimed at the ceiling. Screams rang out. Echoing off the marble walls. Shattering glass came crashing to the floor like razor sharp rain.

"Mr. Slidell," Vader yelled out.

A small, short balding man with thick bifocals standing next to the wall of safe deposit boxes blinked at Vader in a wide-eyed, horrified shock.

Mr. Slidell, the Northbrook Bank & Trust manager, locked eyes on the assault rifle aimed at his daughter's skull. Its smoking muzzle singed her blonde hair. He looked at Vader. Tall, swathed all in black. Sporting a Dark Vader mask. His trigger held steady with a sure hand.

"We are here to rob your bank," Vader announced. "We are not here to kill your daughter." He let the full magnitude of his words sit for a few seconds. That was all the time Mr. Slidell was given for the shock to register. "We're here to take what the government will replace," Vader went on. "We're not here to kill what you cannot replace. Nod your head if you understand me."

The bank manager nodded.

Vader kept speaking calmly but firmly, like they had taken a thousand banks for a thousand vaults a thousand times before. His men took their positions.

Masked Obi-Wan guarded the doors, screaming threats of violence for defiance. C3PO and Jaba were already at the vault. Their rifles at Mr. Slidell's skull while he lifted a shaky hand to turn the combination. Chewbacca and Skywalker were on the bank clerks before they tried to hit the push button alarms. They yanked three tellers from behind the glass, threw them down on the floor, and ordered every banker and patron still standing to follow suit.

Darth Vader checked his watch. C3PO and Jaba should have been inside the vault by now. Mr. Slidell may have been terrified, but his trembling hand didn't add credibility to the mistakes he was making with the combination dial.

Vader was instantly on to him.

"Mr. Slidell!" he screamed. "You turn that dial to trip the vault alarm and your daughter's getting smeared! Do not fuck with me!"

Mr. Slidell's hand froze.

Then he stood there as if he was made of stone.

"She goes home in a car...or a casket," C3PO warned. "Get it open."

Slidell's hand regained its function. He turned the dial, opened the vault, and the men were in.

"How much time?" Jaba shouted out to Vader.

"Thirty seconds," Vader shouted back. "Move!"

C3PO loaded the blocks of money into three large black duffle bags and Jaba poured gasoline over the units of cash they wouldn't have time to take. Just enough time on the clock to make it. Then he heard the yelling.

♛

"Think about what you're doing," Vader said, pulling the girl in front of him.

As predicted the security guard had come from around the corner aiming a pistol at Vader. He looked just as the Retainer had described: like a blacker Bob Marley, only a little shorter, darker, and much younger. If he had to, Vader would use the girl as a Kevlar. Worst case scenario, they'd no longer have a hostage for safe passage.

If worse came to worst, better her than him.

"Put the gun down and let the girl go!"

Vader didn't flinch. "Toss your weapon. I'm not going to ask you again."

"Put the gun down and let the girl go, now!"

"I don't have time for this shit," Skywalker said.

He aimed and fired two shots at the security guard but missed.

The guard fired back, hitting Skywalker in the shoulder, sending blood spraying against the main lobby doors.

Vader pushed the girl's head down out of the way and with lightening speed fired two shots dead center to the guard's chest. He flew back, skidding across the floor, past the elevators. His limp body stopped cold as he slammed into the back wall.

Vader pulled the girl back up onto her feet and shouted loud enough to be heard over her shrill screams, "That's time let's go! Move, move!"

C3PO and Jaba came running out of the vault. Their duffle bags stuffed full. Flames igniting behind them. They sprinted to the side exit and held the doors open. Keeping their rifles aimed at the lobby.

"Nobody move!" Jaba said. "No one else needs to die today!"

Darth Vader snatched the girl out through the doors. Chewbacca held Skywalker upright and walked him towards the exit, dripping blood every step of the way.

C3PO and Jaba waited until they were out and seconds later the Star Wars Takers were gone.

♛

Put her in the back seat and slip the headphones back on," Vader ordered.

The Takers loaded into the van. Tossing the duffle bags to the floor. Obi-Wan slipped the key in the ignition. C3PO sat the girl in the corner behind the driver's seat as the van sped off. He slipped Mozart back on her head then tended to Skywalker's shoulder.

"Keep pressure on that shoulder!" Jaba said. He looked at all the blood Skywalker was loosing. Stripping off his coat, he balled it up and handed it to C3PO.

Skywalker was breathing rapidly, groaning in pain.

Jaba cursed and looked at Vader then dialed a number from a strange phone. Jaba was actually looking at a hand held phone with no cord.

Christ, the man actually had a phone that didn't need a cord. "Where'd you get one of those?" he asked.

"Our Retainer," Vader said. "It's 1984, man. Times have changed. It's in case something goes wrong. He'll send a medevac to get us out."

♛

They're on the way to you now," T-Bone said. "The Assistant Manager just ran off for a phone. You should be getting the call for me any second." He paused for a deep breath. "I already took the digoxin, so I'm about to pass out. My pulse will go weak for a while and my heart will slow but it won't stop just yet. Just get here. And remember what to do the second we're in the air. I'm dumping the phone."

T-Bone hung up.

"T-Bone's in position," Darrion said to Taran. "Stay live, we're about to be inbound."

Taran cocked his assault rifle and the two men climbed into the helicopter.

"Shit," Kincaid shouted, reeling. "I ain't never been on nothing like this before, man! It's usually smash and snatch for me. I haven't flown one of these in a long time. This baby right here is state-of-the-fucking-art, man. Just how I like my women. All it takes is one finger to get 'em going and their cockpit is always open." He turned around, leering mischief at Darrion and Taran, howling laughter at his own joke. "You know, I—"

"Stop talking," Darrion ordered, "turn around, keep your eyes on your controls, and be ready for wheels up when we say." Darrion scowled at him and cocked his Bushmaster. It was apparent. This hillbilly was going to be a problem.

Now it became blatantly obvious to Darrion that Wade "Bucky" Kincaid wasn't the world's finest moralist. His professionalism fell short of up to par. Loud, crude, inborn hicks like him didn't know there was a time and a place for casual conversation. Men like him didn't know when to shut the hell up and focus on the job.

Hiring him was a serious, serious mistake.

But, T-Bone had already made the call and with every second thereafter, his heart rate was beating slower and slower. It was too late to call it off. They would be airborne any second.

Darrion's brick phone buzzed to life. He answered on the first ring. "Are you out?"

"Yeah," Vader huffed. "But one of my men took a hit to the shoulder. He's leaking fast."

"Keep pressure on it," Darrion said. "We're wheels up. ETA is two minutes." He ended the call and nodded to Kincaid. "That's the call. Start her up."

♛

911 what's your emergency?" Lunch asked.

"Yes, we just had another bank robbery here at Northbrook Bank & Trust," the Assistant Manager said. "There were five, maybe six men. All of them had Star Wars masks on. One of them was shot in the shoulder before they escaped and I have a man down. One of our security guards. He's shot center mass, and he's bleeding. I don't think he's got a pulse or if he does, it's really, really shallow."

"What cross street are you on, sir?"

"Um, we're at South Waukegan and Shermer."

"Okay I want you to apply pressure to the wound. The more blood loss he suffers, the more his pulse and his blood pressure are going to drop."

"Someone's already doing that."

"Who?"

"The other security guard."

"Good. Officers and an ambulance are on the way to you now."

Caspar "Lunch" Phoenix Jr. made his seat belt click then put the key in the ignition. "You sound unusually calm in a situation like this."

"Well, believe it or not, we got hit six months ago," the Assistant Manager said. "Our security guard is the one who stopped it. He was a hero. He is a hero."

"Is anyone else hurt?"

"Just one of the bastards who tried to shoot him. Please let him get here in time. This man is very important to us and I would hate to lose him."

"They'll be there in less than three minutes."

Lunch ended the dispatch, turned off the call interceptor, and started up the ambulance. "Time to rock and roll." He pulled away from the curb and sped off, sirens wailing.

♛

Darrion could see the red flair burning to mark the landing as the helicopter descended on the open field.

Just as he was told on the phone, one of the Takers took a hit in the shoulder and looked as if he was bleeding out his last drop. He was barely standing, leaned half over with blood dripping from the mouth of his Skywalker mask, down his black shirt. One of the men stood guarding the bags of cash while two other men waved at the helicopter.

Darrion and Taran slipped their ski masks on the instant they touched down. When the door slid open they leapt from the chopper. Their rifles aimed at the men, they fired tranquillizer darts into their chests.

C3PO, Skywalker and Jabba went down instantly from the force of the darts, but they weren't out cold. Not yet. They slowly tried to stand back up, but dizzily teetered and fell again.

Chewbacca and Vader were still standing. They didn't even sway.

They just stood there, blinking through the eyeholes in their Star Wars masks. "What the hell are you doing?!" Vader shouted, reaching for his weapon.

Darrion re-bolted and took aim to fire another dart. Just as he put a finger to the trigger, he heard Kincaid.

"Payback's a bitch!"

An ear-splitting blast of gunfire cracked the cold night air. Darrion's head snapped toward the blast and the world went still.

Kincaid's arm was extended. The muzzle of his Glock was seeping smoke. Darrion turned back to Vader.

Brains littered the grass of the field and the man lay sprawled on his back. Chewbacca cursed and flew into a rage. He raised his rifle to fire back, but he was too weak from the dart to make a steady aim.

"Too slow, motherfucker!" Kincaid shouted. His eyes went black, he grinned a devil's grin, and shot the man point blank right between the eyes.

In a flash Taran was on Kincaid.

He rammed the butt of his rifle into the back of Kincaid's knee, knocking him off balance, then struck the Glock from his hand and punched him twice in the face.

Kincaid collapsed to the ground wailing in pain. Gripping his nose as blood spewed from his mouth.

"Get up!" Taran shouted, yanking him to his feet. "What the hell's the matter with you?!" He slammed him up against the nose of the helicopter. "Don't fucking move or I swear to God I'm going to kill you!"

Darrion grabbed the Glock, loaded up the money bags, and motioned for Taran to help him with the two bodies Kincaid had just created. Then the two men loaded up the corpses.

Darrion had no choice but to leave the other three men lying in the grass. He spotted their van fifty paces off. Parked in a dark lot. He reached into his Kevlar vest, pulled out a small C-4 shape charge bomb, and set the timer.

"I'm going for the girl," he shouted over the helicopter's engine to Taran. "Watch him. If he moves, kill him!"

Taran nodded and watched Darrion dash across the grass to the lot. Less than a minute later, he returned with the girl. He picked her up and put her in the back with the moneybags and the bodies, then climbed in after her and pulled the door closed.

Taran snatched the hillbilly up and shoved him up into the pilot's seat. "Get us airborne you fucking psycho!" He climbed into the passenger seat, staring rage at Kincaid.

As they lifted into the air, the van exploded into a ball of fire. Seconds later, the men were climbing skyward.

♛

Lunch saw a man waving his hands in the air as he pulled up in the ambulance. He silenced the sirens, made a half-turn near the door's entrance, then slowly backed up and stopped at the curb.

He slipped on a contact precaution mask to hide his face and zipped up his black emergency services suit before he jumped out onto the curb.

Lunch grabbed his medical bag and ran up to whom he assumed had made the call minutes ago.

"Where is he?"

"This way," the man motioned. "Follow me. I'm the Assistant Manager, Burt, by the way."

"Okay, Burt. I have a cold, so excuse the mask."

"Oh, I understand. That's fine."

Lunch jogged close behind and followed him through a crowd in the lobby. Police sirens wailed off in the distance. Getting closer by the second.

"Is that the cavalry?"

"Oh, yes," Burt huffed. "Our manager he hit the alarm as soon as those awful men left. But they made off with his daughter! God, can you believe that? Everyone was in such a panic! The second those men left all the customers started running for the exits. We asked them not to leave. Even though they were scared, we told them it would be better if they stayed around to give a statement. Maybe somebody saw something someone else didn't. At least they can give a statement to the police while it's still fresh in their mind." He motioned to his office and ran through the doorway. "We thought it might be better to keep him in here, on my desk. There's no windows in here. You know, in case they came back."

Lunch worked quickly, checking for a pulse. "It's there but it's slow." He motioned to the guard holding pressure. "Keep pressing. If his heart stops, I'll have to get in there and start CPR. For now, I need to get an IV in him."

Lunch reached into his bag, pulled out his supplies, and went to work. Slipping a blood pressure cuff on one arm, he worked at starting an IV in the other.

He managed to get a good vein on the first try.

"I called for a medevac," he said, pushing the Lidocaine into the IV. "For now this will work to counteract heart failure before it happens."

Burt nodded nervously. "Okay, sure. Let me know if there's anything else I can do."

"You've done more than enough. We'll take it from here."

Lunch looked up when a well dressed woman appeared in the doorway. "The cops are here," she said. "And there's a helicopter landing."

"Let's escort them back," Burt said, rushing her out the door.

Less than a minute later, Lunch and the medevac team rushed past the police, rolling the injured guard toward the helicopter on a gurney. Burt and the other security guard followed close behind.

When they neared the helicopter, Burt ducked low, avoiding wind from the propellers. He waved his hands in an effeminate nervous flutter. "Why are they wearing those contact precaution masks and those plastic glasses?" he yelled over the engine to Lunch. "Should I be wearing one?"

"No," Lunch said, shaking his head. "Sometimes the propellers kick up too much dirt. Some don't like that. They have to be able to navigate and see. Especially at night."

"Oh, that makes sense."

The medevac team loaded up the guard. As one of them started to slide the door shut, he looked at the other security guard. "You can come with if you like."

He nodded a yes and climbed in. When the helicopter was in the air, Lunch told Burt he could go to Vanguard Weiss Memorial Hospital if he wanted to be present for his guard's emergency treatment.

Then he climbed into his ambulance and left the scene.

♛

Darrion checked again for a pulse and nearly felt nothing. He put an ear to his chest and all he heard was a rapid, uneven rhythm.

He cursed in a panic. "His pulse is almost gone! I think he's in V-fib!"

Taran looked back over his shoulder at Darrion. "Didn't Lunch give him the shot?"

"Yeah," Ronald Moss said, slipping off his security guard shirt. "Guess it didn't work."

Darrion pulled a medical bag out of the bottom cargo hold and reached for the gurney then snatched the blanket off. He tore open the white security shirt revealing a fake vest full of red liquid pouches. Darrion knew several of them had been burst open by the Taker's gunfire. He pulled a knife from the sheath of his Kevlar, cut off the vest, and reached into his supply bag for a portable defibrillator and an alcohol wipe.

He wiped the reddened skin and placed the shock pads on. A full charge droned from the defibrillator. But when Darrion reached a finger to press the button, turbulence rocked the helicopter.

"Ronnie, hold the gurney," he said.

Ronald Moss stopped changing his clothes and dropped down to the bottom of the gurney. He got a good grip on the wheels and nodded. "Okay. Got it."

Taran nervously shook his head. "Don't lose him, man."

"I won't," Darrion said, steadying himself.

He pressed the button and all he saw was sparks flying. Dreadlocks thrashed forward, followed by an ear-splitting holler of pain.

Darrion drew back in shock and flinched again when the internal lights blacked out. Then all he felt was the merciless pull of gravity. Within seconds the chopper was in a tailspin.

"The defibrillator must have knocked out the power!" Kincaid shouted. "We're spinning out!"

Darrion moved for the girl and kept her from hitting her head on the hull. He pulled her down to the floor and hollered at Ronnie to get a hold of the gurney.

Taran looked expectantly at Kincaid. "Don't you know how to recover from a tailspin?"

"It ain't no recovering if the torque's gone and the transmission's shorted out. Autorotation's the only way, so hold on!" Kincaid steered the helicopter as he bellowed out his maneuver strategy. "I have to disengage from the main rotor system, then I can force air flow up through the rotors and that'll give us a safe landing."

Kincaid pressed the anti-torque pedal, pulling the helicopter out of its tailspin and kept them in a straight line of flight. The rapid descension abruptly ended and just as they neared a thick of trees and the power bleeped back on. The engine sputtered back to life. Kincaid immediately took his foot off of the anti-torque pedal, letting the blades regain power. He leveled out the helicopter and pulled them back up to a safe altitude.

Drained and terrified, he slumped back in his seat. Soaked dirty blonde hair plastered to his bloodied, sweaty face.

Taran blinked through the shock as the helicopter rose toward the darkening sky. Then he leaned back against the seat. Eyes shut tight.

Darrion sat the girl back upright and flinched when his friend rolled off of the gurney and crashed to the floor. Groaning, rolling around in pain, he flopped onto his back. Now, suddenly wide awake, he sat straight up. Looking down at the shock pads on his chest. Absently drooling into his lap.

Ronnie cursed in disbelief. "It might be a while before he knows math."

Darrion leaned over his traumatized friend, smiling relief. "Welcome back, T-Bone."

♛

Taran instructed Kincaid to land the chopper at a private hangar of Chicago Exclusive Charters, less than 40 miles from O'Hare International Airport.

They were still in Northbrook, yet far enough from the robbery for Darrion to breath a little easier. Taran wasted no time. Before Kincaid could even think about fleeing, he was pulled from the pilot's seat, snatched over to a nearby desk, and hog tied to a chair.

Less than ten minutes after their landing, Lunch arrived in a gleaming black Lincoln Town car. Dressed to the nines in a dark gray three piece suit, Lunch pulled off the black faux wig. His neatly oiled, bleached hair shone like dulled copper gainst his light brown skin. He reached into the back seat and pulled out three tailored suits and coats for Darrion, Taran, and T-Bone. Ronald Moss emerged from the driver's seat with two shoulder holsters complete with loaded pistols and one leather twin back strap which held Darrion's twin Colts.

He walked them over to Taran.

Darrion didn't know Ronnie well enough to trust him. But he knew him well enough to trust he liked money and was willing to work hard on a take to get it. That, coupled with the fact that Ronald could easily be killed should he turn on them, was incentive enough to welcome his expertise of alarm systems into his crew.

Lunch on the other hand, was more than trustworthy.

He was a constant.

Being raised in the DeGrate family since he was a boy spoke volumes for his dependability. Bizarre by a first encounter, to those who didn't know him, many were left with the impression that he was touched by the angels. His cerebral misfires were common among the DeGrates however.

Lunch refused to take his pills mostly because they made him feel 'off inside'. But he never let his psychological disorder take his focus and he was always willing to put in work.

Darrion and Taran placed the moneybags in the trunk of the Town car, changed into their suits, and slipped on their holsters. After briefly discussing T-Bone's condition, they kept him on a monitor for a few minutes longer just to make sure his heart rhythm held steady. Once both men felt satisfied he was stable, T-Bone changed into his suit and coat.

Ron removed the blanket from the girl, kept the sack over her head, and carefully walked her to the car. Darrion checked his Colt 1911s and stepped behind the flight officer's desk. Taran gave instructions for Lunch and T-Bone to watch over Kincaid and joined Darrion at the desk.

Both men went to work on two C-4 bomb timers they'd soon use to torch the helicopter.

Ten minutes later, Darrion pulled out a Newport and took a short smoke break.

Like always, Taran was the first one to say exactly what Darrion was thinking. "We need to get rid of this Appalachian, spit-can fuck," he spat. "He turned our score into his own personal vendetta. For that shit, he earned his halo."

"Agreed," Darrion nodded. "And he'll get it. But right now, we need him to fly us back to the city." He adjusted the pinch of his cuff-links and took a slow pull from his Newport. He glanced across the hangar at Kincaid. "So we go ahead with the plan."

No one else had laid a hand on the hillbilly since Taran punched him in the open field. But, while Ronnie stood by the car, keeping an eye on the girl, Lunch and T-Bone were sticking close to Kincaid, standing not five feet from him should he try to break the ropes and run. He looked quite grated from Darrion's view. Blue eyes afire with rage. His white face stiff, pinched in resentment. Every muscle tensed under his black tactical suit. Old, dried up blood still crusted on his face. Even his long, oily ragtag hair looked pissed.

A take this messy was not what Darrion wanted. But, if they didn't wipe Kincaid off the planet, his double murder would come back to cause more trouble than they were prepared to deal with.

"The second we get back to Chicago," Darrion said, "we unload, torch the chopper, and have Lunch and Ronnie pick us up at the club." He snuffed out his Newport in an ashtray. "Then we kill him."

♛

Taran eased the Lincoln Town car up to the curb and the men released the girl, dropping her off not far from the Ed Rudolph Velodrome where they knew she lived.

Mr. Slidell's home was less than a block away. It was nighttime, but the streets were well lit, so Darrion knew she'd find her way home. But, before the Town Car pulled away, he made sure she understood her release came with a stressed ultimatum. "Don't turn around or remove that sac from your head until you hear the horn blow. If I see you remove it sooner, you'll be dead before your eyes adjust to the street lights. Walk."

He have her a hard shove to get her going. Then they pulled off and left her walking blindly, trembling with unsure steps. Waiting to hear the sound that meant freedom.

When the Lincoln turned the corner, Taran blew the horn.

As planned Kincaid flew Taran, Darrion, and T-Bone back to Chicago while Lunch and Ronnie drove the Town Car to the city. It would take them almost an hour to arrive at City Lights Gentlemen's Club. Plenty of time to for Darrion to torch the medevac helicopter and catch a cab. Then, Kincaid would be taken care of in the basement of the club.

The helicopter landed in an old abandoned field on the southside of Chicago. In an area with no inhabitants, the men were just a half of a mile from an old housing project that had been abandoned for the past five years. No one would notice a helicopter burning straight away. Except for maybe a few squatters who were either dopers, drunks, or both. Either way, Darrion knew they would be too inundated to bear witness to anything seen. Nor would they care. At least, that was the idea. By the time the fire department responded, the helicopter would be burned to a cinder.

Darrion ordered Kincaid to slip on a medevac suit and slick back his hair. He did as he was told. It took his less than a minute to change out of his tactical suit. T-Bone set off the timers on the C-4 bombs then placed them in the helicopter.

The men began the three block walk toward the nearest pay phone. Thirty seconds later the medevac chopper exploded into flames behind them, lighting up the cold November night sky with a bright blaze and the blackest smoke.

Darrion called a cab then exited the booth and stood in front of Kincaid. The hillbilly was flanked by Taran and T-Bone, like a con being watched by two wardens. Darrion looked him in the eyes and saw the insipid face of a man with a quiet nervous tension about him. Kincaid stiffened and his eye twitched but he didn't look away.

"When we get back to the club, we'll straighten you out...give you your cut," Darrion lied. "After that, we don't do business ever again. That means...you don't do business in our city ever again. Are we crystal?"

"Absolutely clear," Kincaid said with a half-sure nod.

Less than five minutes later, the cab arrived. They rode to City Lights in silence. Located on the Magnificent Mile, the strip club was one of the swankiest nightspots that Chicago nightlife had to offer. From wall to wall it was bathed in red light. Regulars never used the front door, the food was cheap, the drinks were strong, and on nights when live performers were not there, the stripper poles were full of possibilities.

Taran motioned Kincaid to a back booth and the instant he sat down T-Bone and Darrion sandwiched him in.

"When Lunch shows with the money," Darrion lied again, "We'll get a call at the bar. You'll get your end." Kincaid nodded and he kept his mouth shut. Thirty minutes later, Darrion noticed the bartender flagging him down. That was the call. He stood, went to the bar, and answered the phone. "Yeah?"

"It's Lunch. We're in the basement. Everything's ready."

Darrion motioned to T-Bone and hung up the phone. Then men took the side stairs down to the basement and went down a long hall. The last door at the end was open. Darrion motioned for Kincaid to step inside.

"We'll count the money out in here first," Taran said. "Then you take what's yours."

Kincaid nodded, walked through the door, and froze.

There was no money. No moneybags. Not even a money counter was anywhere in sight. Just an empty room. Lined floor to ceiling in plastic and a tall Lunch standing bare-chested in a butcher's smock. Holding a handsaw. Swathed from his shin to his shoes in plastic booties.

Lunch cracked his neck and rolled his shoulders, ready to work.

Taran pulled his Beretta from his holster and just as he took aim to the back of the hillbilly's skull, Kincaid hollered out a war cry over the thumping club speakers and rushed backwards, crashing into Taran, knocking T-Bone and Darrion out of the way. He bolted out the back door, running into the alleyway before they were on their feet to give chase.

T-Bone was up and out the back door first, followed by Darrion and Taran. They chased him for the length of the alley, but Kincaid reached the sidewalk first.

He lost it. Running wildly out onto pavement. Knocking pedestrians out of his way. Darting out into traffic. Dodging and weaving between cars.

He made it to the other side of the street before T-Bone reached the sidewalk. By the time Darrion and Taran caught up, the traffic light turned from red to green and cars were moving too fast for them to risk it.

Kincaid was gone.

DUKE

Duke DeGrate stoked coals in the fireplace, grateful for its heat. Then he went over the desk, slipped on his bifocals, and leaned back in his leather chair. He stared at the long awaited letter from his eldest son. Most fathers he knew probably wouldn't have considered two weeks to be a long period of time. Most fathers he knew of didn't have a failing heart. Within two years coronary artery disease had plagued him with two heart attacks. Now, anxiously awaiting news of the surgeon appointed to repair his heart was quite unnerving.

All Derek would say over the phone was he had found the perfect surgeon for the operation and he was convinced Duke would change his mind about refusing surgery once he met...her.

Duke hoped whoever this *her* was, she held far better credentials than the last surgeon chosen. Three days of Dr. Wrobel was enough to make him swear off specialists. Keeping him in the hospital — over the weekend as well as all day on the following Monday — drawing blood and ordering several tests without even telling him why, or explaining what the hell the tests were for, Duke DeGrate had had enough. He pushed the call button, told the nurse he was leaving, got out of bed — plaid pajamas and all — ripped out his IV, popped off his armband, and called a cab. Three days later came the second heart attack that nearly killed him. Duke's wife, Viola, was so distraught over watching them give him chest compressions she fainted in the ER. Resulting in a CT scan of her head just to make sure she hadn't fractured her skull when she hit the floor. For observation, the ER doctor insisted she be admitted overnight.

With both parents in the hospital, the entire family was shaken. That was when Duke decided his rebellion was no longer worthwhile. Derek didn't even bother with pleading and told Duke he was having the bypass. The end. It wasn't up for debate. If he wasn't satisfied with Dr. Wrobel, then Derek would simply comb the country over until he found the appropriate one.

Even with all of his assurances, even though there were hundreds of thousands of successful open-heart surgeries in the country every year, Duke could not ignore the threatening reality of complications. There was a possibility of something going horribly wrong. He knew a triple bypass would never be a one-time cure-all and the recuperation alone would impede his daily lifestyle for months. Viola navigating him through recovery would mean his furrier business would have to be run alone by his brother without him. Duke was not accustomed to resting while Dutch managed his affairs.

As he read the letter, he instantly understood why Derek insisted on writing instead of calling:

Dearest Father,

> *I truly hope this letter finds you still hoping for a second chance at life, because I've finally found the woman who will be just that for the both of us. Her name is Angelique James. She is the best cardiothoracic specialist in the Midwest and her work is well respected at Northbrook Heart Hospital. After reviewing your case several months ago, she has agreed to repair your heart. Not only is she the answer to our prayers, she is also the love of my life. I have asked her to marry me, Father. Much to my amazement, she said yes.*

> *Though we've only known each other for nine months, we have so many things in common. I don't have enough ink to tell you on paper. She even enjoys hunting, if you can believe that. I'd like for her to come to*

*our annual hunting trip this Thanksgiving
if it's alright.*

*It might be nice to bring the ladies of
the family along for once. I know Viola and
DaVita will absolutely love another female
in a family full of DeGrate men. We will be
arriving via private jet at 8:00 p.m. I am
bringing her to the Porter-DeGrate Charity
Ball tonight to introduce her to Mother and
the rest of the family. She says she can't
wait to meet you. I know you will love her
just as much as I do.*

Your loving son,
Derek

Duke folded the letter, slipped it back in the envelope, and smiled then with a pride only a father could know maybe once or twice in the lifetime of raising sons. His eldest, Derek Colton Porter, was getting married. Duke picked up the phone and dialed the number of his secondborn. He looked up at the grandfather clock.

It was just past 6:00 p.m.

Depending on what Darrion and the boys were into on a Friday night, he just might be able to make the drive in time to greet them. Duke left a message with the desk clerk of the Waldorf Towers just in case Darrion didn't answer his phone. Then he asked to be transferred to his loft.

"Hello?"

"It's your father. I'm surprised you answered. I didn't think you'd be home on a Friday night."

"My day wrapped up a little sooner than expected, so…"

"Good, I received word from the Councilman today."

"Oh yeah?"

"He's flying in tonight with a lovely young lady. He's engaged to be married and he's bringing her home. I want you, Taran, Turkell, and Casper to meet them when their plane lands."

Darrion hmmphed. "Married, huh? Derek?"

Duke nodded. "I wouldn't have believed it myself if he hadn't told me. But, he's 34 years old. He's changed a lot over the past four years. I suppose it's time."

"I'm happy for him. What airport are they landing at?"

"Exclusive Charters. They'll park at the same hangar we always rent."

"What time?"

"Less than two hours from now. 8:00 sharp. Don't be late, son."

"Yes, sir."

"And I hope you didn't forget about the charity ball tonight. It starts at 9:00. I expect to see you there. So does your mother. That goes for Taran, Turkell, and Casper as well."

"Yes, sir."

"Good. And son, turn on the charm and make a good impression. His fiancé is a surgeon. She's the woman repairing my heart. I'm sure we don't want to piss her off or give her a reason to fly back the way she came."

"No, sir, we don't. And yes, sir. I will."

"I'll see you in a few hours then."

"Yes, sir."

Duke hung up the phone and stood.

Smiling out the window of his library, Lake Michigan gleamed its small waves. Reflecting the full moon and the city's lights in its dark waters. He went to his bookshelf in the corner of the room and reached for the burgundy suede box. Then he lifted the lid and carefully placed the letter inside along with all the other letters Derek's mother, Patricia, had ever written to him.

DEREK

Derek watched his ladylove look out of the window.

Wide brown eyes filled with anticipation. As the tires screeched on the runway and the plane landed, Angelique smiled like a child full of energy who had just pulled into an amusement park.

What a smile it was to see. She was a beautiful woman. Stately, with pure auburn eyes, dusky brown skin, and the delicate bones of a woman born to an admirable line. Though she had a splendid figure, her supple curves were elegantly concealed tonight.

For the ball she was dressed quite modestly by the standards of Chicago's nightlife: A sleeveless, V-neck floor length Taffeta with a smoothed waistband that hugged her slender waist. Her black ball gown fitted well enough to accentuate her youth.

Derek was more than certain his mother would love her and his father would as well. As the jet steered to a halt near the hangar, he looked out of the window. Tingles shot across his skin. Not from excitement. But from loathing. Derek sat upright.

Oh dear God…not you, was all that he could think.

Darrion, and his three hoods were waiting for him.

Turkell, in all of his dreadlocked splendor, stood perched against whatever black sports car he decided was a must have for 1984. Lunch just looked like…Lunch. Every strand of that blonde-dyed head screamed "Off My Meds Today" and he still had that same black Chevelle which he kept fixed up to a cherry piece of showroom auto. Taran still looked the same except he had seemed to pack on a little more muscle. Still tall, thick in the chest and shoulders, but something was different about his face. Derek thought on it momentarily and then it hit. He had a low trimmed mustache and beard. He must have left his vehicle at home because the only car left near the hangar was Darrion's red four door Mercedes.

Darrion sat with the driver's side door open in a black suit, smoking those Newports. He tossed it to the ground, smashed it out with his shoe, and got out of the car.

Derek suppressed his irritation and the urge to let an expletive fly in disgust. He should have known his father would do such a thing without even asking him first. Commanding that criminal and his blood crew to escort them to the charity ball. He had told Angelique of his younger half-brother on several occasions. Usually over dinner — or when she asked about his family. Most of the stories he'd told of Darrion had to be toned down by omitting the sordid details of the carnage. Perhaps it was because of her profession as a surgeon, but she told him she didn't mind hearing about the blood. Many times over Angelique told Derek she thought he was a man from an unfortunate past making the best of his prosperous circumstances to embrace an extraordinary political future. In the running for Chicago's first black Mayor was extraordinary indeed.

Though it had been nearly a year since Derek had last seen him, Darrion was still handsome. That much he would give him. Same russet brown skin. Same dark eyes and he always kept that low trimmed hair as black as crow's feathers.

Even from the high angled view of the jet's window, Derek could see that small cross Darrion had tattooed just below the corner of his right eye. Just the sight of it — and the gruesome events that inked it there — reminded Derek of the thing his brother could be.

"You look amazing in that suit," Angelique said.

Derek pulled his attention from the window. "Are you sure I don't look like a waiter?" he smirked.

"Only if you're serving me."

Derek stood from the seat, stepped into the isle, and extended his arm like the perfect waitron. "Chi-Town on a silver platter sound good enough?"

Angelique smiled up at him, took his arm, and let him lead the way.

She stopped at the cockpit.

"Thank you, um…" She looked at the pilot, then up at Derek. "I'm sorry, I forgot his name."

"Tu Fang," Derek said.

"Right. Thank you, Tu Fang."

Fang turned around in his seat and nodded.

For as long as Derek could remember, Tu Fang was the strangest Japanese man he had ever known. Not because he was from another country. It wasn't his eyes or his long, pinned-up silvered hair that made him look an oddity. Well into his sixties he wore a wizened face, a lean frame well proportioned to his short height and foreign looks that never begrudged a stranger against a fair first impression.

Still, Fang was just awkward in that quiet sort of way. Since boyhood, Derek was always uneasy when he was in his father's house. As much as he tried not to show it, Derek was put off by him. For a man who never spoke English Fang certainly understood it more than most Americans. He just refused to engage in what he called 'primitive tongue'. Even without a word spoken between them, Derek's child-hood at the DeGrate house was filled with days when those Asian eyes would go from dangerously provoked to simply dangerous in a flash.

He was far too afraid to ask Father why an Asian man lived in their home. But Duke once told him that he worked in Chinatown and he was his master of martial arts. Derek never pushed further than that.

As he got older over the years, he heard the rumors.

Word grew that his father had an assassin living in his home. An immigrant man who was indisputably the best dispatcher in all of Chicago. Or at least from what Derek's mother, Patricia, had once said about the man, the disputes didn't last long.

Fang nodded at Angelique, accepting her thanks.

They deplaned and Derek walked her toward the hanger. She squeezed his arm a little tighter. "Are you sure he speaks English?"

Derek nodded. "Of course he does. But you'll never catch him dead doing it."

"Who is he to the Family?"

"An old friend of my father's. He...helps him sometimes."

"Helps him do what?"

"He...he charms the snakes," Derek said. He couldn't think of a better way to lie about the man being a killer. It was the best he could do off the cuff.

Angelique nodded toward the men waiting for them.

"Who are they?"

Derek followed her gaze to his half-brother and his bandits and repressed the impulse say something unpleasant. "Extended family."

"Extended how?"

"Extended from me to you." He winked down at her. Pure brown eyes blinked up at him in response. If she only knew how much her caution was warranted. Being an only child, Angelique knew nothing of siblings or cousins, or of more nieces and nephews than she could possibly remember to buy presents for without a Rolodex.

She spoke of what little family she had in such a grim tone, Derek sensed she carried secrets that triggered her painful recalls. As her husband-to-be, he felt somewhat delighted to give her a touch of the nearest — if not the dearest — of his line.

Family...Something no daughter should be deprived of before womanhood and love made her a bride. But Derek would make sure his sordid family was kept at a distance. No woman set to marry into the Porter family would be tainted by the likes of the notorious DeGrates. Especially Darrion.

"Hello, gentlemen," Angelique said in greeting. Her mouth spread wide with a smile so magnetic Derek found himself smiling in response.

He gave a nod to the men.

"Noblemen...chaps...grandees," he joked, " please allow me to introduce Dr. Angelique James." He gave another nod to Turkell and motioned to his long, long dreadlocks. "Add dreads, gold teeth, water, and stir...and you get Turkell Julius Scarbone. We just call him T-Bone."

"Hello, Ma'am," T-Bone said, nodding in response. "Welcome to Chicago."

"Thank you," she said, still smiling perfect teeth.

"And to his right," Derek continued, "the high yellow brother from another brother's-mother's-brother, Mr. Casper Phoenix, Jr. But, you can call him Lunch."

Her brow crooked at Derek. Then her smile broadened. "Lunch? Is he hungry all the time? Or is that his favorite meal of the day?"

"Have you had Lunch today?" Lunch said with a fleeting glance to her cleavage.

She thought about it. Then, "Come to think of it, no. I haven't."

"Want some?"

She laughed.

Derek rolled his eyes. "And moving on to the only gentlemen among us who has a modern grasp of fashion and hair sense, Mr. Taran Ellington Carter."

Taran extended his hand. "It's a pleasure to meet you." Angelique shook it and he flinched in surprise. "Firm grip."

"That firm handshake is from holding one too many sniper rifles," Derek said proudly. "She hunts, too. She'll be coming up to the Mammoths to take down game with us this weekend for the Thanksgiving feast."

"Is that right?" Taran asked.

Taran Carter knew guns like Leonardo Da Vinci knew paint. Now his face showed the same initial shock Derek had when he found out she had a passion for stalking wild animals.

He was eager to see how her tactical skills would bump against Taran's. With those two in the same room, with loaded weapons, he knew 1984 would bring the most interesting holidays of his life.

"I'm looking forward to seeing what you're made of," Taran said to Angelique.

"If I'm half of the preemptive genius I hear you are, I'm sure I'll make it back in one piece." She looked to his right. "And you must be Darrion." Angelique held out her hand.

He didn't lift a hand to shake hers in greeting.

He didn't even blink.

He just stood there, staring.

"And I see he's also a selective mute," she said to Derek. "Does he charm snakes as well?"

Derek found his brother's idle tongue somewhat amusing.

She had indeed just said hello. That much his errant brother's brain could register. Perhaps memories of manners would soon tell him to return the hello. Those same etiquettes should have told him it was rude not to. But still his tongue was leaden.

Still he just stood there.

Speech had fled him. Blinking out of his muted tardiness, Darrion looked as if he realized he was indeed being rude. Before he could express regret for his delayed response, he heard the abrasive laughter of his friends.

Lunch clapped him on the shoulder. "Bless him! It happened...the bolt!"

If Darrion only knew how slapped and flayed he looked. Derek almost felt sorry for him and before he could hold it in, he was laughing as well. Of course he understood the initial shock. Derek had endured "the Bolt" when he first met her. But over time, he came to love the benevolent woman underneath the beauty. He was more than certain his family would come to know her just the same.

♛

Derek, I'm not on the list," Patricia Porter spat in a short, affronted tone.

Derek stepped in front of her and skimmed over the guest list. He flipped through the doorman's clipboard. Surely his mother's name may have been listed backwards as Patricia among the 'Pa' last names instead of 'Po' for Porter. He skimmed over it twice. She wasn't on it. One of Viola DeGrate's cruel stunts no doubt. Derek handed the clipboard back to the doorman. "It's not a problem," he said with a hard glare at the doorman. "Write her in. Now."

The doorman nodded, but Derek did not wait for him to do as he was told. He took his mother's arm in his and led her into the main ballroom where all of the invited guests were waiting for him.

Viola DeGrate would not spoil this night for him. Not this time...

VIOLA

What the hell is *she* doing here?" Viola spat.

"Be nice, Mother," DaVita said. She sipped her champagne and watched Derek and his mother cross the room. They stopped at a tall woman swathed in a laced black ball gown. Who is that woman they're talking to? I've never seen her before."

"That is the Alderman's new fiancé," Viola answered, keeping her eyes on Patricia.

"Wow, she's gorgeous."

"Seeing as she's repairing your father's heart, she'd better be more than a pretty face." Viola shook her head in resentment. "I can't believe he brought her here."

"Why not? She's soon to be his wife."

"I don't mean her." Viola took a sip from her daughter's champagne glass and stared a cold stare at Patricia. "That bitch better not start any shit this evening."

"It's a charity ball, Mama," DaVita said. "Why would she start anything here? Not only would it embarrass the entire family it would be bad for Derek's campaign."

Viola glared at Patricia's red ball gown with distaste riddled all over her features. She could spot red silk a mile away. Patricia's naturally curly hair had been straightened and was upswept into lustrous victory rolls secured with the same jewels her gown boasted on the neckline. A beaded empire waist, tulle overlay, lace up the back. That woman knew Duke's favorite color was red. She did that on purpose. The bitch.

"It's a Black Ball," Viola reminded her daughter. "Not a red ball, or a white one, or any other color. The DeGrate-Porter Charity Ball has been the same theme for the past seven years, my daughter. Always black. Every year."

DaVita shrugged. "Well, maybe she couldn't find anything else."

Viola gave DaVita a careful, measured look. If she was trying to slight the obvious, it wasn't working. She was no longer a little girl. If she didn't wise up to Patricia's discreet little ways soon, she would find herself suffering the blunt of her blindness. They would have to have a true talk about the renowned Ms. Porter one day.

Suddenly it struck Viola how much her only daughter had grown. She was quite the attractive young lady donning the perfect gown tonight. Sleeveless satin, it draped down to the floor with a flawless fit. Black beads trailed down her open back, revealing youthful glowing skin above the bow sash. Her light make-up spoke boldly of bygone adolescence. At the green age of twenty and one, DaVita DeGrate was still so naïve. She had thankfully missed Viola's short height. Because of Duke's stature, all of her children loomed over her. Especially Darrion. But beauty was not enough in this life. She was still so young, still so inexperienced to the methods and habits of deceitful people. Lately, Viola had found herself worrying Duke and the rest of the men in the family had sheltered DaVita too much. But what else could a mother do to protect the only girl? She ran her fingers through her daughter's long, dark layered curls. "You're young, baby. You don't know the beast women can be. Not yet." She cut her eyes back to Patricia. "And I know all too well the beast Patricia Porter can be."

"It's all history." DaVita looked around the ballroom at all of the commotion. "I'm sure she's just here to support her son."

"And I'm sure she's just here doing what she does best."

"And what's that?"

"Staying close. And speaking of, where the hell is my son?"

"Devin or Darrion?"

"My firstborn."

"He's probably off with T-Bone and Taran somewhere. Or Lunch."

She handed the champagne glass back to DaVita and made off to see where her husband had disappeared to.

One educated guess told her he was in the private host room, exploring the liquor bar. Rarely did he mingle at gatherings with the city's affluent. Not that he ever thought his aloofness was being rude. Not in the slightest. Though it indeed was.

Duke was an introverted man. Only seen when needed to be seen and he only spoke when he needed to be heard. So the arrangements of tonight's festivities were all left to her. As usual.

The great ballroom of Chicago's Waldorf Astoria was smoke hazed. Filled with the smells of braised meats and freshly baked breads. Every guest stood amidst walls covered in silk. Above them, coffered vaulted ceilings held crystal chandeliers that shimmered with vintage jewelry. Custom black draperies framed the floor-to-ceiling windows. White silk cloth covered tables bordered the entire ballroom floor. All of them were surrounded by black chairs.

Every year, the royal treatment of the charity ball was held at the Waldorf and tonight, city dignitaries—businessmen, philanthropists, politicians, doctors, and judges alike—attended. All of them flocking to meet Derek Porter. Just last month he was placed on *Forbes* List of "13 African Americans To Watch". That raised quite a few brows. Just a decade prior, during the 1970's, no one in the Windy City could have ever thought a black man would grace the pages of a white magazine.

Viola moved through the tables, past a singer lying a top of a grand piano, crooning a ballad. The pianist stroked the keys to a band of horns and percussions behind them. At just an hour past the start of the fundraising gala Viola was starting to feel the weight of her ball gown. Worse over, her feet already hated the high heels and with every step she could feel the heavy pull of her rhombus earrings.

But a good evening of glamour always gave people an excuse to put on the ritz and she had already pulled three contacts wanting an interior design consultation. Business was steady enough with the holidays coming, but Viola was certain she could squeeze in another client or two before the New Year.

She left the main ballroom and walked down the back hall. Her eyes began to burn and she cursed the smoke in the air. Careful not to ruin her make-up, she rubbed an eye and stopped at the door of the host room without giving a knock. If it was closed it was locked.

A slight drift of voices carried through the door's thick oak, but she couldn't make out what was being said.

DARRION

Darrion glanced toward the terrace.

He had to be sure his father was still wrapped in conversation with his uncle Dutch. Both men looked far enough from the sliding glass doors. Hopefully they wouldn't hear this conversation. Just to be on the safe side, he kept his voice low.

"First thing tomorrow we put word out on Kincaid," Darrion said. "That Nazi couldn't have gotten far."

"I already know where to look," T-Bone said. "There's only one place he can run and hide."

"Mount Greenwood," Taran said. He shook his head and cursed.

Darrion couldn't blame him for his lack of enthusiasm. Mount Greenwood was an notoriously racist area just south of where he and Lunch grew up. Located on the far southwest side of Chicago, it was infested with skinheads who enforced their dominance against non-whites in brutal ways.

But there was also a popularity of city workers. Mostly cops and fire fighters. Amongst them, Kincaid would blend well and try to disappear. Greenwood was his only option, but it was a well played one.

"Smart move," Lunch said. "And he'll do anything to set up an out before he gets dead. So that means, we have to find him before he gets ghost."

"I got a few snow bunnies that frequent City Lights," T-Bone said. "I can put them on him. They'll blend in enough to flush him out. All they have to do is set him up and we'll take him out. Give me a few days tops. He's dead, man."

Darrion nodded. "I'll reach out to Pope. He can talk to some of the Aryans in the mean time. They probably know all of his hideouts." He exhaled. "Okay, how much did we tally up from the robbery?"

"1.5 million," Taran said. "Split that four ways, that's $375,000 a piece."

T-Bone wolf-whistled. "I'll take that."

"Not bad for a few hours worth of sweat," Lunch said.

"We'll meet back at the club tonight after the ball and settle up in the vault. First thing tomorrow, we get with our diamond man. This shit with Kincaid is too close for comfort. From now on we keep no cash from our scores. I'm serious about that. Stones only."

"When are we moving on the next score?"

"Not until after the holidays." Darrion went to the bar and poured himself a glass of single malt Glenlivet. "We wait until after Pop's surgery. By then, this mess with Kincaid should be finished. He'll be deep sixed and that worry will be all but forgotten. We'll wait until after the New Year. Hopefully, if the smoke clears, we'll work on the next thing. For now, we stay mute."

Taran looked past Darrion's shoulder when the glass door slid open. Dutch and Duke stepped inside from the cold. A stiff November breeze swept the room as the glass slid closed behind them. Both brothers went straight to the bar and poured themselves a glass of Chivas Regal. Duke's tie was already undone. That was nothing new. Darrion knew he never hid his distaste for events and he never tied a tie until he had to be present for the speeches. He dropped a few ice cubes into his glass and swirled his drink around, cooling the whiskey.

It was easy to tell the men were brothers whenever they stood side by side. They couldn't deny their relation if they tried. Though Duke was three years Dutch's senior, both men were sharp featured and had the same short trimmed graying hair and deep set dark eyes. Both were slightly wide through the nose and they carried the DeGrate height. They each had smiles that cut like a knife.

"I'll make this quick so everybody can get back to the ball," Duke said after a taste. "These next few months are going to be hectic for the Family. We all know Derek's getting married. That won't happen until the spring of '86. That's almost a year and a half from now. Until then, his campaign is first and foremost. Everything else takes a back seat. Making sure he becomes the first black Mayor in the history of Chicago won't be easy for us to do. But, I am more than convinced that Derek has a strong campaign team and with nights like tonight, we can pull massive donations and rally a strong number of voters for February's election. Everything we do and don't do for the next few months will affect his numbers in the polls tremendously. And we will all do our part to make history with this Family. Understood?"

All of the men nodded.

"What about the hunting trip?" Lunch asked.

"That's still very much a go," Dutch said. "Tonight's Friday, we all leave Sunday night. The women too. Three days of hunting until Wednesday afternoon. While we rifle a few deer, the women will stay behind and work on the feast. Wednesday night we have our own family dinner. Then Thursday morning we drive back and after that, all focus is on the campaign. We'll be celebrating Thanksgiving with the church. It'll be a publicized dinner so the media will be there."

"How many votes does he need to win?" Taran asked.

"As of this year," Duke explained, "there are 1,515,000 registered voters in this city. That means we need 757, 501 votes to shut down Mayor Burns. The race to succeed her won't be easy. In running for re-election, to her advantage, she's white and a Republican. But much to her disadvantage, she's a woman and men run this city. She's had her chance to prove what a woman could do in office and none of the political crowns of this town are too happy with the way she's been handling things these past two years."

"But do you think white Republican voters will vote for a black Democrat just get her out of office?"

"They'd vote in an aardvark just to get that senseless degenerate tossed out on her ass. Derek is well versed and high powered. So, she knows she has some serious competition. Tonight Councilman Porter's speech will double as both a charity and a campaign speech. His theme is helping the middle class and the poor.

"Particularly working on a major expansion of subsidized, low-income housing. Also on creating jobs by developing employment in several of the city's successful underused industrial areas. I'll be making the introduction, then I'll step back to the right of the podium. After his speech, his fiancé will present our donation to the church and after that it's all grubs and get down."

"I'd like to talk with her about your treatment plan," Darrion said. "With your surgery being so far away, I'd like to know if — "

"It's all taken care of," Duke said, cutting him off. "My stent from the angioplasty is still holding strong, so no worries. Until then, I'll stay good and medicated." He motioned towards the door. "Shall we? The night awaits, gentlemen. And what a beautiful night it will be."

RENFRO

W hat a shitty night," Detective Brian Bishop spat.

He ducked down against the driver's side door of his squad car.

A bullet whizzed past his head.

Renfro was out of breath. Barely able to speak. He pulled another magazine from his belt clip, slapped it in his Beretta and chambered a round. "Who was the first officer on the scene?"

"Officer Campbell and Officer Sanchez," Bishop said. "They called for back up, and then made immediate radio contact with Robbery/Homicide, then called the coroner and an ambulance. But when medical arrived, they pulled up to a war zone. Both EMT's are dead. They never made it out of the truck."

Renfro's ears began to ring.

Rapid gun fire was the most hazardous noise he could imagine anyone enduring with unprotected ears. On the flip side, going deaf made the likelihood of flinching less significant. A chill crawled up his spine when a hard, cold winter breeze blew his wheat brown hair straight back. Cabrini Green was at war tonight and the sound of gunfire invited Renfro to join the ranks of killers. He never thought in his wildest dreams he would one day live and breath a commonality with violent pushers and dopers. But when it came to vermin, he had to inwardly admit the one thing they had in common: He knew how easy it was to kill. It was the aftermath of creating the corpses that was difficult to bear.

"Where is the most concentrated fire coming from?"

Bishop pushed his glasses up on his nose and pointed skyward towards the top of the highrise buildings. "Everywhere. There's snipers on the roof."

Renfro's brow tented with shock. "Snipers?"

Bishop nodded and took in a deep breath. "With Remington 700s I think. Tactical, and I'm pretty sure they're fitted with night scopes. There's no other way they could pick us off in the dark like this. No fucking way."

Bishop checked his magazine. Three bullets left.

He slid it back into his Glock and cursed.

A bullet flew through the windshield of Bishop's Crown Vick and exited through the driver's side window, sending shattered glass raining down on them. "How many officers down?" Renfro yelled.

"Two dead," he said pointing to the open lawn near a highrise entryway. Two policemen were unmoving. Face down on the grass. Their light blue uniform shirts soaked red with exit wounds. "One injured. I'm not sure where he's hit or how bad, but he radioed from under one of the cars in the lot. If he tries to make a run for it, the Kings will take him out. He's pinned."

"The Kings? We're at the Dirty Deuce. This highrise is Black Cobra territory. What the hell are the King's Disciples doing here?"

Bishop just shook his head. "I guess Zane took it over."

Zane Harris. Now Renfro knew this night would mark one in the history books for the Chicago PD. As the most feared and cold-blooded leader of the King Disciples, Zane's command held brutal authority and blood soaked victims. Just the power of his presence in the Near North projects made him a walking dread of vehemence and a sheer terror to the men and women who lived in fear as common residents.

In the day-to-day fight against sanity, he excelled, even reveled in his madness. Only his brother, Zeno, equaled him in sociopathic ruthlessness. The Harris brothers lived for warfare. They never bowed a knee. These were two men so made for wrath and war Renfro assumed it was a disgrace for a Harris to die in their sleep. "Looks like we got pulled into a push for power," he said. "Pushing the Cobras out of the Dirty Deuce gives Zane total control and power over all of the towers from Chicago Ave. to Sedgwick."

"How many towers is that?"

Renfro held up four fingers.

Bishop shook his head in disgust.

"Where are Campbell and Sanchez?"

"At the far end of the lot, using the dumpsters for cover." Bishop looked down the line of squad cars and shook his head again. "The department is in pure decay. This is bullshit, Renfro! Bullshit! We're detectives. We wear suits and we arrive after, not before the bodies get made. We shouldn't be responding to shoot outs. I should be sipping coffee, bitching at some rookie for fucking up my crime scene."

"You know the routine, Bishop. Everybody responds, everybody rotates in and out of back up." Renfro adjusted the Velcro of his Kevlar vest and looked up to the rooftop, chancing exposure of his head to the shooters. The streetlight revealed two snipers aimed at a rusty Buick. One of them fired a shot into the engine like a trained commando. Renfro assumed that was the car the injured patrol officer was trapped under. He couldn't spot the other two snipers. They were out of the streetlight's beam. He looked to the top floor beneath the gable of the roof. More thugs than he could count were running through the breezeways with automatic weapons. Shooting at Crown Vics. Shooting at each other. So many gunshots coming from so many different directions, Renfro knew the Cobras were making their last stand.

Another bullet ricocheted off of the car's top and whizzed past his head. Renfro ducked down and threw a hand to steady himself against the driver's door. To his right, directly behind a row of parked cars, several more Crown Vics pulled up, screeching to a halt. Every officer got out crouched low, using some portion of their vehicle — doors and fenders — for cover. All of them using their Crowns as a Kevlar. Their weapons aimed ready at the towers.

More shots rang out. Renfro looked to see if any uniformed officers had been hit as they pulled up. None of them seemed wounded. Renfro reached for his portable radio and informed them of the circumstances then looked at Bishop. "I say we draw fire away from the injured officer and the two departed, then we retrieve them and get the hell out of Dodge," Bishop said. "To hell with this war. Let them kill each other."

Renfro put down his radio. "I couldn't agree more." He gave another quick glance to the building and ducked back down. "Here's how we're going to do this. You reach into my trunk and grab the smoke bombs and the launcher and fire two bombs at the roof first. That'll blind the snipers with a smoke screen. Then climb inside the trunk. I'll get behind the wheel and I'll shoot and steer you towards the other officers. I got twelve smoke bombs. When you jump out, have the bombs and the launcher with you. Fire as many as you can at the top floors, the roof, and through any vacant windows. That'll pull them away from the breezeways to eliminate a clear shot. The second they stop shooting and start running, fire everything you've got. The smoke screen will last one to three minutes. I'll use it to get the officer from under the car, then I'll recover the departed and scoop up the other two officers behind the dumpster."

Bishop nodded. "Pop the trunk."

Renfro stayed low and moved down to Bishop's back fender.

When the gunfire ceased, he dashed the twenty foot distance to Bishop's car and popped the trunk.

Bishop loaded the smoke bombs into the M243 grenade launcher, keeping low as the trunk top took on bullets. He waited for another lull in the gunfire then launched two smoke bombs at the roof of the tower. Seconds later red phosphorus fumes galvanized into a thick haze of white smoke.

"Let's move!" Renfro yelled.

Bishop dived into the trunk as Renfro climbed behind the wheel and shoved the key in the ignition. He mashed the gas pedal to the floor and sped straight towards the patrol cars, then slammed the brakes, popped the trunk, and crouched low in the seat.

Bishop climbed out and ran behind the nearest squad car for cover. Then he took aim, firing smoke bombs until the launcher was empty.

Ten seconds later, Renfro sat up, surveying the damage. It was pandemonium. All he saw were black men with over-sized coats and baggy jeans scattering from the white smoke like a thousand roaches on a wall.

What happened next came in slow motion stilted with unnatural silence. Even the air he heaved into his lungs seemed locked in a timeless pause. Renfro could feel every muscle in his body tense. His face switched up calm and composure with furrowed brows and clenched teeth.

Terror and foreboding replaced trained bearings of self-control. As he slammed on the gas, his heart was dancing on his tongue.

He reached the old Buick in less than ten seconds, skidded to a halt, then leaned to the passenger side and threw the door open. "This is Detective Renfro! If you can, climb out from under the car and get in!"

Renfro didn't have to tell him twice. The officer quickly scrambled out from under the car and climbed into the passenger seat so fast he almost head-butted him in the nose.

He ducked down and slammed the door.

Just as Renfro opened his mouth to speak, Bishop executed their plan in full force. The officers were firing off at the building with so much brutality the whole world grayed into thunderous chaos of earsplitting blasts.

"There's two more officers," the uniformed officer yelled, "down by the dumpsters!"

"I know." Renfro instantly noticed the blood trickling from the officer's shirt. "How bad are you injured?"

"I took one through my right shoulder, but I think it's just a flesh wound. The bleeding is minimal and I still have full motion in my arm."

"Good, cause I'm gonna need some help. We're headed to the front lawn to pick up the dead officers. Then we'll get the other two."

The officer nodded and Renfro hit the gas once more, speeding toward the bodies on the lawn. The instant he hit the brakes, both men scrambled out onto the frozen grass and ran to the bodies.

They picked up one, did a two-man carry — tossing the body in the back seat — then went for the other. Suddenly it dawned on him — the deceased officers didn't have their coats, but Renfro didn't slow to ask why they were missing.

Both back tires spun out, kicking up grass and dirt as Renfro backed out off the lawn. He threw the Crown Vic in drive and sped down the lot to the dumpster. Both of the officers were crouched low. Weapons in hand. One of them appeared a tall black man. Thickset with solid muscle. Light brown skin and a clean shaven bald head. His partner was a slim Latino woman that looked a third her partner's size.

They both spun around in a wide-eyed shock when the squad car screeched to a halt.

"Get in!" Renfro yelled.

They scrambled into the back seat a top of the dead bodies.

"Stay down!" Renfro tossed the radio to the officer in the passenger seat. "Let them know we are a 10-24!"

The officer relayed the message that they were leaving the scene and Renfro sped out of the lot, turning down the first street corner he saw like the car was on rails.

ANGELIQUE

Angelique clapped along to applause in the ballroom.

City Councilman Derek Porter had finished his speech.

She admired the theme. Helping the city's middle class and poor with employment opportunities and equal housing approval. It was political apple pie. All of his most interesting ideas were aimed at the liberal Democratic primary electorate.

Angelique knew most of his ideas would take years to accomplish, but those ideas would solely benefit from the city's next Mayor.

Tonight, every foreman of his campaign stood next to him.

The Councilman's campaign manager, Thomas Prescott, stood to his right. He was a handsome man, though not as tall as Derek. Olive skin. Blue eyes. Well trimmed dark hair that shone like deep bronze. Tonight, he looked quite stately in his black suit.

Next to him stood Roth Garrett. If anyone could keep to the financial wellbeing of Derek's democratic crusade it was he. Angelique did not like the man. Roth's love for the dollar ranged his political interests somewhere close to the methods of a bonafide racketeer. His dark complexion nearly matched the black of his suit and his teeth shone as bright as the diamonds of his Rolex. From where Angelique stood on the ballroom floor she could easily see he leaked monetary ambition. Damn, but the man could at least try to hide it.

To Roth's right stood young David Wendell. He was a lanky wisp of a boy. Not quite twenty and one, his natural hair was well oiled. Cut low to deep waves. Youth glowed in those brown eyes—matching the youthful flush of his skin. Angelique couldn't help but to notice the unsure shyness of his smile as he clapped on, as if he knew he was on that stage but wasn't quite sure if he belonged there. But he did belong. Wendell faired well as the coordinator to the Councilman. So well Angelique thought of stealing him away as her personal assistant. Though smart and staid for his young age, she worried Wendell was much too naïve to see all the veracities of policymaking.

At Derek's left stood the head faction of St. Victor Catholic Church. Archbishop Courdenay stood in his colorful sacramental vestments. Looking majestic and regal next to his six episcopal Vicars. Donald DeGrate, Duke's youngest brother and Bishop of the church, stood amongst them, equally robed and ceremonial.

All in all, the men looked quite privileged to be standing so close to the future of the city. They looked more proud of the Councilman than she was. There were times—not many, but a few—when she remembered honored moments that would surely go down in African American history. This was one of them. She was pulled out of her inward observations the instant the applause ended and Derek announced her to the center of the room. "The new honorary chairwoman of the DeGrate Porter Charity Foundation, my beautiful future bride, Dr. Angelique James." Timbres of the band's trumpets signaled her cue. Angelique felt her face flush warm from the prolonged and thunderous applause.

She nervously gripped the lace of her gown and stepped forward. Archbishop Courdenay came to her side and Prescott followed, handing her the giant, ornamented disbursement certificate. She quietly thanked him, cleared her throat as the horns died out, and announced the evening's coveted contribution, "I don't know if I have the Councilman's talent for discourse and formal address," she beamed, "but here goes. For the past ten years, the DeGrate Porter Charity Foundation has done much more than fund medical research and support artistry. Particularly dedicating funds to the disadvantaged and underprivileged of Chicago, the foundation continues to give grounds to the resurgence of every child's hopes and dreams."

She turned to Archbishop, holding the enlarged festooned certificate. "Archbishop Courdenay, here is $10,000,000 for orphans of the Church in the name of the late Octavious DeGrate and Colton Porter. Try not to spend it all at once!"

Gasps circled the room followed by an explosion of camera flashes and cheering ovations.

DUKE

Duke smiled, watching Derek watch Angelique.

She was far off near the center of the room, chattering with Prescott and the Archbishop, amongst the crowd of influential priests, capitalists, moguls, wives, and giddy playful children-- all of them a riot of color. Duke eyed a long table festooned with every delicacy Viola thought would swoon their guests. He sat the Chivas aside, picked up a plate and began filling it with braised bourbon beef.

Derek picked up his father's glass and took a sip. "God, she's amazing, isn't she?"

Duke forked a piece of meat and nodded. "She's lovely. Though I can't imagine why she's with a knuckle head like you."

Derek laughed. "For the same reason Viola's with a stubborn ox like you. Behind every woman is a beautiful woman rolling her eyes."

"From the letter you sent she might be standing behind you with a 12-gauge. She really enjoys a hunt?"

"She'd give Taran and Darrion a run for their money."

"Really?" He took a bite of the bourbon beef.

Delicious. All he could taste was seared meat and a scrumptous sweet glaze of whiskey and brown sugar. In that moment, no other beef he'd ever tasted compared — and Viola was a damn fine cook. Duke would have to personally thank the chef. He picked up a cloth napkin from the table, dabbed his mouth, and took another bite. "I think what you suggested is a wonderful idea. I would like very much for her to come on the hunting trip. It'll be perfect. Have you planned an engagement party yet?"

Derek shook his head. "With the campaign and all of Angie's hospital interviews, I haven't had much time for anything else."

"What hospital is she looking toward?"

"I think she'll choose Scott Joplin. Her final interview was last Monday. It's the best teaching hospital in the country. Also the most competitive. And she's always saying how she loves working with interns, so…"

Duke nodded. "That's a good choice."

"It is. And when she starts up her practice, we'll hardly have time for much else. I don't know if we can swing an enagement party."

Duke waved off his worry. "Nonsense, we'll plan one for you. Viola loves that shit."

"That was quite a speech," Darrion cut in, approaching the men with Viola on his arm. There was a hint of malevolence in his eyes. "Shark any brothers lately?"

"Can't say that I have," Derek said, unaffected. "Have you?"

Darrion smiled dryly.

Duke's was in no mood for their sibling rivalry. Not tonight. "Both of you stop it."

"He started it," Derek said.

"And what are you, twelve?"

Satisfied he'd won that round, Derek shrugged it off with a smirk.

Darrion cut his eyes from his brother to Duke. "There's something we need to talk to you about, Pop. In private."

"Okay," Duke said. "Give us a minute, Derek. And don't go far, there's something important I have to talk to you about."

Derek nodded. Viola left Darrion's arm and embraced Derek in a hug. "Congratulations, Derek." She pulled back and flushed his tie with her hand. "On the campaign, your engagement. Everything. I mean that."

Derek looked taken aback as if surprised she would touch him. "Thank you very much."

Duke knew his firstborn was not used to affections from Viola. Before the awkwardness set in, he led the way back to the private host office. Viola and Darrion followed and waited until

Duke closed the door. He poured another drink and took a seat behind the desk then loosed his tie and spoke. "What's the problem?"

"Ronald Moss is in town," Darrion said.

Duke's brow lifted. "Who's Ronald Moss?"

"The grandson of DaVita's godmother," Viola reminded him.

"Aunt Pearl?"

Darrion nodded. "Mmm-hmm."

Duke thought for a moment longer, then his face took on sudden recollection. "That loose cannon? The one who beat that kid into a coma over ten dollars? When was it…eight, nine years ago?"

"Sounds about right."

"And what does he want from me?"

"He wants out from under Zosa," Darrion said. "Says he can't stand gaming for a selfish Italian anymore."

"I don't need young hotheads with gambling problems. I need politicians, lawyers, judges, accountants. Seeing as he's none of those, he's of no use to me."

A hard knock came to the door. Duke knew by how the wood shook it was Dutch. His brother had a knock that could take any door down if it weren't for its hinges.

"Come in."

Dutch stepped inside and closed the door. "We have a problem."

"What problem?"

"Tommy Zosa's here at the ball."

Duke looked from his brother to Darrion then back to Dutch. "Was he on the list?"

"Don't know. But he got in somehow and he wants to see you."

"Is it necessary?"

"He says he just wants a word. To give congratulations and good wishes."

"I say we bring them both in," Darrion suggested. "Clearly they have their own say of whatever is going on and they both want to be heard. Let Zosa and Ronnie have a little sit down, they can put all of their differences out on the table, air out their grievances. If they can squash their beef maybe you can come up with a solution."

"Why do I have to come up with a solution to a problem that has nothing to do with me? Or you?"

"Actually it does have to do with me. Ronnie is in Zosa's debt. I agreed to pay that debt, but he has to pay me back. The only way he'll walk the straight and narrow to square up with me is if he's working for the Family. Otherwise, he's going to fall right back into the same shit."

Duke grimaced and exhaled a frustrated breath. "How much is he in with Zosa for?"

"Two plus fifty."

"Grand?"

Darrion nodded. "Put a hundred infront of that. And I imagine that's not plus interest."

"A quarter of a million dollars? And you're willing to vouch for Ronnie?"

"I will."

"He's your charge now. I'm against it, but it's your choice. Every mistake he makes, good or bad, is on you."

Darrion nodded. "Yes, sir."

"Alright, send them in."

DARRION

Darrion found Ronnie in an alcove with a flush blonde.

He looked set to be drunk soon if he wasn't already. An hour ago, he had dark brown ale in his glass. After that, wine. Now his drink was the light color of a cognac. Darrion buried the urge to slap the glass out of his hand and tapped him on the arm instead. "Father wants a word."

Ronnie disentangled from the dame, fixed the lapel of his suit jacket, and followed Darrion through the crowd of guests. "I told you I'd speak with him about settling your problem. Now, when you go in there, don't speak unless he speaks to you first. He doesn't like being interrupted, especially if he doesn't know you and a word of caution, Zosa is here. He's already in the office."

"What's he doing here?"

"I just said we're settling your problem." Darrion stopped at the door and wrapped lightly on the wood with his knuckle. "Or did you not hear that part?"

Ronnie swallowed hard and kept his mouth shut.

"Finish that drink and make it your last."

Ronnie downed it in one long swallow and looked for a place to set it down before the door opened. He couldn't find a table so he just nervously held the glass in his hand.

♛

Dutch opened the door and the men stepped inside. Tension sat thick in the office. No one spoke until Darrion severed the silence. "Father, this is Ronald Moss."

"Aunt Pearl's grandson, hmm?"

"Yes, Sir," Ronnie said. "Thank you for seeing me this evening. I really appreciate it."

Duke nodded.

Zosa ran a hand through his chestnut hair then propped a foot up on a knee as if he owned the chair he sat in. Darrion knew faces, but he didn't recognize the dark haired mountain of a man next to him, but by the stern gaze locked on his face and the bulk of his build he could've only been the Mafioso's hired guard dog.

"I understand that you two have a quarrel over an unpaid debt?" Duke began.

"We do," Zosa said with a sure nod.

"I have to ask, what does this have to do with me? Your business is none of my concern. If my son agreed to pay off this young man's debt, then problem solved."

"I couldn't agree more. And I fully intended on taking care of my problem with this man," Zosa said, pointing to Ronnie. "See, in my world, I would usually take a hand for that kind of financial obligation. And the night that I came to settle up for his transgression, he tells me that if I harm him, then my actions would incur the…repercussions of his family. And when I asked who his family was, he dropped your name. The great Duke DeGrate. Or, to put it more specifically, he said, *'Touch me and my Uncle will find you, reach down your throat and pull your nuts out through your fucking pasta hole.'* I didn't make his debt your problem. He did. So here we sit.

"I hire the blacks to show that I have a good heart," Zosa went on. "The coloreds who work for me, I give 'em just enough money to function. This very moment right here is the reason why. I treat one of them differently, I give just one of you a chance to prove you're not all the same and this…dilemma…this gambling drunk is what I get."

Duke did not look pleased.

In that moment, Ronnie's debt took a back seat to Darrion's own temper. To his memory it had been a long time since a man sat before his father and shot prejudiced affronts across the room like poison tipped barbs from a blowgun. Ronnie's analogy was quite in line with what he wanted to do to the man. Duke let out a breath as he came around to lean against the desk. He folded his arms across his chest, and said, "Let us start again, Mr. Zosa. You speak to me as if I'm a well known man of veneration in this city and I'll speak to you as if there's a chance on this side of hell that I'll agree to your terms of a settlement."

Zosa was quiet for a moment. Then he pointed to the gifted commemoration from St. Victor Catholic Church on the desk. "That's beautiful. St. Victor. Did you know that Victor the Third was born the son of a prince? He became Pope in 1086. His own son became Pope Urban the Second. That's who that church was named after. Even after he became ill, he led a crusade against the Saracens in Africa."

"Mr. Zosa, do you —"

Zosa held up a hand, "Please, call me Tommy."

"Tommy," Duke complied. "Do you know who Saint Victor the First was?"

Zosa shook his head. "I can't say that I do."

"Saint Victor I was the first black Pope of the Roman Catholic Church," Duke said calmly. "He was not Italian. Nor was he from Italy. He was a native of the Roman Province of Africa, so is my bloodline. His father's name was Felix. He was a great man who always showed boundless concern for severing ties with those who opposed church beliefs and values. He is known to this Family as the Saint of Reason. That's who St. Victor Catholic Church was named after."

Zosa hmmphed. "I didn't know that."

"Well now you do." Duke motioned a hand. "Your offer."

Zosa cracked his knuckles, then, "Well, that's $250,000...plus interest per annum, equals $425,000. Now, I'm willing to let that debt slide, if you and I can come to terms with a different proposal that would suit us both."

"I'm listening."

"Your current investment with the church is quite a clever move. It's set to make you a mint as one of the richest men in the history of Chicago if you buy out their stock of O'Meravenchi. Class A holding shares in the largest real estate company of the

Midwest are hard to come by these days. My boss, Mr. D'Amico is more than willing to negotiate terms to buy you out."

Duke raised a brow. " Your boss, buy me out? Why do you think I would be interested in that?"

"We both know that your history with Salvatore is less than unsullied. Let's be honest, Mr. DeGrate. It's 1984. These days, a Class A principle shareholder has more voting power on board elections and corporate policy than Class B shareholders, as well as any common dividend payments. One month ago, Mr. D'Amico was set to purchase majority shares of O'Meravenchi from St. Victor in an effort to absolve the papacy's nasty deficit. A Bishop was sent to his house to inform him that the church was no longer interested in his offer. From what the newspapers are saying...the D'Amico Family believes you are the reason why. They believe that you've cut them out. They're unhappy about that. Allow them to buy their way back in, and you save yourself a lot of opposition."

"Opposition?" Dutch spat. "Is that supposed to be a threat?"

"I'm just a man delivering a message," Zosa said with a genteel smile.

"A second ago you were a man who cuts off hands," Duke said.

"You can take some time to think about it if you like," Zosa said. "But my Family, we don't take no for an answer, not very well. Especially when it comes down to what we feel is ours."

"I don't need time to think about it. I decline your proposal. You may leave your account number with my son, Darrion. He will make sure that what is owed to you is in your account by noon tomorrow."

Zosa sat there for a moment. He looked as if he wasn't sure how to take Duke's blunt dismissal. Then he stood and his guard dog followed him to the door. Zosa put a hand to the doorknob, turned, and said, "Mr. DeGrate, it's been a real pleasure speaking with you. I'm sorry we couldn't come to an agreement."

"I'm not," Duke spat.

"I second that," Dutch said.

"I third it," Darrion agreed.

Dutch shut the door behind them and took the seat Zosa left empty. "That WOP pimp."

"He's not going to go away," Darrion warned.

Duke remained quiet for a long moment. Then looked at Ronnie. "We settle your debt, that means you are indebted to this Family for years to come."

Ronnie nodded. "Absolutely, Mr. DeGrate, one hundred percent indebted."

"You are my son's charge. You do whatever he asks without question. Understand?"

"Absolutely."

"Good. Stick around. Keep close, you might learn something." Duke motioned towards the door, signaling his dismissal. "That's it."

"Thank you, Uncle." Ronnie made for the door and turned to thank him again. "Thank you very much."

Viola shut the door behind him and stood beneath a large oil painting. "You did the right thing. I know he's not blood. Not true Family. But he needs to be around strong men. Pearl will be so grateful that you gave him your support."

"Do me a favor, love," Duke said. "Stick close to him tonight and find out everything you can from him about Zosa."

Viola nodded. "It's done."

She was out the door before Darrion could mention to steer him clear of the alcohol, but to his surprise, Duke mentioned it instead. "Son, make sure that he's walking on two legs for the rest of the evening." Darrion nodded and made for the door.

Dutch went to the bar and poured himself a drink. "So, how do we handle Moss?"

"Wait a second, Darrion," Duke said. "You need to hear this."

Duke motioned his son closer.

Dutch took a long swallow and stepped nearer. Duke threw an arm around his brother. "Employ him at Christian Lebarron's. Let him get a taste of the furrier business. Pay him enough to keep his mouth wet, but not enough to drop dice at a table. As a favor to Pearl we do this. But, keep him closer than he would like."

ANGELIQUE

Angelique left the noise of the Grand Ballroom.

The Waldorf's private dining chamber — she found at the end of the long hall — seemed the quietest. She tried not to gawk at everything shiny. The Parisian fireplace, its size mocked a carpenter's hearth and its flames nearly reached the height of her brow. Standing close to the searing wood, she took in the thick aroma of the fire's kindling. Quiet warmth always reminded her of childhood days in the sun. Of Grandmother Eleanor and Mother — what few memories she had of them together. That was more than twenty years gone.

Now, Grandmother Eleanor lived as a retired surgeon in the comfort of Northbrook, Illinois. Still the known legend among black female surgeons. Still hard as stone. Though her only daughter had departed life when Angelique was only nine, she seemed rarely effected by it. If she was saddened, Eleanor Berkely surely never let on and she never let up. Driving Angelique through schooling, always provoking a competitive spirit was everything to her.

Angelique loved her for that. Now, she had finally arrived.

Dr. Angelique Michael Eleanor James.

Offered an attending position at Scott Joplin Cook County Hospital. She hoped it was the right decision. Everything seemed to be happening so fast.

Her residency at Johns Hopkins, over. Meeting Derek at a cardiac conference and falling in love faster than her breath could register. Taking on a slew of accountabilities for terrified interns that would surely kill a patient within their first year.

It all came at a whirlwind's pace. But, life at a slow pace held no existence she would've been interested in living. Still, in coming back to Chicago, to a new family that barely knew her, she worried it was all a mistake.

"Not a camera person either, hmm?" came a masculine voice thick with aversion.

Angelique turned from the fire. Darrion stood not ten paces from her. Nursing a chilled bottle of water. Maybe it was a family thing. She hated it when Derek did that. Standing there for however long before she even knew he was there. Derek had said his younger brother served in Vietnam with him. It made sense of course that Darrion could do the quiet-stalk-thing as well. She hid the irritation of being snuck upon. Her brow lifted instead.

"Ah, so you can speak." She glanced down at his water bottle. "And I see you have the use of opposable thumbs."

His eyes narrowed with derision. "And I see you have my brother's smart mouth."

She smiled broadly, then covered her smile with her hands and laughed. "I'm sorry, when I'm out of my element I make jokes. Sometimes they grate a little. And no, I don't like cameras. So your brother and I don't have everything in common."

Darrion moved closer to the fire and sipped his water. From his profile it was easy to see he resembled Duke more than Derek did. He carried that same stern glare and with that tented ridge of his brow she nearly thought it bordered on menacing. "You look like him. Your father."

He nodded as if the remark did not surprise him. "I get that a lot."

"Are the two of you close?"

"He's everything to me." Darrion capped his water bottle and looked at her . "He's the best man I know. This Family is not ready to lose him."

"His heart's strong enough to handle the bypass," she assured him. "If he continues to take his medications and he takes care of himself afterward, I think he'll be around for a long time to come."

"How many of those have you done?"

"Ninety-nine," she answered without hesitation. "Duke DeGrate will be my big 100."

"How does a bypass work?"

"In your father's case, when the coronary arteries are completely blocked, there is angioplasty that can be done to temporarily widen the arteries and press the plaque—that's causing the blockage—against the artery walls...which should improve blood flow. With your father, the angioplasty was not enough. Even after the procedure, he still suffered a second heart attack. So stents had to be placed to keep his arteries open."

"But if the stents kept his arteries open, why does he need the bypass?"

"You want the truth or do you want me to lie to you?"

"I'll take the former."

"His diet," she said frankly. "He doesn't exercise. Everything he eats is fried, sautéed, and smothered. And with him already being born with a heart defect, it caught up to him. So, now I'm going to have to open his chest, expose his heart, and use blood vessels from his leg and graft them onto his damaged vessels above and below where the blockage is. It's kind of like a quick detour you take down a back street to avoid the congested traffic. Actually, that's exactly what it is."

"How much time will that give him?"

"If he takes care of himself, another 10 to 15 years. Easily. But I have to be clear, it's not just the surgery that will keep him alive. Your mother, Viola, she has to take an active role in controlling what he eats and making sure that he takes his medications. And so do you. It has to be a family effort."

Darrion exhaled. Then, "When is the surgery?"

"He wants to wait until after the holidays and I understand your youngest brother, Devin, has a birthday on January 25th?"

"He does."

"Your father wants to wait until after then, so on the last week of January we'll admit him for pre-surgery tests and keep him for observation. Then we'll do the operation on the first week of February."

"Is it okay to wait that long?"

Angelique shook her head. "No. Not ususally."

"You're against it?"

"No surgeon wouldn't be. I'd admit him tomorrow if he'd let me. But I respect his apprehension. He thinks these might be his last holidays. He wants to see his youngest turn 18. Who am I to tell him no?"

Darrion looked as if a sudden realization hit him. "So that explains it."

"What?"

"Why he's inviting the women of the Family on our hunting trip next week."

She smiled. "Oh I already heard. It's usually no girls allowed."

He uncapped his water and took a long gulp. "Less accidents that way."

That brought a bitter twist to her lips.

Why do men always assume women can't handle themselves with a weapon? She cast a hard glare at him. "That was a bit sexist, don't you think?"

"I hope so," he said bluntly, "because I wasn't talking about the women." He held up two fingers. "Two years in Nam taught me the worst thing a man can have in war, other than a gun that jams, is a woman that makes him forget his side-arm is even there. It impairs judgment. Mars your tactical skills. It's the worst truth in the rules of engagement. That's why you're not allowed in combat. That's why you'll never be a Navy SEAL. That's why you're not allowed on submarines. And that Maritime issue has nothing to do with separate showers and not being able to flush tampons out to sea on your Massengil days when you're feeling…" he flicked quotation marks with a free hand, "…not so fresh. Supposedly they say it might happen in the next ten to twenty years." He waved it off with his hand like that was the most crass thing he'd ever heard. "I don't care what the media said just to shut ya'll up. It'll never happen. Why? One reason, Doc—women make men messy." Darrion punctuated every last word of that sentence like it was testament scripture. He cast a quick glance from her breasts to her glossed lips. "Especially the fat ugly ones."

He turned and walked towards the doors.

Angelique's mouth was agape. It was the most insulting compliment she had ever heard in her life. She didn't know whether to blush or smack the tattoo off his face. But he was already out the door, making his way down the long hall. Since he was too out of reach for a slap, Angelique did the only thing she could do. "I fired my first rifle when I was twelve," she called at his back.

"Welcome to the Family," Darrion said over his shoulder like he couldn't have cared less.

"You sure about that?" she spat back, not making it a question.

He shrugged without a backward glance and kept walking. "Derek is. That's all that matters."

Angelique blazed anger. She threw a hand on one hip and glared at the back of his smug head as he disappeared around a corner. Knowing no one was around to hear, knowing her rant would be wasted, she shouted it anyway, "What an animal!"

♛

Aside from studying for her boards six years ago, closing on a new property proved one of the most stressful affairs of her life. Appraisals, repair requests to the seller, battling the mortgage company, arranging movers for both her and Derek's apartments. These things descended upon her with overwhelming speed. Just meeting for the final settlement and the signing of papers made waiting thirty days for final possession seem like torture. But at last the 4,500 square foot, four-bedroom, four-bathroom domicile was theirs.

What she loved most was its location and history. Constructed in 1928, the stately limestone building stood comprised of 23 full-floor residences. She and Derek now occupied the 19th story. Lake Shore Drive was just two blocks north if she ever wanted to walk to Lake Michigan. Grant Park was even closer.

After the ball was over, after the frantic Saturday that followed of unpacking with Derek, grocery shopping, and packing all day Sunday for the hunting trip, by Monday morning she was glad to be back in a world were things made sense. A world where all she needed to feel sane was a signed consent form, a warm body and a scalpel in her hand.

Today she had chosen a black pants suit and suede loafers. With her hair, she decided to be different. A different life called for a different coif. Angelique had spent nearly an hour in the mirror creating a reverse French braid from the neck up instead of the common French that starts from the top down. That decision kept the hair off of her neck. Then she took the pile of hair left on top of her head and smoothed it all into one tall forward barrel curl and secured it with pins. It looked almost like false bangs, but she kept it back from her forehead. Hair on her skin made her itch, which she hated.

Now, she sat across from the Scott Joplin Hospital Administrator at 9:00 in the morning, inwardly admiring how well the woman carried her weight.

Delores Shaw was a tall, heavyset woman. Her smooth charcoal eyes beamed bright and saw much. Her long dark hair shone beautifully stark against her dusky fawn skin. Today her locks were pulled into in a neatly smoothed French roll adorned with a shimmery gold-leaf trinket, and her wide curves were well swathed in a white cashmere sweater and grey slacks. Pearl earrings accented her lobes and to Angelique, from across the desk, she smelled of sweet plumbs and lavender.

She assumed the boy seated quietly to her left was her son. He carried the same bright eyes and smooth skin. His lanky frame was nearly swallowed up by the short sleeved Polo shirt and the starched Khakis did little to hide his stilts for legs. Thick, naturally curly hair sat thick atop of his head. He pushed his frameless bifocals up his nose and smiled shyly. Dr. James smiled back.

Maybe it was racist, maybe it was biased, but Angelique was glad another African American woman thrived in the world of surgery. She hoped that working under a female hospital administrator would give them an unspoken bond the boys weren't in on.

"I read about the charity ball in the Sunday paper," Delores said. "It looked amazing."

"It was."

"So, you decided to stay with us?"

"Yes, Chicago is my home town. It just seemed right."

"I heard Dr. Berkley wasn't too happy about your decision."

Dr. James gave a nod. "Well, she wanted me to start my practice in Northbrook and I decided otherwise." She broke into a devious grin. "Besides, she's retired. Dr. Berkley doesn't get to tell me what to do anymore."

Delores smiled in agreement. "That's right! If you don't operate you don't regulate. That's what I say."

Her smile broadened. "God, I wish she was sitting here to hear you say that."

"I don't. I'd be peeling myself off the wall if she caught me sassing her."

Angelique laughed. Was there anyone who wasn't deathly afraid of her grandmother?

"I hope you don't mind my son sitting over there next to my vase," Delores said, nodding toward her son.

Dr. James shook her head at the heavy sword-shaped green leaves, admiring its gargantuan size. A snake plant. It had been years since she'd seen one. "Oh, not at all."

"Deon, Dr. Angelique James, she's our new cardiothoracic specialist. Dr. James, this is my only son, Deon."

"It's nice to meet you," she said in greeting. Deon stood like the perfect gentleman, stepped forward, and shook her hand. She almost winced. "Wow, strong grip."

"He plans on holding a 10 blade in those hands, one day," Delores said.

"Really?" Dr. James looked at him with amazement. It seemed rare to her. Meeting someone so young who knew exactly what he wanted. He instantly reminded her of young Wendell. "What specialty have you considered?"

He shrugged bony shoulders. "I don't know, um, I haven't even decided what pre-med I want to attend."

"That's why he's here today," Delores cut in. "He's on Thanksgiving break from school so I thought I'd bring him in here bright and early to meet you."

That brought a wily grin.

"Oh, wow!" Angelique praised, clapping. "Nice, Mom. That's exactly what I would've done. Perfect way to slide that one right on in there."

Delores laughed.

"That's what my grandmother did."

"Really?"

"Mmm-hmm. When I didn't have school she didn't leave me in the house to mess around and sleep all day. Dr. Berkley brought me with her to work, sat me down in her office," she motioned to the book shelf to her right, "and she would pull the books off of her shelf and make me read them."

"Is that right?"

"Yes, Ma'am," Angelique continued, "and her favorite thing to do to me was to put the Stedman's Medical Dictionary in front of me and she would call out a letter. She would say, 'I want you to study the P's today,' and I had to study every medical term under that letter. By lunchtime, she would throw any word of that letter at me. She would drill me just to see if I retained the information and I had better know the answers. That was Grandmother Eleanor."

Delores looked at her son. A scheming gleam shone in her eyes.

Deon shook his head. "Please don't give her any ideas," he said, rolling his eyes.

"Too late," Delores said, smiling white teeth.

Dr. James couldn't help but to laugh at the anguish on his young face. Then she caught her breath and invited inquiry. "So, ask away. Anything you want to know."

He adjusted his bifocals again and said, "Okay...How many years of school is it?"

She shook her head. *God, the young ones, they always ask that one first.* She laughed again. "How did I know you were going to say that?"

He smiled sheepishly. "Well, I heard it's a lot."

"And for once, the rumors are true," she began. "I attended Northbrook Preparatory and I graduated a year early at seventeen. I was accepted at Tulane University for my pre-med studies and four years later, at the age of twenty, I attended Johns Hopkins School of Medicine—"

"Graduated top of her class too," Delores chimed in.

"Really?" Deon's brow lifted. "What year did you graduate?"

"In 1978," Angelique answered. "I was twenty-four. I chose to stay in Baltimore for my internship and my four-year residency. In '82 I chose to extend my residency for vascular and trauma surgery. With my residency now over, here I am."

"And how many years is that total?"

She watched him half-wince like he didn't want to hear the answer.

"Sixteen."

His eyes went wide with shock.

"Sixteen! How old are you?"

"I'm 34, and in April I'll be 35."

"She's still young, son," Delores said. "She still has her whole life ahead of her. And if you work hard enough, so will you."

Angelique nodded in agreement. "She's right."

"Was it hard for you?" Deon asked, "being black and going through school? I mean, how many black female surgeons are there in this country? Let alone in this hospital?"

"As of today, here, you're looking at the first," Delores said.

"And yes," Angelique said, "there were times when I found it difficult. There are far more African American male surgeons out there then there are female. But, I accepted the rarity of being the first at Scott Joplin with open arms."

"Was your grandmother really the first black female heart surgeon in the Midwest?"

Angelique nodded. "And she never let me forget it."

Deon winced. "She sounds mean."

"Deon!" Delores said. She shook her head, blinking wide-eyed at Angelique. "I'm sorry, he's sixteen and sometimes he forgets to put a filter between here," she motioned a finger from her own forehead to her mouth, "and here."

Delores had no kind of patience for ill-thought remarks, Angelique knew. All she could do was lighten the sudden serious mood with a laugh. It was true after all. Grandmother Eleanor was walking wrath. Deon was not off the mark, so how could she be offended? Delores seemed to be relieved by her humor.

"I'm not offended at all," she said with the wave of her hand. "And yes, she was a beast. She was so mean they all used to call her Mein Kampf...Dr. Swastika...and my favorite was Lady Hitler. It had that feminine swing to it." She smiled at her thoughts. "Oh yes, she was dread. But back then she had to be. We're talking the 1940's when my Grandmother was young. She had dreams. Her father, my great grandfather, had high hopes for her. But, when she was fifteen she met a boy. Then she had a baby by the time she was sixteen. Poof! Dream gone, right?

Wrong. Adofilus Berkley would not give up on his daughter. He pushed her through school. He pushed her to become a surgeon.

"It was hard times then. This is when segregation was still apart of our society. She had a lot of opposition on her back. The odds were stacked against her. Black. A woman. With a baby, mind you, and a father who was illiterate. According to the standards of society and the signs of the times, she wasn't supposed to make it. She was supposed to fail. So, the only way she knew how to be successful and persevere was to be as hard as nails."

Deon looked disturbed. "It's not still that hard now is it?"

"Oh, Lord," Delores said, shaking her head. "Did you see any crosses burning on our front lawn this morning, boy?"

Realizing how ridiculous the question was, Deon smiled a mouthful of braces as the women laughed at his foolishness.

DEREK

So, I hear you're our new surgeon," Dr. Yu said, smiling.

Dr. Yu was a tall man. His thinned eyes were as dark as his straight black hair, and he carried the flat cheeks and wide nose of Peking. From what Angelique had said during their drive to Dr. Yu's office, the dermatologist was a forty-six year old golf enthusiast who spoke better English than Chinese. He looked no older than twenty one, which made Derek inwardly question the man's expertise. Knowing better than to let his apprehension be known, he stood quietly at her side, the ever rock-solid support.

Angelique nodded at Yu's icebreaker statement and nervously pulled at her loose fitting patient gown. Derek could tell that, for an MD, she did not like being a patient.

She readjusted herself on the exam table and intertwined her fingers on her lap. "I start my practice next week, after Thanksgiving. And after the New Year," she motioned to Derek, "we'll be married in August of '86."

Dr. Yu smiled, surprised. "Oh, congratulations!" He looked at Derek. "I'll be voting for you by the way. Burns," he shook his head," that tool has got to go!"

Derek laughed and shifted the weight of his wool long coat to the other arm, then rubbed his tired eyes. "Oh she is definitely a tool and thank you. Your vote is much appreciated." Now that he was out of the cold and in the heat of Yu's practice building, he wanted to roll up his sleeves and loosen his tie, but he knew that wasn't appropriate. It was barely 11:00 in the morning. His day wasn't even half over yet. A man loosening his tie and rolling up his sleeves before 5:00 in the afternoon was just wrong. It just seemed slothful and it gave the impression of lassitude. Derek folded his arms under the drape of his coat.

"So, why have you come to see me today?" Yu asked.

"I have scars," Angelique said, pointing over her shoulder. "On my back. And with the wedding coming up the year after next, I was hoping that...maybe there was a new procedure that could be done. To fade them before then."

Dr. Yu nodded, slipped his glasses on, washed his hands quickly at the sink, and reached for a pair of latex gloves. "What happened?"

"It was an accident. When I was little." She paused and went silent. Derek could tell her dread was rising. "I got attacked by a wolf."

Yu looked startled. For a brief moment he didn't stir.

He didn't even blink. "A wolf?"

Angelique nodded. "When I was nine. On a hunting trip."

Dr. Yu sat on a stool and moved closer on squeaking wheels. Then opened the back of her gown and studied the old wounds closely.

From what she had told Derek, she took over 200 stitches and the scars looked like it. Three flat, thin lines skewed across the entire width of her back. They were smooth and slightly lighter than the pigment of her brown skin.

"I apologize for my cold hands." Yu reached up and lightly touched each of the slanting scars like a blind man reading brail, then he moved back around to the other side of the table, reached up for a pamphlet mounted by the door, and handed it to her.

Angelique read the cover page in silence. Then, "DermiScar Silicone Sheet Technology...What's this?"

"What you are holding is the latest scar management product. It's of high interest to plastic surgeons and burn centers. Even at Scott Joplin, the burn unit there is using them to help reduce the appearance of severe scarring."

"How does it work?"

"Each sheet is lined on one side with medical grade silicone gel. You have to wear them for twenty-four hours a day for a period of eight to twelve weeks."

"But I'm a runner," Angelique said, "won't they sweat off?"

"If you find them coming off after a work out, just shower and pat your skin dry then gently wash the silicone sheet and reapply it immediately. Try not to get lotions on them. If you keep the sheets washed and clean, they should last for a three month treatment."

Angelique let out a deep breath and nodded.

"Please understand, the scars will never go away fully," Yu said.

Derek knew those words were like the coldest draft through her heart. Angelique said nothing right away. She just glanced down helplessly at the pamphlet in her hands. Derek wanted to hold her just then. But he knew that even his embrace would not fix her pain. He'd told her time and time again that her back didn't matter to him. Yet she would always answer in a tone that would harbor no comfort. She hated the scars.

He pulled at the cotton of his shirt collar. For some reason it began to irritate the skin of his neck.

"They happened when you were very young," Dr. Yu continued, "and though they're old and not as discolored as they once were, they're very deep, penetrating every dermal layer. I don't want to give you false hope. As a surgeon I'm sure you understand that even with modern technology, there is no sure fix for deep set scarring. But, I guarantee that if you're diligent about using them, by your wedding day they'll be looking a lot more forgettable."

Angelique nodded but his last words didn't seem to lighten the disheartened look on her face. "Thank you."

"You're welcome. I'll write your prescription today."

♛

After Angelique's appointment, it was close to noon.

Under the gaze of the midday sun the winter cold refused to ease. When Derek put the key in the ignition snow began to fall. Coming down like a thick curtain of white frost.

"Are you okay?" he asked.

Angelique pulled the passenger door shut. "I'm fine." She made her seat belt click and looked out the window to the falling snow.

Derek regarded her melancholy expression and found himself holding his breath. Since the charity ball, signals had passed between them which he found difficult to interpret. Maybe it had to do with the move or taking on a new residency at one of the most competitive hospitals in the country. Perhaps the wedding was too much on top of the campaign. But even so, Angelique never lost her temper. Not once in the nine months he'd known her.

"Are you hungry?" he asked her.

"Starving." She looked at him and the corners of her mouth went up in a slight grin. "I haven't been out to a good restaurant in my hometown in a long time. Surprise me."

Derek drove to Le Perroquet. He thought dining at the French sanctuary would lighten her mood. But he also chose it because the restaurant was on the Gold Coast, which meant that it was close to home. He had a 2:00 meeting with Prescott, Garrett, and Wendell. By the time they ordered, ate and he dropped her off at home, he would make it to his office just in time.

He parked at 70 East Walton Place and escorted his fiancé inside. There were plenty of restaurants in the city to feed anyone's cravings. Le Perroquet was the one place to get the best French cuisine the Windy City had to offer.

Angelique commented on being surprised by the elevator ride to the restaurant's third floor and the instant they were seated at a back corner booth, Derek could not help but notice her brown eyes taking in all of the lighting, paintings, and antique embellishments.

This time of day was the loudest and busiest. Every table was filled with suits dining for business lunches or spending what time they could with their spouses before heading back to their offices. But it wasn't just the lunchtime rush that had every seat occupied. This cold outside, no one felt like cooking for anything other than Thanksgiving dinner, so every restaurant in the city swelled with patrons before the holidays. Today Derek knew he was guilty of the same time crisis. But tonight they would all be heading out on the road for three days and two nights of quality time at the Mammoths.

Their waiter appeared in seconds with two menus and an ice-cold pitcher of water. Angelique shrugged up at him, admitting that she had no idea what to order. Derek ordered the Perroquet duck with apples for himself and a glass of Chateau Haut Brion wine. Catering to Angelique's love of seafood he ordered the traditional French bouillabaisse for her and promised that she would love it. When he offered a taste of the wine, she declined, opting instead for a slice of lemon for the water.

Derek took a sip of water and leaned back in his chair, enjoying the atmosphere. Letting the live buzz of conversation drift around him. When the server left, he spoke. "What's wrong? You seem sad since we left the office."

Angelique shrugged nonchalantly. "I'm fine. It's just been a busy weekend, that's all. I'll feel better when I settle into my practice."

One of Angelique's most outstanding talents was staying in content spirits in front of anyone, no matter how bad she was feeling. He had seen her turn on such charm in front of a four year old little boy in less than ten minutes the child had all but forgotten he had a mother not ten feet from him and the boy was perfect content with abandoning her all together. Elderly men were no exception to her charms and they often found "old school" ways of hitting on her in some way or another. Derek had quickly become well familiarized to this however, so her graceful little shrug off bore little effect on him.

"You want to tell me what's really wrong?" he said. "If it's the wedding, we can —"

"No," she said, cutting him off. "It's not the wedding. I don't feel pressured or rushed. I just…" She went quiet and absently reached a hand to the hemp napkin next to her plate. "Do you ever feel overwhelmed by all of the people that know who you are?"

"No," he said without a pause.

"Do you ever feel overwhelmed by all the people who don't know who you are?"

That paused him. A question like that only meant one thing. On only two occasions had Derek ever discussed the Big Family Secret. At the age of nine, he asked his mother why his father never came to see him. That question sparked summer visits at the DeGrate household—but Derek was always introduced by Viola to house guests as the son of a family friend. Almost ten years later, at his high school graduation, with complete shock all over his face, he asked his mother why Duke had actually come to see him. That sparked the letters. His father always loved it when Derek wrote to him. Over the years, the older they both got, the closer they had become.

He imagined their bond was because Viola had little power to stop it once her husband's bastard son had become a full grown adult. For the past ten years, Derek spent every Thanksgiving with the DeGrates and every Christmas Day with Patricia. But his biological father was never discussed. His mother had once told him Duke's name wasn't even on his birth certificate.

Now, looking into the curious eyes of his future wife, Derek was happy for the secluded corner booth they sat in. Was it so wrong? Her wanting to know the truth of the family she was marrying into? He could not blame her for wanting the answer to the same question he had asked himself as a boy. He could suddenly see a different Derek Porter staring back at the beautiful woman who sat across from him—a Derek Porter who was no longer a roving ladies' man. For all of the women who had lain in his bed, he had remained a bachelor and one of the reasons why had just come spilling out of Angelique's mouth. There was never a woman whom Derek felt at ease with—and trusted enough—to bring into a family that was built of so many defamations and sordid details. But he intended to marry her. With that affirmation, Derek knew she had to know the truth. Because it was a secret that would jeopardize everything he stood for in the city, should she ask the wrong person.

"I once told you about our family secret," he began, keeping his voice calm and low, "and that there is a lot of mystery shrouded around who my father is. Now, I'm going to tell you why. My mother married a man named Charles Matthews. He died just before I was born."

"I remember you telling me that."

Derek shook his head. "He was not the man my mother's side of the family was led to believe."

Her brow lifted. "Who did they believe he was?"

"My father."

Angelique blinked, stunned.

She leaned forward and lowered her voice. "They don't know who your father is either?"

Derek took another sip of his water. When he opened his mouth to speak, their waiter arrived with the Chateau. He waited until the glass was poured and the server was gone before he spoke. "Duke is a very important man in this city," he began. "He's also a very feared man. Years ago, when I was a boy, he ruled a very powerful street mob. The King's Disciples. He was the ultimate voice and he comanded them in all things. All actions and inactions were meted out through him. The Disciples were erected to protect the southside from hate crimes. To protect the children and the elderly and the mothers from the violence of the times. In the 60's, no black man could walk down the streets of Chicago without being in fear for his life from a white policeman. But the southside was differrent. Anywhere the Disciples lived, the police were kept in line and their people were kept safe. Parks were clean. Graffiti was removed from the school walls. Old churches were renovated. That spoke volumes to the disadvantaged who felt locked out of society. And so, Duke was revered as the King Of The South.

"Over the years what he created became the very same monster that they were supposed to protect their people from. Duke's Disciples were lost to him. Even though that broke my father's heart, he didn't give up on this city. He gave up his crown and set his sights on the legitimate way of life. As a furrier. A decade later, he is well on his way to becoming a real estate giant, he has the most successful furrier trade in the country and Viola, runs a well-heeled interior decorating business. Be that as it may — in spite of how hard he's worked to clean up the Family name — his days as a gangster still follow him. In my world of political affairs, if certain people ever found out who my father is..."

"They would make things very difficult for you," she said, finishing his sentence. Derek regarded her with a look of sudden ease. He caught himself holding his breath.

A moment of silence passed between them. He was nervously waiting to hear what she had to say next. It's not every day that a man tells a woman his father is known as a notorious criminal. But she didn't look in the least bit surprised. She looked quite accepting if not empathetic.

"Your image would be all but destroyed," she said quietly. "That's for sure. Not to mention your livelihood. I know the feeling. Every family has its secrets, Derek. Even the most prestigious. And if anyone tells you otherwise, trust me, they are so far flung from the truth." She slowly shook her head. "They either don't know their relatives at all, or they're lying right to your face." Angelique took a deep breath. She'd stopped playing with the napkin and looked down to her lap.

Her words came without an ounce of judgment. In that moment Derek couldn't have loved her more. "For all his faults," he said, "he's still my father, Angie. In spite of all evils that darken the streets, Chicago is still my home. I love my father. I love my city. And I love them both enough to protect them."

She looked at him and smiled. "And that's why I love you. At least you have a father. And I can tell he loves you very much."

There was a muted sadness in her smile. It made him sorely aware Angelique was taken from her father as a child and raised by her grandmother. Just as he opened his mouth to lighten the mood, their waiter reappeared without warning holding a bottle of Chateau Haut Brion, Cru Classe Des Graves 1855. Wrapped in cloth to protect his hands from the chill, the wine was unopened. It was not the wine he had ordered.

"Sir," the waiter said with a genteel nod. "The gentlemen at the far table to your right send their best regards."

They both looked past their waiter to a corner booth on the other side of the restaurant. Derek did well in hiding disbelief. Two men nodded promptly in greeting at him.

"Who are they?" Angelique asked.

Derek motioned a hand for the waiter to sit the bottle on the table and thanked him. Their waiter opened the Chateau, let it breath, then disappeared into the kitchen. Derek raised his wine glass to the men then looked at Angelique.

"The taller, gray haired man in the dark blue suit, sitting on the right side of the table…The one with the cruel eyes who looks like no stiff wind from hell or heaven could knock him over…that's Ugo Brassi."

"Lawyer?" she guessed.

Derek shook his head. "Industrialist and former head of the Ugo Corporation. And the short, fat man sitting across from him, with the receding hairline, is his lawyer. Calvino Cironei."

"What kind of industrialist?"

"He used to be one hell of a big fish in steel, textiles, mines, and metals."

"Used to be? What happened?"

Derek gave a sniff to the wine then sipped it. "Same thing that always happens when a war ends," he said. "After World War II, there was vast competition from Japan — which caused a decline in exports and from there, interest difficulties arose and a decline in production caused a massive tank in stock. Their company is still family owned by Italians, but the Brassi's haven't been the corporate power they once were in more than 30 years." Now Derek's mind was reeling. Explaining who Ugo Brassi was to her made him extremely curious about why the man would send a $2,000.00 bottle of wine. If that was a baited hook, Derek bit it. He took another sip of his wine and stood from their corner booth. "I'm going to say hello," he said. "I'll be back in a few minutes."

Angelique nodded and watched him make his way through the tables and the hectic bustle of waiters.

ANGELIQUE

Angelique looked up when Derek returned to their table.

It had only been minutes, but from where she sat watching, their brief chat seemed pressing. With a nod in the direction of Brassi's table, he said, "Care to meet a corporate legend?"

"Does he bite?"

"Only if you sign a non-disclosure consensual sex agreement. I heard Cironei is quite good at those."

She smiled, then stood and followed him through the tables. "What about our food?"

"The maître d' will take care of that."

Derek led her to a table near the center of the restaurant where Brassi and Cironei had been reseated. Another waiter brought the Chateau and began placing serving dishes. Angelique spoke hello to the men and Derek gave them a proper introduction. From up close, Brassi's frame looked lean and fit. He easily looked Duke's age of fifty-four — if not older. His thick gray hair lay straight back and shone like silver spun silk. Cironei looked even more like the typical Harvard grad up close. Unhealthy, with a protruding belly, a pockmarked nose, and a half balding head shining with beaded sweat.

Just when Angelique's stomach let out a low growl she hoped no one heard, two servers arrived with their meals.

A thick smell of sauces and broiled meats wafted up to her nose. It took less than a minute for them to serve up the dishes and disappear back into the kitchen. Angelique wasted no time delving into her seafood. When the men were a few bites in, Brassi spoke.

"I'll get straight to the point, Councilman. I have quite a proposal for you. Once you've listened to what I have to say, you can take some time to deliberate on it before you make a decision."

Derek nodded. "Alright."

"I heard a voice on the wind recently. That you're having problems with the *Chicago Sun Times*. Problems which put your *Chicago Eagle* at risk."

Angelique knew the *Chicago Eagle* was once owned by Derek's grandfather, Colton Porter, who had acquired the parent company, Windy City Newspapers Inc., in November of 1945. When he passed away, Derek inherited the ownership and responsibility of protecting its interests. Angelique fairly enjoyed reading the *Eagle*. It served as her megaphone for views on taxes, national security, politics, business, and local news on sports and entertainment. She couldn't help but to feel thrown off by Brassi's sudden accusation that Derek's paper was in difficulties.

"My newspaper is in no more jeopardy than any other newsprint in this city," Derek said. "So your source is mistaken."

"Feuding editors and journalists — who've gone public with their disputes — are my source," Brassi answered. "There is no being mistaken about that."

"In time, I'm more than confident we can repair the situation with our writers and publishing staff."

"I doubt it," Brassi disagreed.

"And why is that?"

"Well, let's see, several of the journalists, who once wrote for the *Eagle*, expressed outrage that their reported articles on city-wide racial injustices were being down-played and flat out overlooked by the editors. Articles on unequal employment opportunities...redlining and sub prime loans and the lack of grant funding for minority education — these stories were often rejected by your editor in chief. During a recent ASNE panel discussion tempers flared when several editors complained about *Eagle* reporters constantly covering the difficulties of racial strife instead of focusing on the positive endeavors of the city. Then, one of your own editors, Halbert Algrin, took the floor and actually had the gall to comment on the inferiority of minority issues compared to the overall grand scheme of mass majority success. I have to say, it was a well versed and clever spoken way of telling blacks to go fuck themselves."

Angelique's fork froze as her mouth paused mid-chew. Suddenly she was acutely aware that knives were on the table. Derek was not a physically violent man and the instant she thought about their discussion ending in bloodshed she knew it was absurd. But if she could think it then Derek certainly wasn't above contemplating several good places to plant sharp steel in Brassi's flesh.

Her fiancé did not look pleased.

His expression was no less than goaded and before he had a chance to retort, Brassi continued, "After that nasty incident, eight journalists left the *Eagle* and went to write for other publishing factions. Six of whom now write for the *Chicago Sun Times*. That's quite a blow since each of them have thousands of devoted readers who bought the *Eagle* just to read their columns. A daily newspaper with a print run of 400,000. No one at this table has to be a genius to do the math here. Ink and newsprint accounts for 25 percent of production costs and just this year alone your average price per paper had to increase by more than 50 percent just to keep your head above water and make a profit.

"Last year a man could go to the newsstand and drop two quarters down on the counter and walk away happy. Now he has to pay more than a dollar. The *Eagle* was raking in $460,000 daily from sales. Those sales have declined significantly from the loss of your journalists and I'm sure several advertisers have pulled out as well. With salaries...print and distribution costs...lose your readers and you're set to face falling revenues, falling circulation, and a devastating collapse of goodwill and support that can not be recovered. You're running for Mayor. Do you really think you can afford to lose the voice and the ear of the people? With the election less than four months away, Alderman, I truly don't think you have the time to find out. You need to reclaim the readers of this city. And you need the minority vote as much as you need the white ballots."

Angelique caught herself regarding Derek in the long silence that followed with a wary expression. It was too late to retract it. Cironei looked impassive as ever. Sliding another forkful of steak into the plump jowls of his mouth like Brassi had simply made a blasé comment on Derek's tie. He must have been used to Brassi's bluntness when proposing business.

Derek chewed mechanically.

Using the time to think.

While he said nothing at first a slight smile tugged at the corner of his lips. It must have been in that moment Ugo Brassi knew he had him. In that moment, the corporate contender didn't let up.

"I've done my homework," Brassi said. "I know you're bleeding." He took a sip of his wine and continued. "You and I both know it's politically advantageous to have the muscle of the media behind you. I once ran the *Chicago Sentinel*, a very prominent magazine in the 1960's and 70's. I was an influential publisher once. I can be so again. I still have contacts and associates in the press. So, either you can choke softly on the wad of debt you're soon to incur or you can take me on as an investor and partner." Brassi paused. Then, "To hold sway over readers of your newspaper and a reemerging quarterly magazine would give you a power of speech not even the *Sun Times* or the *Tribune* could contend with."

Derek calmly took another bite of his duck, took his time to swallow, and said, "Why would a pure born Sicilian magnate like yourself want to invest in a partnership with a black-owned newspaper? Knowing full well what this sort of unanny association would do to your, how should I put it...clandestine connections?"

Angelique may have been unfamiliar with Derek's careful wordage. But she was sure "clandestine connections" referred to the Cosa Nostra, so the question seemed just. Why would any Italian Mafia mogul want to help the black community?

Brassi let out a slow breath. "I'm a deep-rooted man, filled with regret. Deserving of redemption. I have friends I should have helped more and enemies I should have fought harder. That dream is not gone from me, Councilman. But my proposal comes with one trivial condition."

"And that is?"

"You must alter your editorial policies and let your advertisers jump ship."

"Absolutely not!" Derek spat.

"Oh, but you will," Brassi said, equally curt. "You will if you want to win this election. You know that you need the black vote. You know you need the white vote." His brow lifted and his eyes went stern. "But there are shades in between you have not considered...Little Italy...Chinatown. Pilsen. La Villita. And that's just to name a few and I have employment relations with all of them.

"Your competition, Jayne Burns, has the backing of the *Chicago Sun Times*. Her husband owns it. She would have a stroke if she read a press release stating the Ugo Corporation was backing you and the *Sentinel* was re-emerging. There is no better way to send a message that this election will not be easily won for her. Once that hits the streets of this city, Burns' enemies will flock to you faster than bees to a berry."

♛

Angelique kept quiet for the drive home. She could tell Derek was still irritated by the tight knuckled grip he held on the steering wheel. Ten minutes later, they walked through the front door and she broke the silence once she'd made it past the foyer.

"What the hell was that all about?"

"Just business, love."

Angelique watched him slip off his long coat and hang it on the coat stand, and walk towards the bar. He loosened his tie and took an empty glass from the overhead shelf.

Angelique sat her foil duck on the hall table then hung up her coat and went over to the bar, watching Derek in silence as he poured a glass of bourbon. As far as she knew, he only drank when the stress hit him. She inwardly hoped it wouldn't become a hard habit in the next few months. "That didn't seem like just business to me," she pressed. "And they didn't seem like they liked you very much."

"Oh, but it was business," Derek said. "Because business has nothing to do with like."

She cut her eyes away to the floor and exhaled. "Let me see if I can wrap my head around what just happened back there. Ugo Brassi just offered to bail you out of financial straits with the newspaper, in exchange for a partnership, and the chance to crush Burns come February? Derek, clearly he has ulterior motives that you don't know about. Did I miss anything?"

He took another long swallow and sat the glass down on the bar. "No. And that's why I love you."

DARRION

The DeGrate family hunting trip left for Galena at 1900.

Tradition demanded deer meat for Thanksgiving and because Duke demanded tradition, the entire family gathered at his estate in Highland Park, piled into several cars, and headed north.

Darrion drove his father's Mercedes with Duke riding passenger. Devin and uncle Donald chattered with each other in the back seat while Fang sat quietly beside them, gazing out of the window. All of the women — Angelique, DaVita, uncle Donald's wife, Mary, and uncle Dutch's wife, Melody — climbed into Viola's Range Rover.

Derek drove Roth Garrett's Jeep Cherokee, which had plenty of room for Prescott, Garrett, Wendell and Duke's sibling pit bulls, Legend and Luna. Much to Donald and Mary's pleasant surprise, Derek had volunteered babysitting their twins, Olivia and Donell. Last in the DeGrate motorcade was T-Bone's Chevy Suburban — its roof piled high with hunting gear and camping equipment. Taran, Lunch, and Ronnie rode with him. Watching over a chest filled with enough weapons to conquer Manchuria.

Darrion would have much preferred the women and children be left behind, but it was his father's wish. Viola was no stranger to guns but she knew nothing about hunting and had openly voiced she would take no part in running around in the bushes getting her ass cold. Mannerly as ever. DaVita said she would be helping cook dinner and had better things to do than shooting guns. However, Derek's soon-to-be was utterly thrilled to take down game for the holiday feast. Rumor had it the good doctor even brought her own sniper rifle.

Olivia and Donell were only nine years old. Accidents could happen, no matter how cautious the hunters. Two years in Vietnam taught Darrion that much. Nothing was more gruesome than the meeting of a child with a bullet. With Donald as the religious spear of the family, Darrion doubted the twins had ever seen a gun, let alone watched their father — reserved Bishop of St. Victor Catholic — use one to kill.

Darrion never had the luxury of being untried with guns. By the age of eleven, steel become more familiar than his own skin and by now their names were a song to him. Smith & Wesson. Hecklor & Koch. Springfield. Mossberg. Colt. Remington. They each told a story of violence and death. To have children around them at such a young age. If uncle Donald was fine with that, then so be it.

The Family arrived in Galena just after 2200 and much to Darrion's surprise, they had managed to unload all of their belongings and settle into the grand lodge cabin in under 30 minutes. From what Duke told him during the drive, the massive brick house was built in the 1890's. In all it had 8 bedrooms, 4 bathrooms, a large dining area, wide kitchen, a wrap around porch, and a second story deck for star gazing and nature viewing. Darrion planned to do neither. Less than 200 hundred paces away stood a small two-bedroom guest lodge. Every room was well furnished. Every wall festooned with mounted skins, paintings, brass sconces, and the skilled work of taxidermists. What impressed Darrion the most was the carpenter sized fire place which spread wide enough to lay on and tall enough to stand in.

Everyone's sleeping arrangements were yet to be decided, but he assumed they would all mete it out themselves. Darrion and Fang planned to head out before midnight and take to the forest before their cover of darkness lost its advantage. If they found a high enough branch to post by dawn any white tails passing their aim would be well spotted before they were alarmed enough to flee. Taran and T-Bone could lead everyone else out in the morning.

Rural landowners offered the hunting of white tail and mule deer, Merriam turkey, elk, bison, and antelope, but it was only white tail that they would be stalking. Tonight, Fang looked like the Japanese Ainu Ezo warriors in the stories of his boyhood. The old warrior wore a thick gray wolf's fur coat over silk black robes. Each layer of his ceremonial dress bore bold red and white swirling patterns. Boots made of embroidered salmon skin spared his steps from the ice and snow. Detailed carvings of the animal Gods decorated the bamboo scabbard of his katana, as well as the necklace that hung low over the strap of his furred arrow case. Fang had pulled up his silvered hair to a tightly coiled bun and secured it with what looked like a set of chop sticks at first glance. Darrion knew they were a pair of sharp poisoned daggers. Fang had long lived a life in Japan Darrion could scarcely imagine. He hoped to go there someday and learn the culture. Fang teaching him to speak Japanese and Chinese stood as hardly enough.

Tonight, Darrion's own gear was more like his father's. A stealth hunter snow camo vest and pants. A heavy white snow camo coat. Matching gloves and boots.

A week before the hunt, Darrion had placed his clothing in a compact tightly sealed bin with sage brush, pine needles, and wood bark from the preserve they would be hunting in. When it came to scent, there were two types: those that attract and those that mask. Fang specialized in mixing his own *doe in heat* recipe. He never explained how he made it but it mirrored both doe and dominate buck urine. Somehow his mixture of lures formed a soft clear balm, which he had put in small jars for everyone to use. Like Fang had done, Darrion rubbed some of the doe lures on his right boot and buck lures on his left—to mimic the scent trail of an eager buck following a willing doe. He often wanted to ask why Tu Fang never sold his formula. It worked like magic and every hunting season he had kills to show for it. Last year Darrion took to using arrows for the the buck he brought for the feast.

This year, Darrion would try Taran's latest steel obsession: the Italian Benelli M1 Super 90 12-gauge. According to Taran's animated description, you could go pump or auto. With a pistol grip and dedicated weapon light, six saddle shell holders ran flush with the stock. Taran even went so far as to have it painted to snow camo. It was an early Christmas gift. While everyone else in the family gifted clothing or books or some other mark of current times, Taran Carter always gave him guns.

Darrion strapped his knife sheath tight to his left thigh and made sure the gun holster held tight to his right. He could feel the weight of the Desert Eagle it braced but it wasn't near enough to cause a limp. Most live game enthusiasts would deem a pistol of that magnitude overkill but anything that could strike back and take his life was worth a powerful side-arm. Several cougar sightings had been reported in the last few months and Darrion was taking no chances. He even had it modified with laser sighting. Just a slight touch of the trigger and the beam came alive. A bullet always hit where the red dot marked.

While everyone dressed for sleep and filled the cabin with the loud chatter of politics and religious convictions, Darrion and Fang slipped away unnoticed into the night. It was still hours before dawn and the night sky was silent and gray enough to keep their footsteps lit.

Fang set the pace, trekking away from the south end of the grand lodge towards the thick of the Mammoth's forest. For an old man, the Ezo could move when he had to. Darrion had to push hard just to keep up. By the time they neared the Mammoth's wood, they were more than a mile south of all the lodges and snow began to fall.

Fang looked flushed and exhilarated.

His Asian eyes round. Keen with a subdued eagerness that only hunters — trained to wait for the kill — knew.

"Kon'ya wa tokubetsuna kikaidesu," Fang said with a sure nod.

Darrion looked at him in surprise. "Why is tonight a special occasion?"

"Yumewomita."

"What dream?" Darrion was aware he sounded like an eager child. Never had Fang discussed his dreams. Many occasions Darrion had come to him with questions about a strange sleep or nightmare he'd had. Always Fang told Darrion what his nightmares meant. But the warrior never spoke on his own dreams.

Not once in the twenty-eight years he had known him.

"Kon'ya no kami wa anata ni jibun jishin o akiraka ni surud-
earou."

Darrion didn't know if it was the hard wind or the old Ezo's
words that sent a chill racing up his spine, but there was
foreboding in him. He didn't know if Ainu Gods were real. But,
if Fang dreamed of the Gods revealing themselves, tonight
would be the time for the core of his spirituality.

An *iomante*, from his studies, meant to worship in ceremony
then kill an animal in order to send their soul to heaven as a
blessing from mankind. Each animal represented a powerful
God. All Ainu of his tribe coveted him as a great seer. Darrion
held reservations as to whether or not he was ever wrong. If Fang
did, in fact, just say 'Gods,' then there would be much killing on
this night.

A killing of more than one beast.

♔

Angelique frowned at the window. Watching Darrion and Tu
Fang disappear into the distance. A shiver from the cold of their
bedroom made her want to put her coat back on. When they had
chosen the upstairs room on the south end corner of the lodge,
she had no idea it would carry all the chill of the grave. She
shivered again. At her back Derek unzipped the luggage on their
bed.

Harsh winds rocked the trees below and far off into the
coldness. Both men walking toward the Mammoth's wood now
looked so small. So vulnerable as their frames began to white out
in the storm. They disappeared into the thick trees like ewes
amidst unseen terrors of the night.

Angelique couldn't help but to wonder what two men meant
to seek in the dead of dark away from food and fire. Their family
hunt had yet to begin. They hadn't planned to leave out until 4:00
in the morning. It was barely past 10:00 the night before.

"Where's the quilt?" Derek asked. "The one your
grandmother gave to you? Tonight we're going to need it."

"It's in the large Louis at the foot of the bed," she said,
keeping her gaze out the window.

Derek reached for the Louis Vuitton and unzipped it. "It'll take hours before the fireplace warms the entire house." He unfolded the heavy quilt and held it up as if he were admiring its embroidery. "This'll do just fine."

"Where are they going?"

Derek lowered the quilt and looked up at her. "Who?"

She gave a nod to the window. "Darrion and Tu Fang. They made off into the trees. Alone. It's practically freezing out there."

"If those two are with each other trust me, dove, they are anything but alone and I have seen Fang make a fire hotter than hell's waiting room, so they'll be fine."

"But what are they doing? Fang looks like he's dressed for some kind of ceremony."

"Ah," Derek nodded with a smile. Her inquiry suddenly made sense to him. "Every year, before the hunt, Fang and Darrion have a worship sacrament for the Gods of the Wood. They go out into the middle of the forest to pray for protection for the men and the safety of the women who await their return while they're away."

"Women aren't allowed at this sacrament I suppose?" She could hear him sliding an empty suitcase from under their bed. He set to moving back and forth from the bed to the dresser. Placing clothes and toiletries in the drawers.

"You suppose correctly," he answered. "But even if you were invited, would you really want to be out at night on an empty stomach and pray in the dark snow around animals that could easily fill their bellies with you instead of the other way around?"

He had a point. Just the thought of being mauled in the dark by some pissed off beast made her cringe. Though it had been years since the accident left her back marred, the terror was still too near. Most nights Angelique slept well, but on rare occasion the wolf came like it always did. Its yellow eyes and storm-grey fur stalking closer. Drowning out her whimpering cries with its dooming low growl and bloodstained teeth.

"No," Angelique finally said, turning back to Derek. She went to their bed. Sliding off her boots, she slipped under the cold sheets, fully clothed, then pulled the quilt to her chin. "Take a nap with me. We can go downstairs and eat later."

Derek put the last of their things in a drawer, pulled off his boots, slid in bed, and pulled her into his chest. Angelique closed her eyes to the rhythm of his breathing and hoped sleep would be free of the wolf tonight.

♕

The hunt was underway just before dawn. Darrion waited patiently as everyone gathered at Fang's pyre and quietly set to snuffing out the flames with clomps of dirt. Duke brought the dogs and kept a firm grip on their leashes. Legend looked eager to break free and give chase to anything. A strong gust rippled his sleek white coat and he narrowed his eyes and stared off into the trees as if he could see all of the wood with one glance. His wet nose twitched at scents the winds blew his way. Luna was absent of a hand reaching down to stroke her black coat. She held true to her namesake and stood with her bright yellow eyes staring up at the moon as if it would drop out of the sky and come to her.

Darrion's father looked alert and healthy in spite of his heart sickness and he sounded more alive than ever as he howled laughter and joked with uncle Dutch and Angelique. Fang kept quiet as always. His eyes to the trees. Off into the distance. Uncle Donald had his rifle draped over his shoulder and stood filming everyone and everything that came into focus with his video camera.

Darrion was surprised at the rifle Angelique held. Just last year, Taran had told him the PGM 338 was completely sold out. How she had gotten a hold of one — a snow-camo painted one at that — was beyond him. Even still, it was a good choice for a hunt, especially with a silencer. Because of its lightweight; loaded with a scope it was no more than seven kilograms. A few hours of lugging her steel around in the snow she wouldn't be exhausted. Darrion knew he wouldn't end up carrying it for her.

T-Bone, Taran, Lunch, and Ronnie huddled amongst themselves thirty paces off. Too far off for Darrion to catch the focus of their conversation. He could tell by the animation of Taran's hands they were talking guns. Derek, Prescott, and Garrett stood together, equally dressed in hunting gear. Darrion could tell Garrett wasn't as experienced a hunter as he had let on to be. The extra slugs for his 12-gauge were slipped into his vest backwards. He'd have a hard time reloading if he grabbed them red first instead of brass first. Darrion thought of telling him, but then looked down to Garrett's side-arm and decided he didn't care to. A Smith & Wesson 39. Poor choice, but to each his own.

Devin had Wendell's undivided attention, explaining features of their rifles like a hired gunsmith. He looked well clothed in snow camo hunting wears and Darrion couldn't help but to notice his lanky frame stood a little taller. Perhaps how he held his rifle gave off the look of maturity. Their last hunting season had been his first close brush with death, even observing it. Watching Duke shoot a white tail left a shock on Devin's face that reminded Darrion of the sheltered Gold Coast up-bringing he had.

Viola had given birth to his younger brother after the family made good on acquired property and their Cabrini days were nearly over. Devin never knew the slums like Darrion did. He never knew the cruelty of beings. Darrion was grateful for that until Devin's first hunt. He looked at the dying deer like he had just found out all at once that Santa, the Easter Bunny, and the Tooth Fairy did not exist. But with their father's careful coaxing, he overcame his initial shock of death quite easily. Now, he looked hardened somewhat. As if any innocence in his eyes the last time he had stood in the Mammoth trees was gone. Darrion felt proud of him for that.

Every snow covered tree loomed over the frozen ground like a white great wall built to blot out the sun. In the Mammoth's wood, not even moonlight could penetrate the far reach of the branches. Taran decided to lead the group with Darrion and Fang stalking behind as watch. With eleven men and one woman trailing them in the near darkness, they would need all of the visual scrutiny they could get. They would leave the pyre then head southeast towards Mammoth River.

Darrion stood and wiped his gloved hands on his camo pants then drew in a lungful of air. A light sound of mechanical whirring caught his attention. He looked about and almost drew back from his uncle. Donald zoomed in, moving at his face with a camera. Darrion hated being filmed.

"Get that camera out of my face, Uncle Duck."

Like paparazzi, uncle Donald smiled mischief, ignored him, and kept filming. Then shifted his lens to Dutch's loud beckoning. "See this?" he boasted. "I want everybody to watch me get stealth." Gliding a black war paint stick on his face, Dutch smiled at the camera. "Be ready so you don't have to get ready."

"You're blacker than a cave full of crows without the paint," Duke spat.

"Kiss my ass, Duke."

"And you need to put down that camera and make sure you know how to shoot that thing," Duke said to Donald with a quick glance to his weapon. "You remember what happened last time."

"What happened last time?" Angelique asked.

Donald put the camera down and lifted a finger in self-defense. "That was my first time shooting a double barrel. I wasn't used to the recoil. It could've happened to anybody."

Duke rolled his eyes. Dutch grumbled low in his throat. Angelique looked at both men as if she knew they had a different take on things.

Darrion shook his head and kept his mouth shut.

She didn't. "What happened?"

"The gun left him," Duke said.

"And that steel had a motor on it," Dutch said, giving a flipping motion with his hands. "Spun off clear back over his head. Scared off every white tail we had in our sights, too."

Angelique lifted a hand from her rifle and covered her laugh. Then she looked down at his weapon. Her laughter came to an abrupt halt. "Wow. That's a L96. Bolt action...Are you sure you know how to use that thing?"

Donald pointed to the barrel's tip. "Last time I checked the bullets come out of this end."

She reached a hand down to his rifle and flipped the safety switch at the rear from white to red. "They do now."

Duke and Uncle Dutch burst into loud laughter. Fang even smiled at her. Everyone else must have been listening because they were laughing moreover.

Uncle Donald looked as humiliated as any embarrassed man could look. "I know that," he spat, trying to mend his dignity.

Angelique took a step back as if bowing out gracefully, but held a sly smirk on her face. "Alright then. Please excuse me."

"Swing that camera back my way," Dutch ordered. He picked

up where he had left off. Smearing his face with the paint stick. "Watch me get incog-negro." His features twisted to mock a war face. Donald resumed filming Dutch's cocky grin.

Everyone's laughter was stilted at the sound of a low growl in the distance. Unless reality cheated his mind, Darrion never knew deer to make such a sound. Cougars were indeed out there, however large cats gave a different grumble of a threat. This sounded much bigger. Another growl pierced the darkness. It came just as menacing. Sounding much closer than before.

Fang moved closer and slightly unsheathed his sword, pausing the steel as the blade collar cleared the scabbard. Angelique moved forward a few paces then stopped, dropped to one knee, and put an eye to her riflescope. On instinct, Darrion released the safety on his Benelli, taking aim into the darkness of the trees.

"What is it?" Devin asked, blinking fear.

"Quiet," Darrion said.

Legend and Luna padded close to Darrion's boots and growled back at the threat approaching in the underbrush. A sharp wind swirled a foul smell around them. It seemed to make the sibling Pitts growl louder. Even more fiercely. All went silent when the wind paused abruptly. Too silent. Now the darkness seemed to grow and draw out.

Just as Darrion thought of firing a warning shot just to scare off whatever neared them, he heard Angelique's breath catch in her throat.

"100 meters and moving fast!"

"Your scope's got infrared," Darrion said. "What is it?"

"There's too many bushes in the way! Whatever they are they're right on us!"

"They?" Wendell nervously pushed his bifocals up his nose and stepped back behind Derek. His voice came so squeezed and tight, the words left his throat in a thinned whisper. "How many?"

"50 meters!" she said. "Shit, they're fast!"

Darrion narrowed his eyes at the underbrush. "If you have never fired a weapon before, get back."

Garrett, Wendell, and Devin fell behind the rest of the men. Catching a bullet in the back of his skull from the wayward aim of a startled trigger finger was the last thing he needed. He knew

Taran, T-Bone, and Lunch were secretly thanking him for that one. They didn't want to take an errant slug anymore than he did. Vietnam was riddled with dead soldiers killed by a fellow comrade's panick-shooting in the dark. Dreadlocks came into his peripheral. T-Bone had moved up to his side. Lunch and Taran did the same.

Darrion barely saw the first wolf. In a flash bushes parted, bursting snow, and Darrion saw hell. Before his brain could function to count how many wolves were racing towards them, he felt the air being knocked out of his lungs at the first trigger pull of his Benelli. If a slug didn't kill one of them, the muzzle flash alone would have set it's pelt on fire.

Wolves sprinted towards them, snarling and roaring. Angelique had already fired three bullets from her rifle. Everything around him was bullets, more bullets shouts, screams, and confusion.

Darrion shot down one wolf, took aim at another and kept firing. All that pierced his dread and panic was the harsh smell of gunpowder and blood and Devin's screams growing further and further away.

♛

Angelique heard the click when she squeezed the trigger. Ten bullets were gone before she could blink. She pulled another magazine from her thigh pouch, reloaded, and just as her finger neared the trigger, Devin screamed.

She put an eye to the rifle scope and spotted him running for his life through the trees but the wolf was gaining speed. If she tracked it, if she timed the shot just right, the bullet would miss the trees' bark and strike the predator gaining fast on Devin's heels. More predators were coming at her. She hoped the other men aimed well enough to kill them before they got close enough to strike.

Devin was fast, but four legs were faster than two. Just when his doom couldn't be any more real, he tripped and fell face down in the snow. He flipped over, wide eyed and trembling, his face full of dread, and crawled backward, screaming into the night as the wolf leaped for his face.

Now. She pulled the trigger, lifted her eye from the scope, and watched the wolf fall unmoving. Devin's scream was cut short with a face full of blood. The dead wolf skidded to a halt at his feet. Wiping the blood from his eyes with the back of his gloved hand, Devin blinked through the shock and scrambled to his feet.

When he looked in Angelique's direction, his red stained eyes grew even wider with fear. "Look out!"

Angelique didn't even see it.

The wolf came at her so fast the force of the blow knocked the wind from her lungs and hurled the rifle from her hands. Before she could grab at it, the weapon went spinning off into a thick of nearby bushes. Gray fur and yellow eyes ablaze was all she saw. One of its paws slammed into her as it nearly leapt clear over her head. Razor claws slashed through the dirt and snow as the wolf turned and came for her again. Angelique righted herself, pulled her side arm and her hunting knife, and took aim.

Her nightmares became reality. She was facing the one wolf of her dream terrors with shocking vivid clarity.

"No," she said through clenched teeth.

She fired again and missed. Molten eyes stalked closer. Fearless. Unflinching. The beast licked its yellow teeth and growled as it neared the kill.

She kept firing. Not thinking to count the rounds until she heard the dooming click of an empty chamber.

♕

Darrion heard the click.

His Benelli was empty.

No time to reload. He pulled his Eagle.

Fang unsheathed his sword.

Its steel made a piercing chime as it cleared the scabbard.

He aimed ready to strike. Three gray wolves were on them. Darrion only had time to fire at two before the third flew at Fang. He dodged claws and teeth then swung the katana with such force, the gray wolf was relieved of its head before it hit the ground.

Darrion looked left, right and locked eyes on T-Bone screaming out like an unleashed psychopath, firing his Uzi. Taran and Lunch were nowhere to be seen. Duke and Dutch were shooting a wolf tearing into Donald's leg. Derek had flung his rifle and was shooting his pistol at an angry gray giving chase to Wendell.

Everywhere Darrion looked blood, dead wolves, shell casings, and barrel smoke owned his vision.

Then came the worst of it all: Again Devin's screams.

♛

Angelique cursed. Slamming down her knife into the frozen ground, she reloaded, snatched her knife back up, and kept firing off more rounds. Now the wolf was close enough for a good aim. All of the bullets found flesh, but it was too large an animal. This time her mind sparked through the panic to count the rounds.

Five shots gone.

She tripped and fell on her back but kept firing.

Six. It kept moving closer. Angelique cursed and inched back farther.

Seven fired off but the beast still wasn't down.

"Shit!"

Eight. "Goddammit!"

Nine. Not only was it not down, it looked even more enraged from taking rounds into its flesh. If nine rounds failed to kill it, ten wouldn't save her from a bloody, brutal end. This night she would suffer more than a clawed back. Angelique did the only thing she could do. She lifted the gun to her head, shut her eyes tight, and as the wolf leaped to seal her fate, she screamed at the sound of the gunshot.

Her eyes leapt open.

Darrion stood over her. Before she could think of where he possibly could have come from, he fired two more rounds into its skull. He ejected the magazine and quickly slapped in another. Angelique blinked up at him trying to register the shock.

She should have been dead. She was supposed to be dead. But by some reason, she couldn't pull the trigger.

To slow her breathing, Angelique shut her eyes and took a deep breath. Seconds later she felt somewhat relieved it was over. Then a roaring flew past her ears and in a blink Darrion was on the ground fighting another wolf. Glittering steel spun off. His Eagle was knocked from his hand. Darrion cursed, pulled his long knife, and stabbed the wolf with all the strength he could muster.

Angelique fired the last shot from her pistol but the bullet struck snow. She looked in a panic for the Eagle and locked eyes on her rifle under a near bush. She sprinted for it, snatched it from the undergrowth, and took aim just as Darrion threw the wounded gray wolf off of him.

It was severely wounded. But not enough to stop it from striking for a kill.

Angelique fired. The wolf let out a sharp high-pitched yelp when the round struck right through its heart. Blood sprayed the snow and the wolf skidded sideways, breathing ragged, dying breaths. When the last pant of winter vapor escaped its nostrils, its chest went still.

Its eyes went unseeing.

♛

A familiar barking sounded out in the distance.

Darrion put a hand to his back and saw blood. He stood, grunting in pain, and looked down at the dead wolf. At the sound of another loud animal, he looked up. Legend was running from another wolf giving chase at his hide.

"Hold on, Legend!" Duke shouted.

Darrion spotted his father to his left at what seemed to be no more than one hundred paces away. Duke dropped to one knee to reload his rifle. Then his hand left the steel and clenched his chest. Duke cursed and fell over.

Angelique ran to his side and took aim. Darrion watched her first shot splinter the bark of a tree. Her second shot struck the wolf dead on. Instead of slowing, Legend kept running.

Darrion noticed suddenly all of the gunfire had ceased.

All around him white snow had fouled to red with blood. Another low growl came from a bush. Darrion readied his blade.

As the wolf came from the bushes he prepared to fight. But he didn't get a chance. What he mistook in the brush for another dead wolf, was Fang. His fur coat mocked a pelt of gray fur. Red silk from his garb mocked blood in the dark and snow and as he lay faking death next to a dead animal, Darrion never saw him coming.

Fang sprang to life, spinning out of his mock corpse and swiftly struck a deathblow to the airborne wolf. It landed with a high pitched wail of agony. Its entrails spilled out before the old Ainu. Raw, slick viscous lining coiled into a steaming red pile on the snow.

DUKE

Duke was in pain.

He coughed unhealthily and rubbed his chest.

Two heart attacks followed by angioplasty and stents. Every medication he was on, every ER visit, every close brush with death he'd ever had, it all came rushing to mind. For a short spell it was a sharp pain that quickly eased to a dull throb. It felt as if his heart might not forgive him this time. He had been given enough chances after all.

A dizzy spell rocked his skull and his vision blurred. Duke inhaled a lungful of cold air and blinked out of it.

"What the hell just happened?" Garrett spat to no one in particular. He stood bent at the waist with both hands on his knees. Breathing rutted huffs of vapor.

"What does it look like?" Darrion said, pointing his knife at the bloody intestines of the dead animal. "We just got attacked by a pack of wolves."

They all regrouped and stood encircled around the last wolf Fang had put down. Duke had counted fifteen slain. Not including the wolves that had run off. He gave thought to answering Garrett's question, but his tongue was leaden. Fighting off the ebb and flow of chest pains took the will for speech from him.

Remain calm, he thought. *Stay calm.*

One of his brothers was wounded. Donald was on the ground. Groaning in pain and clutching his left leg. Derek put a hand on his chest to keep him lying still on the ground. Devin was at his side as well. Looking on. Eyes wide. Angelique worked to stop the bleeding. Her hands moved at cutting away the shredded cloth of his pant leg with her hunting knife. Folding the cloth, she used it to apply pressure to his leg. A wound bleeding so profusely Duke looked on him, amazed Donald was still conscious enough to shout out in pain. It made him wonder how much blood the human body could carry.

"Devin, help me," Angelique said.

Devin stepped forward. "What do you want me to do?"

"Unlace the shoe string from his boot and tie it as tightly as you can above the wound, we need a constricted tourniquet above the bleeding. Derek, hold him down to keep him from moving." She looked up at Donald's pained face. "This is going to hurt. A lot. Take some deep breaths."

Derek leaned on Donald's chest and gave a nod to Devin. He moved quickly. Tying the string around the wound. Donald thrashed against Derek's weight. Screaming out in agony. Wendell and Garrett stood over him. Both men looking queasy from the sight of his blood loss.

Angelique grabbed Devin's hands and placed them on the cloth where her hands had been. She pulled off one glove and pressed her hand to the inside of Donald's thigh. "I can feel a strong pulse," she said. "It looks like the bleeding is starting to slow." She exhaled. "Worse case, it's deep puncture wounds, but we need X-rays to make sure teeth didn't knick the bone. Keep applying pressure, I'll be right back."

Angelique walked a few paces over to Duke. He was on the ground. Fang helped lean him up against the bark of a tree. Angelique knelt down before him.

"How's the chest pain?" she asked. "On a scale of one to ten? One being slight and ten being the worst pain you've ever had in your life?"

Duke coughed and rubbed his chest. "About a five."

"Is it still coming and going or is it more constant now?"

"Still coming and going."

She cleared her throat and nodded. "Okay, we need to get you back to the lodge and give you a Nitro pill. Just to be on the safe side." She glanced at the animal corpses. "Every lodge within earshot heard that shootout. Soon the land rangers will be here. We'll use their jeeps and get your medicine, then get you and Donald to the hospital."

Duke gave an irritated grunt. "For their sakes, Gilroy better have a damned good explanation for how wolves slipped onto his land and how a lodge house occupied by an unsuspecting family wasn't even notified."

"He better get a good lawyer," Derek added.

Dutch wiped sweat from his brow. "They probably slipped onto the land for the same reason we're here. Plenty of white tail to feed off of and a water source that'll last all year round." He unzipped his coat, pulled slugs from the holder of his vest and reloaded his shotgun.

"They probably wandered in," Prescott said. His dark eyes looked down at Fang's kill with a traumatized haze. To Duke he sounded like he was talking to a ghost.

"Stay with him," Angelique said to Fang.

She stood from Duke and moved over to the carcass. Pulling out her hunting knife, she knelt down by one of its claws and carefully slipped the blunt side of her blade under one of its nails to inspect it.

Prescott just rambled on, "I read that sometimes, when they move in packs, they'll migrate during the winter months to the caves of the mountains. They'll drive out cougars, fox, anything that lives there. Even bears. Christ, that thing alone is the size of a Grizzly."

Angelique searched its frame from nose to hide. Then looked up at Prescott. "That's a nice theory. But there are no mountains in Illinois." She pointed at the carcass with her knife and went on, "From teeth to tail this is twice the size of an ordinary wolf. The one that attacked Darrion is just as large. Look a few feet to your left and you'll see the rest of them are much smaller."

"They're alphas of the pack obviously," Darrion cut in.

Angelique shook her head in disagreement. "I don't think so." She motioned her knife over to the lesser wolves. "There's only two alphas of a pack. The male and the female. With these wolves, their claws are longer and more blunted. Like they don't move around much. It's the terrain and the constant movement that keeps them trimmed and sharp."

She knelt down and slipped the blade under one of the its claw nails again and held it up for the men to see. "These are shorter and almost blade sharp. Sometimes, they'll use rock to sharpen them or even the bark of a tree if it's frozen enough to take the grinding." She stood, exhaled a white cloud, and looked at Darrion. "This might sound crazy, but I think the larger wolves that came for the two of us were wild. The rest of them…were domesticated."

"What?" T-Bone touched a hand to a small cut on his neck and looked at her like she really had gone mad. "You mean like pets?"

"No, I mean like your local *petting* zoo." She looked at the trees to her left. "The smaller wolves, they came at us head on. Like they didn't know any better. And we heard them coming. If they had been true wolves from the wild, like this one, wolves that know how to kill, we never would have survived that attack. We wouldn't have stood a chance. These two larger ones came at us from the side. I didn't even know they were there."

"Fang had to fake a corpse just to out fox this one," Darrion said.

"Wait a minute…" Prescott said to Angelique with an apprehensive leer in his blue eyes. "…what are you saying? A pack of wolves escaped from a zoo somewhere and then just…stalked in and started attacking people? And what do you mean '*never would have survived*'? You almost make it sound like it wasn't an accident."

"That's because I don't think it was."

♛

After nearly an hour of waiting, the land rangers arrived in their Jeeps. There were only two men. One ranger bore much older features than the other. Reddened cheeks. Red, thick brows mirrored the red of his graying hair. He owned dark eyes, a full moustache, and a thick chest to match his wide gut. The other was a little shorter. Thinner. With trimmed, dark hair, and the youthful freckles of a hatchling no more than twenty and one. Both were swathed in thick black coats and gray fur collars. Matching black uniform pants. Steel toe weather boots. To look on them, it was immediately clear to Duke which one held charge. Both badges read Illinois Parks & Wildlife Department.

Though only one badge belonging to the older ranger read: Game Warden.

Both men looked alarmed at the sight of the wolf carcasses. Duke expected them to know the view of the carnage got no better up close. He couldn't remember the last time he was so angry. He gave both men a terse report of what happened, demanded Gilroy be brought to him, made a few solid threats of a lawsuit, and demanded his family be immediately taken back to the lodge.

Angelique made demands of her own. Both Duke and Donald needed to be taken to a hospital. Duke objected, arguing his chest pain had completely subsided. Donald rose to his feet and walked over to his brother's side, agreeing they would both be fine and even his own bleeding had stopped. Dr. James regarded them with irritated suspicion for a long moment, then relented. But the doctor made it clear if either of their conditions worsened, they were leaving the Mammoths for a hospital without dispute.

♛

They found the lodge ransacked.

Lamps, chairs, end tables had been knocked over. Blood sprayed the walls. Darrion had burst through the doors. Duke, Dutch, Derek, and T-Bone flowed in after him just in time to see Legend pulling off of a dead wolf by the fireplace. The pit sprinted up the stairs to the twin's room — his white coat red with blood. Darrion made for the stairs. T-Bone and Derek followed. Before he reached the second story, Duke heard shots ring out and Viola's screams.

"Viola!" He ran to the twins' room to find Taran's barrel wafting smoke. He had put down another wolf. Viola sat huddled in the far corner with the twins cradled under her arms. Legend had the wolf's throat still clutched in its teeth. The beast was fading but not fast enough.

Duke ran up to Taran and took his shotgun from him. "Put another one in the damned thing and end it!" Its head exploded from the shot as he pulled the trigger sending blood spraying the walls, smearing several paintings.

Donell and Olivia screamed, but Viola was a silent as a mouse. Looking at the headless wolf with a deadpan gaze, she didn't so much as blink. Not even when her face was splashed with red.

To Duke it was a look so distant and filled with horror a pang of fear rushed through him. He opened his mouth to call her name and talk her back to him, but shouts from the land rangers cut him short. Duke handed the shotgun back to Taran and rushed down the stairs to find their shouts coming from the back porch. He rushed outside to hear them arguing.

"What the hell is going on?" Duke demanded, looking between them.

"Two of the women with you have gone missing," the older ranger said. "The tall fella with the bleached out hair, he radioed the emergency about ten minutes ago, but we were already responding to the gun shots fired. So, we told him to stay put and we would be there as soon as we could. I think he said his name was um, breakfast or something."

"Lunch," Casper corrected. He and Ronnie stepped out onto the back porch. "Aunt Mary hid in the bathroom. But DaVita and Melody got chased off." He held up a slender gold watch. "I found this."

Legend scurried past his leg just before the back door shut and stopped at Duke's side as Lunch tossed the watch. Duke caught it mid-air and recognized it instantly. Diamond rimmed onyx face, jade inlay, gold banding. An Omega. DaVita's gift for her eighteenth birthday. Legend trotted off a few paces, ran back to him, barked loudly, looked off into the trees, then back up at him and barked again. As if an invisible leash were around his neck.

Legend growled. Pacing from side to side like a raving fox waiting for a squirrel.

Six years ago, Luna had run away from home. She was gone for three days before she decided to return. That was the last time Duke had seen Legend so wound up and beside himself. Now, Duke could hardly have missed what Legend was trying to tell him. "They're off south into the same wood we just came from. And I think my dog's already been there."

"How do you know that?" the younger ranger asked.

"Because he just told me." Duke shot a quick glance down to his nervous dog. "He's covered in blood and my other dog is missing. So when you two are through pissing down each other's throats, you can swallow and set out to finding them."

ANGELIQUE

Are you alright?" Angelique asked.

Viola said nothing at first. She just stood there at the window of the back den. Stonefaced. Watching the sun break day above the horizon. "What kind of question is that to ask a mother whose daughter is off in the woods," she finally said, "lost to a pack of wolves?"

"A very stupid one," Angelique replied, "if I meant your heart and not your health." She stepped closer and joined mother DeGrate. It felt easier to watch the sunrise. Somehow the view eased the sound of dead wolves being dragged across the floor by the men. All of the carcasses were being kept in the pantry. Duke had already made plans to have them skinned for their fur. A tacit agreement had been struck between Gilroy and the men. Duke would keep the unpleasant incident from the press and withdraw the threats of a lawsuit if every wolf they killed could be kept for skinning and profit.

Angelique knew no owner of a game preserve wanted to lose business because of a wild attack in the media. So Gilroy humbly agreed and ordered his rangers to go with T-Bone, Dutch, and Lunch to collect the corpses — as well as give the family any aid they needed in finding DaVita and Melody.

"Are you injured? Even if it's just a scratch I need to — "

"I'm fine," Viola said, cutting her off with sharp finality.

That set Angelique to wariness. She realized Viola looked just like Darrion when her face flashed anger. She carried the brown skin and intense dark eyes all of her children bore. Derek had warned her on more than one occasion about Viola's cold bite of a temper. Though Mrs. DeGrate was short in height, her stark voice raised her taller than any other woman she had ever met besides grandmother Eleanor.

Even if her next words earned her an evil glare or harsh words, they needed to be said. "I'm concerned for everyone's health because I don't know where the wolves have been. And if their brain is tainted with a communicable disease...that could be life threatening for all of us. Donald's been bitten but I stitched him up okay. Darrion took a few claw marks. Taran and T-Bone are a little banged up as well. Duke had a few chest pains. I'm worried for him the most. He and Donald refuse to go to the hospital. I've tried to convince them but—"

"I know." Viola cut her off again and blinked absently out the window, her eyes still set on the brightening skyline. "My husband is going to have his feast and his Thanksgiving...And he won't be spending it in a hospital bed. Not his doctor or his wife or his sons will be convincing him otherwise."

Viola looked miserable. Nothing shy of grief-stricken.

Rightfully so.

Her entire family had nearly been killed and her only daughter was out there somewhere, alone in the cold wild, fighting for her life with no weapon or any means to call for aid. If she was still alive. Angelique tried but failed to lend a single word of comfort. So she just nodded quietly, turned, and walked away.

In the main family room, the men were discussing the best plan of action to look for DaVita and Melody. Darrion was absent to their discussion which Angelique found odd.

Donald looked just as worried and miserable as Viola. While the men argued and fussed amongst each other, the Bishop stood silently by the side window holding a bible. His lips moved inaudibly in prayer. Or perhaps he was speaking audibly, but no prayers would be heard over the men and their racket and commotion.

For the second time in less than a minute, Angelique wound up feeling helpless and it made her want to step outside and breathe in the morning's dawn. She went over to the coat rack, slipped on her camo, and left the lodge.

A deep lungful of cold air brought an unexpected thankfulness. She was still very much alive. No wolf would be grinding teeth on her bones tonight. She headed west from the main cabin. Snow crunching under her boots like thick sugar crust. Not a fast stroll, yet she kept a good pace. Angelique did not realize she had walked upon the guest lodge until it came into view.

Fang and Darrion had set up their own secluded quarters separate from the rest of the family. As if their private world was one they'd rather not share.

Curiosity drew her nearer. She could see flickering light coming through the side window. A queasiness waved through her stomach as she stepped closer. Growling and snarling and loud chanting billowed through the glass to her ears. It was a strange tongue, thick with Asian foreign words and calls she could not pretend to understand.

A few steps closer and she realized the window was too tall for her eyes. She looked around for a large rock. A pile of chopped wood for the fireplace. Anything hard would be sturdy for a boost. She spotted an empty wooden crate under a snow-covered thicket ten paces away. She quietly pulled it from the small twigs, brushed the snow off with a gloved hand, then placed it upside down on the ground for a boost, and peered inside.

"Oh my God," she whispered.

Fang was killing a wolf.

Stabbing it with his sword over and over again.

But it was a different kind of killing.

Not a reaction from self-defense. The wolf couldn't move past the sword to attack back. Still, it lashed out with its claws and growled with whatever resistance it had left. But it was no use. Soon it was helplessly slipping on its own blood until growls diminished to weak whines and cries of agony and torment.

Darrion sat stone-faced and bare chested on a wide table with his legs folded. Surrounded by a circle made of candle fire. Watching the animal die without so much as a blink. When its suffering was over and it was finally dead, Fang took up three strange, misshapen glasses and filled each one with blood of the dead wolf.

He then went over to Darrion and he spoke something to him. Angelique could not make out the words. He must have told him to lay prone on the table because moments after, he did so. Fang poured the blood of the dead wolf over Darrion's wounds then chose a lit candle from the circle of flames and blew a strange black powder from what looked like a blow gun onto his back. Darrion groaned aloud through gritted teeth but he held still.

It looked so painful, Angelique found herself wincing in response. She thought back to the attack that happened just hours ago. When the wolf had come at him, she knew he was injured, but Darrion never let on that the wounds were that deep. Though she was a child when the claws of a wolf tore her back open, just looking at his slashes sent the pain rushing back at her as if she were still bleeding.

Fang touched the candle to the strange powder on Darrion's back and his wounds burst into flames. Immediately the old man turned each cup rim down, placed them over the flames and Angelique watched in horrified wonder as blood pooled up into the cups, lifting the flames as each glass was nearly filled. When no more blood pooled up from his skin a strange blue smoke rose from the wounds of his back and the flames in the glasses went out almost instantly.

A loud, solid snap under Angelique's boot gave her a start. She looked down from the window to the crate.

 Snow did tend to wet anything it touched, including wood. Before Angelique could shift her weight off of the weakened spot on the crate, it gave with a loud crack and her boot broke through. Wood scraped her shin, sending pain shooting up her left leg. She grabbed the windowsill with a firm grip and bit her lip to keep from yelling out. With her right foot holding steady on the crate, she was still eye level with the window.

On instinct she looked through the glass to see if the stumble had been heard. Fang and Darrion were locked on the window. Staring right at her.

Angelique froze. She was so startled she lost her grip on the sill. Everything happened at once then. She fell screaming and landed hard on her back in the snow. She felt the world go dim but she didn't faint.

Angelique wrenched the crate from her boot, scrambled to her feet and ran back to the main house.

A flash of vertigo threw her off balance when she flew through the back door. She ran through the family room, up the main stairs and made for the nearest bathroom. She barely heard Derek ask what was wrong as the door slammed shut behind her. She locked it, went to the sink, and turned on the cold water. After a few splashes to her face and neck things began to clear. But she was still panting, unable to control her breathing.

Derek called through the door and knocked.

"Just a minute," she panted. "I'm alright. It's just a panic attack. It'll pass."

"Are you sure?"

She turned off the faucet, sat on the stool, and rubbed her temples.

"I'll be fine."

"Okay." Derek sounded less than swayed. "When you feel better come downstairs. We're about to head out and look for DaVita and Melody."

♛

Duke was ready to punch Gilroy Moiyay.

Instead of agreeing to send out a search party, the self-seeking bastard stood at the table and spoke his worry on the other renters becoming frantic. While Gilroy tried to sound concerned for the wellbeing of his lodgers, Duke was well aware the landowner was more afraid of his game preserve losing business.

He was a tall, brash looking man with hard blue eyes, pale sun-chaffed cheeks, a muscular build, and a square yellow-haired beard. It took all the restraint Duke had to keep from reaching across the table and snatching him up to ram a fist down his arrogant throat.

"While the prospect of your office being flooded with calls is of foremost concern to you, Gilroy, I couldn't care less." Duke said. "My daughter and my brother's wife are out there somewhere and the longer we wait here playing rural politics with you and your rangers, the less likely it'll be that we find them alive."

"Then you best move quickly," Gilroy replied, unmoved. "Sounds to me like you don't have much time. My rangers are more than willing to help you search for them. But calling out a search party will cause a panic no one needs. You already said yourself that you killed all of the wolves, both out there and here in the house. So, if they're lost, chances are very high they'll be found soon."

Gilroy gave Duke a perfunctory nod and walked away from the table. His two rangers followed him to the front door. "I'll have my rangers drive around the property. And they will radio me if they spot them. I'll call you the moment I know anything."

"Perhaps they could give a call out to all of the surrounding lodges?" Dutch said, tersely. "It is possible they made it to the first house they saw. Or is that too much to ask?"

Gilroy stood there with his hand on the doorknob, mulling over an answer.

"All you have to say is that there are two women who lost their way back to their lodge," Derek added. "You don't have to mention the attacks. If anyone's let them in out of the cold, all you have to do is let us know."

"I don't think that would be too much to ask at all," Gilroy said.

"For the record, Gilroy," Duke added, "your lack of effort has been noted."

Gilroy looked less than affected as Duke watched the men leave, cursing them as soon as the door closed.

"Racist bastard," Taran spat.

"We're on our own," Darrion cut in, approaching the table. "He made that clear."

Duke had not heard Darrion enter the family room but there he stood at the table. He sat his Benelli in one of the empty chairs, slid it aside, and looked down at the map of the reservation. One of the rangers had provided it. At least they weren't completely worthless.

"And with the agreement we struck for the pelts in exchange for our silence," Lunch put in, "we just cleaned up his dirty little mess for him."

Duke felt lightheaded. He took a seat at the head of the table, hoping it would pass. Even with the Nitro in his system, his heart was still ailing him and he was drained. Viola had brewed a fresh pot of coffee and brought the men a steaming hot cup, but caffeine and heart trouble didn't mix, so Dr. James strictly forbade Duke to take one sip.

At least the caffeine would have kept him more alert. Now, he was ready to have a fainting fit. Things were bad enough. Duke refused to make matters worse with his own ailing complaints. So he sat quietly, watching his second-born son look over all of the guns sprawled out around the map. Some had been taken apart for cleaning. Others were trigger ready but the magazines had been pulled out for reloading. He slid a rifle out of the way, opened a box of bullets, and pulled the map closer.

"Who said it was *his* mess?" Duke asked him. "I think the good doctor was dead on with what she said."

"If someone wanted to kill your family there's less messier ways to do it," Garrett said. "Who would want to kill someone like that?"

"Start with who wouldn't," Prescott added in. "The list will be shorter."

"Fuck you, man," Taran spat.

"Alright," Derek cut in, ending the fight before it started. "We'll hash all of that out later. We're alive, that's all that matters. Let's work on finding who may not be for much longer, shall we?"

Prescott looked at Taran as if his tongue held choice words, but he kept his mouth shut. T-Bone laughed at the look of detained irritation on the man's face. Duke was well aware Taran, T-Bone, nor Lunch ever cared for politicians and it came as no surprise there was a clear rift between them at the table. Derek did what he could to keep the peace between them. Duke loved his first-born for that.

Darrion remained as detached as ever for the moment. Disconnected from the conversation of ill plots. His eyes never left the map. Duke loved his second-born for that as well.

"We're here," Darrion said, placing a bullet on the map to mark the main lodge. "If we move southeast, along the river, we'll cover all of the forest ground along the way until we reach the edge of the preserve." He marked the outer ridge of the reservation with another bullet. "From there, we'll sweep back west and move up deeper into the forest until we reach the edge of the trees. If we still haven't found them, we'll keep moving back east and further north, we'll sweep from east to west until we've covered all the woodland. If they're out there we'll find them."

"Sounds like a good plan," T-Bone said. "But what if there's more wolves out there? I don't think we got 'em all."

"If we didn't, however many are left, they're not strong enough in numbers to come after us like that again in the daytime. The few that are still there, if we cross paths, we'll take 'em down."

"You might be wrong about that," Angelique cut in.

All eyes looked her way. She blinked back at them, suddenly mindful that no one was aware of her presence until just then.

"How so?" Darrion asked. He looked less than pleased at her difference of opinion.

Duke could tell that his son's annoyed expression intimidated the doctor. She dropped her eyes for a moment then blinked up at Derek. Something was wrong. There was no way of knowing why she flew up the main stairs in such a panic. Whatever had happened, with everyone standing around, now was not the appropriate time to ask. Though she did look much better, Duke knew some unease still lingered and his son's tone of voice wasn't helping. "If you have something to add," Duke said, "please do."

It was an effort to put a dent in Darrion's overbearing manners and make her feel welcome to the conversation. It worked. She stepped closer next to young Wendell and folded her arms across her chest.

"All of the wolves we killed except two were domesticated," she said. "There could be another pack out there somewhere. Large packs could be anywhere from 20 to 30. Smaller packs could be less than 10. I don't think the larger ones were alphas. I think they were betas."

T-Bone's brow lifted. "So, there's alphas still out there? Bigger than the two you and Fang took out?"

Garrett backed away from the table. "I don't know about this shit."

"Maybe we should let the rangers do a sweep with the jeeps first," Prescott said.

"If there are more," Darrion said to Angelique, "and they're a pack like you say, again I say, if they cross our paths, we'll take them down."

Dr. James looked down at the map and slowly shook her head. "I don't think they will cross our paths. We won't be so fortunate. Not on this side of the river." She reached for the map, careful not to knock over the bullets Darrion used for markers, and slid it closer. "When I had the wolf that was chasing Legend in my crosshairs, I could see water kicking up from under its paws. I didn't give much thought to it then. Now it makes perfect sense. Legend was soaking wet when he made it back to the house. Most packs keep their den near a water source because enemy predators can't track their scent across water. If there were any cougars around in the area, they wouldn't be able to pick up wolf pups on the opposite side of the river. Any alpha worth his pack would have his betas on the other side of the water. Stalking the perimeter, closer to where we were, to take out any immediate threats should they get too close. But when we were attacked, something drew Legend away from us towards the river."

"And then a beta picked him up and tried to chase him down," Derek said.

"Exactly," she nodded. "Those rangers won't find anything. If the girls got chased from here, we should have seen them on the way back in the Jeeps. But we didn't, so they were already gone before we got back. Which means the wolves that got into this house must have come right after we left out for the deer hunt."

"What are the odds of that." T-Bone said, not making it a que-stion.

Now Duke was convinced their attack was deliberate. Not only was it premeditated, it was well calculated. The DeGrates had enemies. No denying that. Prescott's remark was rude, but it was no less true. Sorting through who had no motives to murder his family would have been an easier task. D'Amico and his bulldog, Tommy Zosa, came to mind first.

"You're saying someone put wolves on us and everyone in the house at the same time?" Garrett asked.

"Nothing else makes sense," Angelique said. "If we didn't spot them in the wood it was because we were busy trying to save our own lives."

"If they were trying to find us, they could've ran right past us and we wouldn't have known," Dutch said.

"Let's hope like hell we didn't accidentally shoot them," Lunch said.

"Oh Christ," Derek said.

"It was almost pitch black out there," Wendell said. "I couldn't see a thing."

"Me either," T-Bone agreed.

Darrion threw a hand up. "We don't know that. There is no way of knowing if both attacks happened at the same time."

"I think she might be right, man," Taran said. "When I stopped to reload, I heard shouts coming from the house. So did Lunch. We both took off and when we got back here…blood and screams."

"She's right," a voice cut in.

Everyone looked over to the far end of the family room.

Viola stood leaned with a shoulder against the doorway. Duke could see the worry on her face. She looked as exhausted as he felt. He stood from the table went over to her and pulled her into his chest.

"It happened not long after you were gone," Viola said.

"How long?" Duke asked.

She looked up into his eyes. "Ten minutes, maybe less."

"If the dogs knew they were in trouble that's what pulled them across the river," Derek said. "And that's where we have to go."

"I don't swim so well," Garrett admitted. "Especially with a weapon in my hands."

"Then stay your ass here," Taran spat.

"I'll go with you," Angelique said to the men. "If Legend crossed that river, so can we."

"Yeah, she'll come," Taran said, not taking his eyes off of Garrett. "You can keep the Queen Bee company. Babysit the kids…Make sure the fireplace stays lit…Have my slippers nice and warm when I get back."

Garrett's dark brown features stiffened and his eyes bristled at Taran but he kept his mouth shut.

"I don't want you going back out there," Derek said to Angelique.

"If something happens to one of you out there then what? I can bring my field kit. If the girls are badly injured I can help."

"If they're badly injured, we'll bring them back. What if something happens to you out there? Who's sewing us up if you're dead? Who's fixing Duke's heart?"

She cut her eyes to the floor and shook her head. "Fine, I'll stay."

Derek's face lightened to a smile. "Thank you."

She didn't smile back. "You're not welcome."

"Maybe they're not injured," Wendell said, trying to break the tension. "Let's just hope they made it to a nearby lodge."

"The nearest lodge is just two miles from here," Darrion said. "If they were there, they'd be back by now."

"He's right," Taran said. "We would have heard something already. If they're across the river, if they're not dead it's because they're still being hunted."

"Then so are we. Starting right now."

INTERVIEW

F or this interview," Zella said, "I'll be asking several questions."

"Yeah," Renfro said. "Is all this makeup necessary?"

Zella pointed skyward. "It's for the lighting."

Renfro frowned as the make-up artist dusted his face from forehead to chin with powder. This was new for him. Being interviewed by superiors in an office setting was different. Their questions always came short and to the point. Captain Delgado chewed him a new one if need be and it was done. There were no cameras or long microphones hanging over his head recording every word that came out of his mouth. Words that would be regurgitated on television once the episode aired.

Renfro hated cameras. He hated questions. He hated interviews. All he wanted to do was the job. But there was a reason why he agreed to take part in the documentary when Zella Rice had called him three weeks prior. From what she had told him, the interview would be a part of some Chicago segment for a TV show dedicated to gangs across the nation. Renfro had said yes so fast, it scared him and after Zella hung up, he spent the rest of that night thinking of all the things he would say and how he would say them. Knowing it would be gratifying to speak on all of the fouls in the police department, and set the record straight once and for all, kept his mind reeling for days. There would be backlash for this day, but any repercussions would be in no way worse than the last ten years he'd spent fighting the deadliest street war ever to hit the city.

The fall of the King Disciples Nation gave his superiors—
who launched his career to Detective First Grade on the joint
state and federal gang task force—confirmation that their
decision was no mistake. The downside of that promotion was
the cost of his third marriage down the drain and living a
neverending nightmare as the hunter who had become the
hunted.

"You're welcome to answer these questions however you
like, Mr. Renfro. But we do ask that you refrain from too much
profanity. Particularly the 'F-word' and the 'S-word'. They have
to be bleeped out if you use them. When the show airs, you'll
only see the comments and remarks of yourself and everyone
else that we've interviewed, mixed narration and documentary
footage. So, basically, what we're expounding on here today is
what we've already been covering on film throughout the city,
but with your own personal experience added in. Do you have
any questions before we begin?"

Renfro shook his head. When the makeup artist had gone
Zella gave the cameraman the cue to start filming. Renfro cleared
his throat and took in a deep breath. She told him not to look at
the camera. It was a pointless instruction as far as he was
concerned. Even if he had been instructed to stare into the lens he
wouldn't have.

"In your opinion when would you say the worst years of the
gang wars were in this city?" Zella began.

Renfro answered without hesitation. "From 1984 up 'til now.
Because even twelve years later, the streets are just as lethal as
they were back then."

"What police rank were you back in the 80's and what was
your role in the Chicago police department at that time?"

"Back then I was a Detective, Third Grade. My partner and I
worked the Robbery/Homicide division. But we all rotated out
for response calls from dispatch because of the massive shortage
of policemen and to cut back on all of the overtime pay the
uniformed officers were getting."

"When did it all start? The street wars seemed to take the
media by storm all of a sudden. But you and I both know that no
war is just waged out of nowhere."

"You're asking the wrong question. The media caught on
after the war had already begun because politics were involved,

Mayor Burns was on her way out, and the then Councilman was running for office. So, it's not when, but where it started is what you should be asking. All over the Westside and the Southside...the Near North is where the gangs were. But the war started in Cabrini."

"When did you find yourself in the middle of it?"

"The night Bishop and I responded to a call for backup. Officers were pinned behind a dumpster in a shootout. Back in 1984. November was the month. Two officers who were on a routine patrol of the area were called out there to one of the highrise towers for a supposed rape of a teenage girl. It was bad timing. Unfortunately the officers arrived right at the eruption of a building war between the King Cobras and the King Disciples. They were shot and one of them got killed right there on the edge of the front lawn. They never made more than ten steps from their squad cars before snipers on the roof shot at them. Two more officers responded but their vehicles got shredded by gunfire. They had to abandon their squad cars and run behind a dumpster for cover. It was Officer Campbell and his partner Officer Sanchez. I'm sure that was a night they'll never forget."

"Then what happened?"

"After those two were no longer a target the snipers could hit, both gangs started shooting at each other. It was a push for power. A notorious drug dealer Zane "Mad King" Harris was in the take for Cobra territory. If memory serves, twenty-eight Cobras and fifteen Disciples died in that barrage. The next morning, I had to sit before a shooting board at the precinct. Explain what I saw, what happened, and I sat there while my superiors decided whether or not my actions were justifiable in the situation."

"What actions did you take?"

"I had Bishop bomb them with smoke grenades. Whenever an officer or detective uses any weapon of any kind, they're called into face the board for review. It's standard procedure. After that, my captain had ordered me on two weeks vacation while the incident was investigated. Also standard procedure. I didn't realize it at the time, but those two weeks would be the last peaceful days of my life."

RENFRO

How do you feel, Renfro?" Captain Delgado asked.

Sitting across from the Captain's desk, Renfro still couldn't decide what Delgado was. He never cared to ask, but with the sunlight beaming in through his office window, it was easy to see hard eyes of an Aztec Indian and the steel demeanor of a Spanish Conquistador, so there was no telling the truth of his heritage. But the rest of the man was recognizably Hispanic. Tall and dark haired with a tinge of gray whiskered on the sides, and skin like bronze clay.

Rumor had him at older than fifty but nowhere near seventy and since no one in the precinct had the gall to ask how old he really was, every year a birthday cake was brought to him with a big question mark candle.

More than twenty years in the police department made Renfro ready for a day like this. One thing that he learned about being a detective was to never answer the 'Are You Okay' question honestly. Not after a shootout. Since last night in Cabrini, it did not seem possible to feel numb to it all nor was he ready to crack. Still, drug dealers, hookers, dead bodies, sometimes they were all one in the same and they all began to look alike after a while. There were days and nights on his job where he had been scared. He had been on the wrong end of a gun a time or two or three and he was disturbingly familiar with what the sharp end of a blade felt like. But was he okay? That's what an old captain, judging a shootout from an armchair, had to ask. He could tell the truth. Say he was burnt out. Distraught with a severe case of insomnia that kept him suspended in a zombie-like state for months. All that would earn him was a demotion—for the betterment of his emotional well-being.

"I'm fine," Renfro lied.

Delgado rested his arms on his desk, picked up a pen, and rolled it with thick fingers. "Well, you handled the shooting board well. It'll take a few weeks for them to sort out all of the details of what happened. In the meantime, you are required to take two weeks with pay. Upon your return, counseling is available and it's advisable you take it."

"So, it's still voluntary, huh?"

Delgado nodded. "It is."

"I'm good."

"Renfro, you were just in a hail of bullets last night. Two officers are dead. Officers you pulled off the ground after you drove into massive gunfire just to retrieve them. Any badge who's faced Cabrini and survived to walk this earth another day are rarely unscathed by it. I strongly suggest you take the counseling."

Renfro exhaled, glanced out the window, then looked back at his captain. "You ever wonder why it's not mandatory anymore?"

"No one in this division is forced into seeing a therapist. If you feel that you need it, then it's there. If you don't, from our end, it was offered."

"That would've been the perfect answer if I had asked why counseling is voluntary. But why it's no longer mandatory, nobody around here wants to talk about that. But here's why." Renfro leaned forward in the chair. His eyes narrowed as he spoke. "There's more than sixty detectives who have been out on the streets investigating gruesome chaos for more than a decade. Everyday they take it in and every morning when they wake up they come back for more. They dedicate time away from their families to rid the streets of murderers, drug dealers, and the thieves. Then comes the cop's worst nightmare. That one day when you have to pull your weapon and shoot it. And then comes the shooting board, then the investigation of your actions which may or may not result in the declaration of laxity on your part and or charges brought against you.

"Then, once your mandatory vacation is over, you're required to receive mandatory counseling in your department…after you've come back to work to find yourself demoted and pulled from the streets to a cubicle. Now, be it anger or humiliation or the fear of repercussions, that badge is dealt with altogether differently. You've been transferred out of your unit. Blasted by heavy media coverage and Internal Affairs. Scrutinized by your fellow law enforcement peers. It's like all of a sudden the one who once upheld the law now has the Ebola virus. Like the man behind the badge doesn't even exist. Oh, but he's in counseling though. So he'll be okay. Sound familiar?"

Delgado just looked at him.

"Lieutenant Michael Diaz," Renfro answered. "Blew his brains out after he was demoted to Fleet Services for ordering the shooting of a 13 year old kid, even after it was found the kid was a known gang member who was implicated in five murders it didn't matter. He was pulled from duty and suspended until the charges against him were dropped. His department clipped his balls for ridding the streets of one less drug dealing punk. But after his suicide, then the department came into question. '*He was in counseling,*' his wife cried. '*So what went wrong?*' When the Deputy, the Sup., the Chief, and when the Commander had to answer to the Mayor for that, poof! Policy changed. No longer mandatory."

Delgado stopped twirling the pen. Renfro could see his muscles tense under his uniform shirt. His badge even jumped a little on his chest and his nametag went a little crooked.

"This department made a conscientious effort to reduce suicides," he said. "It's not as though your superiors take a nonchalant attitude towards counseling. But…at the end of the day, no matter what positive efforts towards mental health are made, some individuals are going to act. Regardless of what is done to prevent it."

Renfro thought on his captain's words for a moment. True, his superiors may not have taken a nonchalant attitude towards Diaz's death. In fact, they did anything but dismiss it. From the backlash that his suicide had caused, they took 'Cover Your Ass' to whole new heights. Even the rookies took the Lieutenant's demise as one cautionary tale against agreeing to seek counseling within the department.

Renfro took in a deep breath. It was time to end this conversation. It was 8:00 in the morning and all he had had so far was coffee and a dose of his wife's Lorazepam. He needed to eat. "Well, as much as I appreciate the offer, Captain, I decline." He stood and spoke over his shoulder on the way out the door. "I'd rather be brought up on charges and fired before I let some shrink into my head only to be stuck washing the bird shit off Crown-Vics for the rest of my career."

ANGELIQUE

I didn't mean to snoop," Angelique said.

Darrion said nothing. In the lighting from the ceiling fan, he had more of his mother Viola's sorrel coloring than Duke. Now he looked much taller than he had out in the Mammoth wood. She realized why when she gave a quick glance down to her knitted socks and noticed she had removed her boots. That easily knocked her down a few inches from his brow. She felt nervous in his presence and Angelique hated being nervous. She tightened her grip on the leather bag.

His brow stiffened into an accusatory glare. Now Angelique was well aware the lie wasn't working. Her resolve faded into guilt. "Okay fine," she said, giving in. "I meant to snoop. But not for the reason you think. My world is medicine. Any form of healing is interesting to me. In my world you don't see that type of holistic therapy every day."

Darrion slipped on a pair of latex gloves, grabbed a box of .50 bullets from his black duffle bag, and reloaded the magazines for his Eagle. Angelique stood quiet for a long moment watching his hands work. After the pistol was loaded, he holstered it to his thigh, pulled a stone from the pocket of his vest, and set to sharpening the long knife.

Angelique glanced around the bedroom. Legend lay on the children's bed with his front paws tucked under his massive head. His blue eyes locked on Darrion. Watching. His white tail wagging from side to side like a pendulum of vigilance. As if he were his appointed high guard for the day. His coat was spotless. Scrubbed clean of all the blood. Angelique assumed that was Darrion's doing.

She looked past Legend to the children's suitcases. They were still open on the leather bench at the foot of the bed, most of the clothes were stained with blood. This was the room where Viola had huddled the twins into her body. Here is where Taran had killed the last wolf.

That was a kill Angelique understood.

Every dead wolf in the red snow they had shot dead, she understood. But the wolf Fang killed in the guesthouse did not fight back. It was in such suffering, all it could do was growl until the growls became howls that became yelps of pain. What she witnessed through that window was no justified act of self-defense. All she saw was a sadistic, calloused cruelty.

After mulling over how to speak her thoughts for a moment, she swallowed hard and finally said, "Why did Fang kill that wolf?"

Darrion took his eyes off the blade long enough to see the confused dread on her face. He went back to sharpening the steel and said nothing at first. "For the Ainu, pain of death is the only way to set the spirit free. Releasing it to return to its realm, that's a great honor for the wolf."

Angelique wished she could understand his reasoning. But there had been no mistaking the torture that poor animal had suffered before it died its horrible death. "It didn't look honored when it was wailing its last breath and slipping on its own blood," she said.

"What you see as torture," he said, almost gently, "warrior men of his kind see as a right of passage. Through its blood is the path to the other side."

She looked down to his hands, sliding the blade across the sharpening stone. Swift lashes. Shhling. Shhling. Shhling.

Darrion paused the sharpening and ran a thumb along the steel, testing its edge, then went back to it. Now was the best time to interrupt him before the men set out into the wood. If she delayed, there was a chance none of them would make it back in good health. Even if the wolves had not found them again.

"I know your mind is on other things besides what I'm about to say," she said, "but it's important."

Shhling. Shhling. Shhling.

"If it's important then you better say it."

There was something about the sound of that blade. Shearing across that stone. It made her think of what the Manson family probably did on family night. Instead of going out for pizza, all of them probably sat around in the living room. Lost in some sick, twisted circle-jerk trance. Meditating on how sweet the next victim would be while they all sharpened their steel. She could feel gastric juice rising in her throat.

"Could you please stop doing that?"

Darrion paused the knife and looked at her.

Not kindly.

She inwardly winced at his terse glare. "I'm sorry," she said. "It's like a goddamn fork on a metal pipe."

He turned his attention back to his knife and picked up right where he left off. Slashing at that steel like her aggravation was a fleeting little outburst a child gives. Nothing more. She found it hard not feeling affronted by his disregard. That noise threatened to drive her mad. So, all she could do was switch tact.

"I'm pretty sure most of the wolves were domesticated but that doesn't mean the wild ones weren't infectious."

Shhling. Shhling. Shhling.

"The virus is highly transmittable, so your wounds might be infected."

Shhling. Shhling. Shhling.

"I need a skin sample and some of your saliva. You might have rabies."

Shhling. Shhli… "What?"

Angelique crossed the room to the leather bench and moved the children's luggage to the part of the floor that was clear of blood stained wood. She sat on the bench and opened her leather bag. "Sit please," she said, taking out the contents: a small bag of ice, betodine, sterile gauze, a roll of tape, a disposable knife in sterile packaging, one sterile eye dropper pipet, a small sterile container, lidocaine, and a needle. She blinked up at him and her hands paused. Darrion slid the knife back into his thigh sheath, slipped the stone in his vest pocket, and just stood there looking at the needle.

Angelique followed his gaze to the contents of her bag. She had to consciously keep from rolling her eyes. "With all of those tattoos, don't tell me you're afraid of needles?"

"I'm fine," he protested. "You don't need a sample."

Dr. James folded her hands in her lap, leaned back against the foot of the bed and smiled roguishly. *So the lion has a weakness.* "Wow really," she said, looking him up and down. "Shaft's double-y chromo little half-brother is afraid of a teensy-weensy-wittle needle stick. Just so you know, a skin sample and some saliva doesn't involve needles. But the lidocane I'm going to use to make it painless does. And you don't want me taking skin from a pissed off wound without numbing you up first. Trust me."

Darrion grimaced at that.

Just then she noticed a small gleam in his dark eyes revealing a man who refused to be outshone. He walked over to the bench, sat and looked off towards the dresser at a box of ammunition. She pulled up his long john thermo. Three large wounds ran diagnally down his back. They were well cleaned. Slightly swollen but no redness remained. His ink was ruined. Whatever healing methods Fang had used they looked just as well cared for as any surgeon would have done in the OR. Darrion's wounds looked so similar to her own she almost got lost in a spell of Deja Vu. She reached in her bag for a pair of sterile gloves and filled a syringe with licocane, picked a wound, and set to numbing his skin.

"This'll only take a second," she said. "You can think about stabbing furry little animals to death in the meantime. It'll be over before you know it."

Darrion shook his head at her witticism and kept his eyes on the dresser. Then he mumbled something she could only assume was Japanese. Her eyes narrowed. "Since I am the one holding the needle," she warned, "for the next minute or so, if I were you, I'd keep my smart remarks in English."

"I wouldn't expect someone like you to understand or even agree with what a man like him believes in."

"And what God does he believe in?"

"Many."

"What God do you believe in?" She slipped the needle into his swollen skin. Darrion held his breath and closed his eyes. Then he slowly exhaled and looked off again to the dresser.

"A cynic often strikes with humor," he said. "Until the laugh is over and their jaundiced view of the world is exposed for the soul rot it is."

"Soul rot?"

Darrion hmmphed. "So let me ask you a question. Do you go to church?"

"I do."

"Why?"

"Because...I was raised to."

"Because you're expected to."

"I suppose."

"If you don't believe in it...why do you do it? And don't bother denying it. I know an atheist when I see one."

She couldn't think fast enough to justify his accusation with a defensive lie. Instead she pulled the needle and waited for a moment. Then pricked the wound, testing for numbness. "Do you feel that?"

"Feel what?"

"Good answer." She opened the sterile knife and cleaned off his skin with betadine. "Do you think they're still alive? Your sister and Melody?"

"Fang says yes."

Dr. James carefully removed 5mm of skin from the wound and quickly placed a sterile gauze over it to catch the bleeding. "How does he know?"

Darrion looked at her and in looking back at him, she saw nothing but steep honesty in his eyes. "He says he does not feel their death."

She placed the skin into a sterile container with saline. Without warning her eyes burned and welled with tears. "Whatever God you believe in, please ask him to bring Derek back to me."

"I'll bring him back."

"That would be easier to believe if I didn't know what's out there."

"I will bring him back."

"What if you can't?"

"If it costs me my life, Fang will bring him back."

Angelique nodded. In the most unexpected way that came as a comfort to her. "When the storm breaks," she said as she gathered up the supplies, "I'll drive back to Chicago and phone the Rabies Lab at the CDC and send the samples to the Public Health Lab. If any of the wolves test positive...we're all at Scott Joplin getting shots." She stood and left him alone with Legend and his weapons.

♛

She could have allowed her fears to drive her to another panic attack, but instead Lunch was kind enough to help and found a mini power saw and a pair of goggles for her in a storage closet. She set up a collection table near the doorway. Lunch looked on with humored awe as Dr. James grabbed the medical bag then took to cutting craniums open. Lastly she took brain samples from each of the wolf carcasses in the kitchen's walk-in pantry.

She stepped carefully on the black tarp — mindful not so slip on the blood. In some way being so close to what had nearly killed her and removing bone became a surprising source of therapy. Seeing their exposed brain, their bullet wounds as permanent marks of fatal mistakes. How they had lost the last fight...How they wouldn't be dining on her bones. Survivor's vanity was a strange thing. A prideful thing.

She removed tissue from each cerbellum and brain stem, taking care to label each sample as: Canus Lupus. After packing them in ice and placing them in the refrigerator, she went into the family room where the men were gathered, making ready to leave for the search. Like an assembly line, anyone who had a nick or a scratch had his or her skin sampled at the wound site.

Viola busied herself all over the lodge as well, using Wendell and Garrett to help her clean up as much of the blood and overturned furniture as she could. Donell and Olivia helped only so much as their mother, Mary, would allow. She warned them in a harsh tone to stay away from the broken glass. While her round frame busied fixing breakfast, she watched every move they made from the kitchen counter. Angelique knew she could do well to take notes from a woman like her. Her wide frame aside, she made her way around the kitchen with the energy of an athlete. Lustrous thick curls flounced at her neck with every step as she wisped back and forth from the cabinets to the refrigerator to the stove. Mixing and seasoning. Pouring and slicing. Flipping and sautéing. Her round eyes missed nothing. Not one slice of bacon got burned nor did her spoon lift a clump from the Cream of Wheat. On the island, every biscuit sat fluffed to perfection, brushed with butter. A tall stack of flapjacks stood next to a pitcher of maple syrup and freshly squeezed orange juice.

Mary worked every pot and every gas burner like she had spent the whole of her life in the kitchen. Angelique felt a pang of failure seep in as she moved past her and placed the men's skin samples in the refrigerator. With her livelihood taking a constant front seat, she almost never cooked. If Derek lost his love for fine dining, Patricia Porter would soon be blaming his wife for starving her only son.

In spite of the tragedy the family had suffered, everyone ate like they never knew food tasted better. Mostly the men ate hurriedly, downed their coffee, slipped their weather wears on, and made for the back door. Donald limped into the family room and called everyone to gather for a prayer before anyone set foot out into the storm.

While Fang and Darrion lingered at the back door, Angelique found it difficult to escape the bishop's call of devout supplication. She stepped between Derek and Donell, held hands, bowed her head, and the words just flowed through one ear and out the other. Amen.

Less than a minute later, she found herself at the back door, standing next to Viola. Watching Derek set out in the morning snowfall with Darrion, Fang, Dutch, Taran, Turkell, Casper, and Ronald.

All of them headed southeast.

When the men were all but a whiteout in the distance, Viola left the doorway and took a rest on the couch, relaxing into her husband's chest. Angelique could tell his devotion to her was an unwavering comfort to her guilt.

They both watched Prescott tend the fireplace while Mary put the children to cleaning up the kitchen. Wendell and Garrett busied themselves with mopping the red stained floors.

Angelique did not move. Even though Derek was long out of sight, she stood there as if at any moment he would come walking back towards the lodge and it would all be over. Just then the sound of Donald's voice drew near and he was at her side. Watching the storm. Praying the prayer of Psalms 23.

She felt a push at her leg and looked down to see Legend at her side. Docked ears perked. White tail wagging. Sniffing the wind. Staring off into the snowstorm.

He, too, was anxiously awaiting their return.

An ache took hold then. A deep, daunting ache that brought to mind the yellow eyes of the wolf. Even now, it was watching her. Somehow she knew it always would.

Perhaps Legend knew too.

DARRION

Darrion burst through the front door with Luna in his arms.
"We found them!"

Duke and Viola rushed to the door.

DaVita, Melody, and Dutch came in after him.

Derek held the door open for the rest of the men, letting sleet and snow flurry in past him, then he closed it behind them and locked it. The men looked like they had been through a war.

Fang stood by the window. His furs coated with a layer of snow. Looking out on the storm with impassive old eyes, he appeared unaffected by the weather. T-Bone cursed the cold and shook the snow out of his dreadlocks like a dog glad to be out of the rain. Taran cracked his neck, pulled his gloves off and sat his shotgun down against the door.

Lunch pulled the cap off of his head and plopped down on the couch as if the last of his energy had been utterly spent. Ronnie moved past him and made straight for the fireplace.

Without his coat he looked well stung from the cold.

Viola pulled her daughter into a firm hug. "Are you alright?"

DaVita nodded meekly. "I'm fine, Mama. Just a little scratched
up and cold. But I'm okay."

Wrapped in a camo coat, she looked well enough despite hours in the cold alone and unfed. Her white sweater was slightly torn and her denim was frayed. Scraped red skin and old crusted blood flaked on her thigh. Viola squeezed her tighter then cupped her face in her hands. "Thank God you didn't freeze to death."

"Me and Mel, we wrapped up in the blankets. We knew somebody would come for us sooner or later. After the gunshots went away. So we just waited. When they found us, Ronnie gave me his coat. But if it wasn't for the blankets, we probably would have froze to death."

"What blankets?" Duke asked.

Darrion laid Luna's limp body in front of the fireplace and snatched off his gloves and camo coat. "We found the cages on the rock bed of the river. For the wolves." He gave a nod to DaVita and Melody. "That's how they stayed alive. They used animal blankets from the floor of the cages and locked themselves in. Where's the doctor?"

"She's upstairs with Mary and the children," Wendell said.

Donald limped towards Luna.

His eyes went wide with horror at the mangled sight of her. Long claw slashes ripped the length of her rib cage nearing her hide, revealing lacerated flesh and bone. More claw marks marred her face. Luna wasn't dead, but by her short labored breaths, Donald must have known she wouldn't be alive much longer.

"Go get her," Darrion ordered. "And tell her to bring her bag."

Wendell made towards the staircase but Devin was already half way up the steps, unbuttoning his camo. "I'll get her. I have to use the restroom anyway." Devin hurried to the children's room. Moments later, Mary and the twins came down the stairs. Angelique ran to her bedroom, retrieved her medical bag, and rushed down to the fireplace.

"There is no way we can drive in that weather," Darrion said to Angelique. "When the storm breaks, get the samples, and I'll drive us to the hospital. In the meantime, you can work on Luna."

Angelique nodded. "Okay, just give me one second." She went over to Derek and embraced him. "Are you alright?"

"I'm fine," he said. Still, she looked him over, making sure he was not injured. "I'm not hurt," he assured her. "Really, I'm fine." He motioned to DaVita and Melody. "You might want to check them out and make sure they're okay."

"Okay," she said, giving both women a quick once over with her eyes. "They seem okay. Just let me see about the pitt, then I'll check them out after. I'm not a veterinarian...but I'll do what I can." She crossed the room to the fireplace and knelt by Luna's side and shined pupil light in her eyes. "Her pupils are fixed and really, really dilated." She pulled out a stethoscope and checked her breathing. "What happened to her?"

"She fought off two wolves," Melody said in tears. "And all we could do was just sit there in a cage and watch them tear her to pieces." Dutch took his wife's hand. Her deep blue eyes found his and he could see how hard it took her. Dutch brushed her blonde hair back with is hand and kissed her lightly on the forehead. Melody had the high cheekbones of a stunning Italian beauty and full lips made for smiles, but she was not smiling now. Though she was wearing Dutch's coat, her soiled clothes were easily seen under the camo. Her blue shirt held muck and dirt and wet snow. Her white jeans would never be bleached the same color of clean again, but her left hand looked far worse than her attire. Scraped from a hard fall, the palm of her hand was skinned raw and one of her acrylic nails had cracked in half. But the blue diamond on her ring finger shined as bright as clear waters.

"All I can do," Angelique said, "is dress her wounds as best as I can, and keep the bleeding to a minimum. I have a couple of saline bags and I can start an IV drip to keep her hydrated. Other than that, we'll keep her comfortable until the weather lets up. Just try not to move her anymore if you can help it." She looked up at all of the men. "Who has an electric razor?"

Several of them spoke at once, "I do."

"Is it charged?"

"Yes," they said.

"Okay. If someone could please go get it. I need to shave one of her forelegs for IV access."

"I'll grab mine," Lunch volunteered as he stood from the couch.

"I just want to go home," Melody sobbed.

"We're all going home," Duke said as he crouched down by his dying dog. "First thing in the morning. We'll pack tonight. After everyone is clean, fed, and settled, I'll work on taking the wolf hides and make arrangements with one of the rangers to pickup the remains. Until we figure out exactly who's responsible for this and why, we're not safe in our own homes." He touched a hand to Luna's head. Her breathing calmed just then as if she knew he was there. Duke looked up at his firstborn. "Derek, you'll have to keep the engagement with the church for Thanksgiving."

Derek nodded as he wiped sweat from his brow and pulled off his gloves. He looked worn and tired. "I know. I'll make arrang-ements for private security."

"Good," Duke agreed. Legend brushed past him then and leaned a wet nose down to Luna. He gently sniffed over the wounds of her face, brayed a hard breath, and gently licked the blood away. Duke looked at every silent, sullen face staring back at him in the room. "Until further notice, no one goes anywhere alone. We all move as one. Which means we'll all be at my house for the holidays."

"Wait a minute," DaVita said. "What do you mean find who's responsible for this and why, Daddy? Are you saying this happened on purpose?"

Viola rubbed her back and spoke calmly. "Your father thinks it could have been intentional." She looked, Darrion. "So does your brother. But don't worry, honey. They're going to find out who did this and by next year, I promise you, the only memory of this nightmare will be another Christian LeBarron fur hanging in your closet with the rest of them."

♛

Most of that afternoon had been spent keeping Luna stable and seeing that everyone had eaten and settled into some form of calm relaxation. By dinner time, everyone ate in silence, but the women quickly cleared out of the kitchen when Duke announced the carcasses couldn't wait any longer before they would begin to permeate the entire cabin with the smell of mortality.

Viola suggested tea by the fireplace and the women gave no objection, but Donell begged to stay and watch. Darrion couldn't blame him for not wanting to sit and listen to the thoughts of women in the family room, while the actions of men were only paces away in the kitchen. To everyone's surprise, Mary consented.

Olivia would have no part of it and trotted off to slip into her bedclothes. Angelique saw about Luna's condition. Melody and DaVita set to packing up what they could for the trip home. Darrion knew Fang would've taken no part of skinning what was not his kill. No Ainu would stoop so low. Lost in meditation somewhere close by. Either in the guesthouse or on the back porch, would be where Fang could be found should Darrion need to speak with him.

Lunch and T-Bone pushed away the table and stacked the chairs flush against the far wall. Dutch lined the floor with black tarp and laid out his tools. Taran pulled all of the dead carcasses out into the center of the kitchen floor.

Darrion planned to spend the last two days before Thanksgiving gutting a few white tails and curing the meat. He never expected to be at his father's side, skinning the hides from a pack of predators. Crouched next to uncle Dutch, Lunch looked more excited than he had been in a long time. Moments like these, Darrion knew, his close friend lived for. Any gutting of flesh from sea, land, or air, seemed to ignite him. Father concluded with certainty long ago that there was a special God for Casper "Lunch" Phoenix. Knowing how much he enjoyed death would have made most men worried to gooseflesh in his presence. But always it put Darrion at ease. Lunch held a capability of doing things to nemeses of the Family that no DeGrate ever could. Unfortunately that meant father took pains to keep his volatilities reigned in at all times.

Devin's eyes were also filled with excitement, but his gaze bore an interest quite different from Lunch's enthrallment. His look came from learning something new. It took over his young features and his brow crinkled with focus. Instantly Darrion became aware of this year marking Devin's second hunt. Yet after all the family had suffered through in the past twenty-four hours, he felt quite proud of his younger brother. Not one tear rolled down his cheeks. For a seventeen year old boy, Devin took all the horrors of the past night's catastrophe like a soldier.

Even uncle Donald limped into the kitchen with a little less pain in his step. Darrion knew he wouldn't join them, but just his presence meant to say, '*Here I am. Here I stand*'. In truth, he knew his uncle hated guns as well. Still, he always held one whenever his brothers did. This was a strange act of camaraderie coming from a bishop of a coveted church. Yet it reigned true that whatever father and uncle Dutch did, uncle Donald would not be ousted from his brothers. That reminded him of his bond with Devin, though he could not say the same for Derek. His older half brother was nothing like a DeGrate. All Porter, the man would show with every bit of himself. Though he stood by Taran and Ronnie with the look of a man ready to take part in a hunter's burden of evisceration, Darrion knew that after the holidays were done, he would go back to his life of legislations and publicities. Yes, a Porter would always be a Porter; never a DeGrate. As Wendell, Garrett, and Prescott stood next to him, that fact rang all the more true. They looked utterly nauseous. Garrett most of all. That made Darrion want to laugh at their weakened stomachs and he would have, if it had not been for the everpresent foreboding in their hearts that matched his own.

No one had purchased tags for a gray wolf or set out to take down one. They had all been schemed upon for a painful, bloody end. All of the possibilities, every enemy who could have had the ambition for such an attack set his thoughts awhirl. Unfortunately, his father and uncle Dutch and even his mother had amassed more than enough foes to keep him guessing. Duke was set to finding who was responsible. Darrion hoped he had a smarter grasp on motivations and resources than he did at present. Kincaid was the first one to enter his mind. But the hunting trip happened only two days after their botched job in Northbrook. *That hillbilly would never have been able to take a piss without wetting his shoes, let alone coordinate a lethal attack in less than forty-eight hours.*

That left only old foes.

Enemies with reach. But their attack was flawed.

Leaving the cages behind proved slack and careless. Angelique certainly found ease piecing together the incident as no accident at all. She saw much for a privileged alumna.

Of all the things left unknown as of yet, he knew one thing for certain. When he found out who set them all to die, he would pay them an exclusive visit.

"Keep the heads," Darrion heard himself say.

Then every eye was on him in the kitchen. But the only eyes staring back at him that mattered were his father's. Duke's dark gaze studied him carefully. "Plan on a little taxidermy, son?"

"I have plans for them, Pop," he answered, "so we'll have to keep them frozen."

"A nice mount would look good in LeBarron's," Dutch added. "In Predator's Apparel too. We got every head mount in that store except a gray wolf."

"That would look nice," Devin agreed.

They had misunderstood his intentions. No matter to him. They could keep a few heads for display. So would he.

"Mind if I join you?" a woman's voice spoke as soft as a song. Darrion turned to see the doctor standing in the doorway.

"I don't know," Duke said, smiling his gentlemen's smile. "Can you? It's about to get a little, uh…crimson in here. If you catch my drift."

Almond eyes roamed over the kitchen at all the men looking at her. Their stares left her unfazed. She leaned against the doorsill. Arms folded. "After years in the OR, I'm more comfortable with a knife in my hand than a cup of tea…if you catch my drift. So a little crimson's fine with me."

"You ever gut game before?"

"No," she said, honestly. "But I listen well and I learn quick."

Without so much as a blink, Duke flipped the knife in his hand from blade out to hilt first and held it up to her in approval. Darrion was intrigued to see if she could stomach it. For dressing game, Duke always used Mr. Mayhem. Forged to a pattern of welded steel, its hilt was a rare custom make of jade, deer bone, marbled flint, and obsidian.

It cut like a guillotine.

Angelique left the doorway and took Mayhem in her left hand as she went down on one knee before the carcass. Duke moved to her left side and instructed with a father's patience. It reminded Darrion of his first gutting and Devin's as well.

"Most game, regardless of the size is done the same way. Most important to remember is you never puncture any of the vitals with the knife while skinning and cleaning. I'm sure you were taught something similar in surgery. Also, you never want to contaminate the pelt or the meat with urine or feces. First thing we'd normally do is tie off the penis with a string or cord." Duke motioned to the animal's genitalia. "As you can see, we've already done that. Now, starting at the tail, make a cut just beneath the skin all the way up to the chin and around the base of the neck." Duke gripped her knife hand and carefully guided Mayhem. Cutting all the way upward until the knife stopped at the jawbone. "Next, cut down the inside of each leg to the joint above each foot." Once again, he slowly guided her hand, making sure cuts along the fur. "Now, it's just like peeling a grape." Duke sat the knife down then took her hands and gave her a firm grip of the pelt. With a yank, she gave a firm pull and the skin came peeling off like a bloody toupee.

Then the gagging followed. A wet choked cough. Before Darrion could spot where the noise came from, Roth Garrett was at the sink, losing Mary's wonderfully baked lasagna. Little Donell looked just as queasy. Poor Wendell never made it to the sink. Lunch had to jump out the way just to avoid the spew.

Darrion had to smile.

DEREK

Everyone in the family did as Duke bid.

Things went as planned on the following morning. To Derek's surprise, Luna survived the drive back to Chicago. After spending three hours in surgery at Durham Animal Hospital she was kept overnight. Duke and Viola brought the tough old bitch home on Wednesday evening, just one hour before the family Thanksgiving dinner. Derek made sure Angelique packed well enough for an extended stay in Duke and Viola's home and he arranged for men from his private security company to escort him and his campaign team to every obligation from Thursday until further notice.

His first obligation required his presence for the festivity at St. Victor Catholic Church. Though Derek loved his father, there were some days he was glad to be a Porter. Suddenly he became aware that this day could be one of them. He smiled for the cameras. Shook Archbishop Courdenay's hand.

Tonight, the Great Hall was filled with guests surrounded by the thick smells of the holiday feast. For some reason, Derek never noticed the architecture before this night. Massive wooden collar beams and carved arched braces lined the roof. Every wall stood sculpted with 14th century tracery. Massive banners streamed from floor to ceiling. Crimson, gold, and white. Three rows of pews, which usually sat arranged in U-shape, had all been removed and replaced with five-chair table seating for the publicized gathering. This modification did quite well to accommodate all 281 guests. Including his security team.

He hated private security. Whenever he walked into a room flanked by broad-chested suits donning dark sunglasses and earwigs, everyone with wary eyes on them went rigid. As if at any moment shots would ring out, blasting through the nearest window. Derek much more preferred his company at ease in his presence. But his father was right. Until the threat was put down, the nuisance of bodyguards would have to be endured. Though discretion had to be used, Derek placed two guards outside of his mother's home as well with specific orders not to be seen or heard unless their defense was necessary. At least the men of Executive Protection were top brass selection when President Reagan had charmed the Windy City with a visit four years ago.

The merriments of the church gathering went on for hours. But for Derek it only lasted until 6:00 in the evening. After the reporters had their questions answered and the photographers had their fill, Derek and his three man campaign team took their leave.

With the security sedan waiting behind them, they piled into the limousine and the driver made for the Gold Coast. Viola had agreed to hold Thanksgiving dinner until they arrived. No doubt some heavy pleading from Duke was the cause of that little bargain. Viola didn't bargain, not for a Porter, and certainly not for a Porter in her own house.

His motorcade made the drive to the DeGrate home in less than a half hour. Derek gave orders for his security team to remain in the foyer. This night would be a draining one, he knew. He could hear the arguing coming from the library before the maid opened the doors. They were all bickering so loudly, no one heard them enter. Wendell gave a loud sneeze and Garrett accidentally knocked into a tall, wooden floor lamp. But not even the flicker of lighting his clumsiness caused made the men so much as glance their way. Roth Garrett quickly uprighted the lamp and the foursome took a seat on the couch in the center of the room.

Derek stared into the flames of the fireplace and let his thoughts drift. He should have been home. Instead of the distant faint warmth of burning wood, he would be enjoying the thickness of a featherbed right now and the heat of his fiancé's body beside him.

As much as it left him grated, he had to keep her here. With her grandmother living in Northbrook, sending her there would've left her more vulnerable than he would've allowed. Selfishness aside, Derek knew she would be safe in the company of DeGrate men.

"Well, Councilman," Duke said. "You'll be happy to know the results for the rabies tests came back negative."

Derek knowingly nodded. "Angie told me this morning."

Duke sat forward and folded his hands on the desk. "And you also have a new opponent for the election...Joseph Caruso."

Derek blinked back to reality. "Since when?"

"Since an hour ago. It was just announced on the news."

Derek looked at Prescott. "Who's Caruso?"

His campaign manager shook his head as if he couldn't believe it. "He's the US Attorney for the Northern District of Illinois. In '79 he ran as candidate for both the Republican and Liberal parties. He lost by the closest margin in the city's history. I guess he's going for it again."

"And this time he just might win," Darrion said. "Seeing as he has his own personal hit squad working for him."

Derek blinked at Darrion. "What?"

"Zosa was behind the attack."

"How do you know that?"

"We can't prove it," Duke said, "and we don't think Caruso is even aware of Zosa's attempt on your life. But here's what we know so far." He reached into the drawer of his desk, pulled out a strip of fur, and held it up for everyone to see. "The USDA mandates any zoo in this country use a marking system for a particular species. From the captive pelts we took, all of them have this same small white patch of fur on their left hind leg near the tail. This is from a form of cryobranding. Zookeepers use a mixture of dry ice and alcohol or liquid nitrogen to supercool a branding iron. After the skin is marked with either a series of numbers or a symbol, the skin heals and the hair grows back but without pigmentation. We're used to seeing V or U clipped ears on the animals we work with, but this is the new wave of tagging the wild." He carefully pulled at the fur, exposing the branding mark: an upper case B in a circle. "These wolves weren't numbered, they were marked with symbols. Northern grays from Brookfield Zoo — which is owned by the Forest Preserve District of Cook County." He put the skin down and rubbed his tired eyes. "Zosa is on their Board of Commissioners as is Caruso. Also an Italian. That many wolves go missing from a zoo, somebody got a handsome ransom to keep a tight lid on it."

Dutch shook his head. "I'm not surprised in the least, Duke. He made himself crystal clear the other night."

"I wouldn't put shit past Zosa," T-Bone agreed.

"Zosa is an enforcer," Derek said, "he's a bull dog. He's nothing."

"Agreed," Duke said. "But I think he acted on his own. Without sanction from the D'Amico Family."

"I'm not sure how much of that sordid history you're aware of," T-Bone said to Derek. "But it's been all negativity with the D'Amicos and Zosa since the Kings cut the Italians out as a main supplier and went straight to a cartel. Zosa didn't want to lose the profits from the powder. D'Amico thought otherwise. He wanted to pull away from drugs. So, they've been at odds for years. Now all of a sudden they're seeing eye to eye?"

"And just because Zosa forgave Zander for cutting him out," Darrion added, "doesn't mean he forgot."

"Same goes for Zane and Zeno," Taran said.

"All of our old ties to the Kings were cut a decade ago," Duke said. "When that business got severed so were any illegal ties to the Italians. That all went to Zander and Pope. After Pope got locked up, his power was diminished and after Zander's untimely demise, his sons took over Cabrini. Even if they're still raw about it all, those two hoods don't have the reach or the muscle to pull off that attack. No business that we're involved in is affecting them. So, with what happened up at the Mammoths, that wasn't old bad blood. That was new. And there's only one person in this room who stands as an immediate threat to a common enemy."

Duke looked at the Councilman. All eyes in the room followed his gaze to the couch. That didn't surprise him near so much as the lengths his enemies would go to in bringing about his end. So Derek sat there blinking back at his father.

"The Italians sent one hell of a message."

"I'm all for sending one back," Darrion said.

"Retaliation is not an option," Duke said. "We can't jeopardize the peaceful accord we have with the church."

"But he was right, Duke," Taran said. "They're not going away. And Derek's event at the church today was all over the news. They know the Councilman's still alive so they now know they failed. It won't be long before they come at us again."

"We're not gangsters," Duke said firmly. "Those days for this family are long gone. We're real estate investors. We own a furrier business. An apparel store. We've had ten years of peace. And I intend on living ten more."

"And yet after a decade of peace," Dutch cut in, "here we are again. Now, I'm not suggesting all out war here, Duke. But Darrion's right. A hit like that can't go unanswered. It wasn't just about knocking off Derek. D'Amico is pissed because the church pushed them aside to do business with you. If you're out of the picture, St. Victor will have no other choice but to consider their terms. Having an Italian in office is just icing on the cake. So retaliation is not about looking weak if we don't. It's about staying alive long enough to see all of your ambitions come into fruition."

Duke shook his head. "Bloodshed is not the answer here."

"Then what is?"

"We call a meeting. I want no futher conflict with him." Duke sat silent and still for a moment. "No one in this room is to retaliate against my wishes. No one."

♛

Derek watched as Angelique learned quickly that in the DeGrate family, food was important. This was new territory for her. Usually her holidays were spent in the OR or watching television. Celebrating wasn't something she or her grandmother did. Thanksgiving turned out to be quite the feast for Derek's kin. For them, the moon revolves around the earth, the earth revolves around the sun, and the DeGrates revolve around a table full of soul food.

Derek joined her at the sink. They washed their hands then went into the dining room and took their place at the dinner table. It all could have been torn from the page of a magazine. A colossal baked turkey. Cornbread stuffing. A stone dish full of braised candied yams. A massive glazed ham with carmelized pinneapple rounds. Two steaming bowls of collard and mustard greens and ham hocks. Macaroni and cheese. Sliced cranberry sauce. Chilled potatoe salad. Warm, flaky biscuits brushed with melted sweet butter. Black eyed peas. Baked beans. A plate piled high with thick squares of cornbread.

Everyone was already seated and there were people Derek knew she hadn't met yet. All of the children were seated at a separate table near the back corner of the room. Quite the convenient spot for the adults to keep an eye on them. Duke stood at the head of the table and led the family prayer. Like at the cabin, Derek knew Angelique went with the motions. Head bowed as a courtesy. He honestly didn't mind marrying an athiest. Love wasn't bound by church. Not to him.

Then Duke carved the turkey. Everyone chattered loudly, taking heaping spoonfuls of every dish on the table. While heads were bent over plates, relishing the enjoyment of eating, Derek sat quiet through dinner with the look of a man with the weight of the world pressing on his mind. When Angelique asked if he was alright, she got a nod and news that a liberal candidate, Caruso, was running for the Mayoral office as well.

Angelique did not understand all of the encumbrance of campaigning, even so she must have kown that meant opposition he didn't care for.

She fiddled with her fork. " I'm sitting here, inwardly wishing there was some way to help you. But I don't even know where to start. Politics remains my constant weakness; nevertheless, I do understand what all liberals have in common. Their focus always stands on regression."

"Correct," Derek agreed.

"Just aiming to one-up their opponent."

"Also correct."

"No speech a liberal ever gave had mass appeal because doing better than the other guy never meant a thing to voters. So, if you're going to win this election, you have to have more than tongue-in-cheek dogma." She went quiet. Thinking. Then, "What you need is epic purpose, because unswerving drive trumps ideology every time."

*Epic purpose…*Derek thought. Those two words swam in his mind.

"I don't know how," she said, "but I'm going to find it for you. A solid advantage no one can challenge, undermine, or outplay. Epic purpose…"

ZANE

Darrion hated shopping.

Worse, he hated Christmas shopping.

On Black Friday.

Among the rush of thousands of Chicagoans.

When Angelique mentioned the notion of catching sales for gifts, Duke didn't hesitate in tasking Darrion with chauffeuring her around. The good doctor became his personal charge for the day. While he would rather have been elsewhere, after the incident at the Mammoths she couldn't be allowed to go anywhere alone.

Darrion could tell she had little experience with the nightmare of retail on the day after Thanksgiving. Before he grabbed his keys to leave the house, she mentioned wanting to get some sleep and leave first thing in the morning. He scoffed at her and said, "If we don't leave before midnight, by the time we get there every store will already be raided, the aisles will be trashed, and the checkout stands will be flooded. By sunrise, there'll be nothing left."

Angelique offered to drive her Firebird. Darrion gave no objection to riding passenger. So, there he was — at half past midnight, on the Magnificent Mile. Following her around in the cold of November. In and out of any store displaying a front window item that caught her eye. All he could do was light a Newport in between stores and hope she'd give up. Of all the items she looked at, only a few purchases were made. A pair of leather gloves for DaVita. Ann Taylor: $85. A nice tanned brown wool coat for Viola. Eddie Bauer: $475. An antique adjustable folding cane of sterling silver with vine inlay and a black beech wood shaft: $1,345 — courtesy of a new antique store he had never heard of, Dolce Lucenti. But the walking stick came with gift box and carrying case included. When Darrion asked her whom the cane was for, Angelique replied with a warm smile, "Your uncle Donald. Even after his leg heals, he'll favor a knee for the rest of his life. If he has to walk with a limp, it'll be a fashionable one."

That left him with a charmed smirk at her thoughtfulness. For a fleeting moment, he couldn't wait to see what she'd bought him on Christmas morning.

A few Newports later, he found himself in Bloomingdale's. Listening to Angelique's frustrated sigh as she passed a section of ties in the men's apparel section. She looked around at all of the clothing racks as if unsure of which way to go next.

"Are you okay?" he asked.

"I'm fine," she said, dryly. She adjusted her grip on the gift-wrapped presents and walked out to the main aisle. "Thank you for bringing me out here today. I'm sure you'd rather be sleeping in. I really appreciate it."

"No problem. You're welcome."

Angelique exhaled another frustrated sigh. "I have no idea what to get Derek or his mother. Any suggestions?"

Darrion shrugged. "You know them better than I do. You're the one walking down the aisle with him. You don't know what he likes?"

"Of course I do. The problem is everything he likes he already has. What do you buy for a man who has everything?" She looked at Darrion. Searching his face for some insight. He said nothing. "You don't know anything about him? I thought you two were close?" She lowered her voice to a whisper. "If I'm not mistaken, he is your brother...The family's big dirty little secret."

"Ah...that he is."

Angelique nodded.

"Was Duke with Viola when that happened with Patricia?"

"Yes, he was."

"Oh," she said sheepishly. "I guess those two ladies won't be exchanging Christmas cards this year."

Darrion laughed at her sadistic humor and cocked his head to one side. That sounded exactly like something he would say. "No...they won't." Then a threatening wave of cautiousness took over, his laugh faded, and his voice turned serious. "We don't talk about it much. And if he told you, then you are in the circle of trust. It's a small one." He stopped walking and turned facing her. His gaze fixed. "We'll be keeping it that way."

Darrion didn't mean for it to come off as a warning. But it did. He could tell she picked up on it straightaway. Yet, by the look on her face she didn't seem offended.

"I know," she said quietly.

After a long silence between them she asked him a question he did not expect. "Your family history with the streets is that bad?"

So bold a question he couldn't think of a lie fast enough to appease her. What else could he do but tell the truth? If he didn't she would just ask Derek. His telling of the truth would be far more explicit than he would like. "Yeah," he finally said. "It is."

She gave him a wary look. He could tell the answer frightened her. "Bad enough to hurt his campaign."

Darrion corrected her. "Bad enough to smear his name and his political career for the rest of his life."

Her brow lifted.

"But...isn't his spending the holidays with the family suspicion enough?"

Darrion shook his head. "No more than his spending time with the church's Archbishop or any other friend or associate he knows. Socializing with a political investor who's financially backing your campaign is one thing. It's another entirely for that investor, who has a notorious past as a gangster, to be his father. Public knowledge of that would hurt him, Angelique. It would hurt us all."

Glass shattered towards the store's entrance. Four security guards were running towards two women in a fist fight over a red scarf. A scarlet and some blonde. Curses were being screamed in between thrown punches, pulled grips of hair, and wild kicks. The red head got the better of her opponent and all but body-slammed her onto a display table. More glass ornaments crashed to the floor. The scarf was all but forgotten by the time security had pulled them apart.

A small horde had gathered to watch the disorder and Darrion blinked in surprise when he spotted Anton Smith and Calvin Forte among them. Just to look on them and see how much they'd grown, it had really been ten years since the last time he'd seen them. Anton was only seven then. Calvin was near the same age when Duke gave up his crown and walked away from Cabrini and the King Disciples. When they were young boys Anton and Calvin favored one another. But now, the baby fat had gone from their faces. They both looked distinctively older.

Anton still kept his hair trimmed low. Light brownish skin like his late older brother, Amari, and eyes the color of copper. Though basketball season was long over, he stood swathed in a red Bulls coat. Ever the basketball fan. Calvin was slightly browner and he still had that lay of hair that smoothed flat with close waves from his short cut. Even after ten years, it didn't matter that he was in the midwest; he still wore his native NY Giants coat. Oblivious to Bears fans who might have a problem with that. Their voices carried out over the crowd, rabble rousing the brawling women.

Darrion inwardly contemplated saying hello. A swell of guilt and remorse rose up in his gut and without warning he was flung back to 1974 — the year the Five Founding Fathers of the Kings had fractured forever; the year Xavier Pope was incarcerated; Zander Harris was dead, as was Casper Phoenix Sr., Pastor Troy had found God, so he turned his back on the gang. Duke's dream of empowering African-Americans fell to drugs, death, and domination, leaving his vision to reign as a nightmare.

Darrion left Amari to lead the Disciples after Pope was imprisoned on the hopes of one good man soldiering on to fight against the trail of violence and drugs Zander had brought to the community. But he was ill used to Zane's treachery. Even now, it was widely speculated that Zane used the lack of control to his advantage, betraying Amari to his death. Though never proven, Darrion knew Zane ordered the kill.

Amari's death had weighed heavy on him. Now, he knew it always would. For that reason, he decided to see about Anton.

"Are you okay?" Angelique asked.

His reluctance must have shown on his face. "I just saw a couple of cats I used to know."

Angelique's brow lifted. "Are you gonna go and say hello?"

Darrion looked down at her. "You don't mind?"

"Depends," she said, smiling. "Am I invited?"

"Sure."

They walked towards the commotion. On reflex, Darrion caught Anton's hands. While security wrangled with the brawling women, he snatched up the red scarf and slipped it into his shopping bag. Ever the pickpocket, Anton had quick eyes and even faster fingers.

"Ant," Darrion said. "Long time, no speak."

Anton blinked at him in disbelief then laughed off the shock. They knocked knuckles. "It's been a long minute, KD...Or should I just call you Darrion?"

"What it is, Son?" Calvin looked him up and down, eyeing the black suit and long coat draped over Darrion's arm.

"Punchy," Darrion nodded.

"Hi," Angelique said.

Darrion suddenly realized he'd forgotten his manners.

"Ant, Punchy, this is Angelique James. I brought her out to do a little Christmas shopping."

"It's a pleasure," Ant said, holding his hand out.

Angelique pulled a hand free from the weight of her gift boxes and shook it. "Nice to meet you."

"Uh oh," Calvin said with a sly grin on his face. "Got yourself a petite little D-Queen, huh?"

"Naw, man. She's a friend of the family. The soon to be wife of Councilman Derek Porter."

"Oh!"

"Dabbling in politics now, huh?" Ant asked. "Mr. DeGrate done moved on up like the Jeffersons." Calvin laughed. All Darrion could do was smirk and shake his head. "So, what you been up to for the past decade?"

"Working for my father. He's still running Christian LeBarron. Everybody wants a fur coat, so..."

"Right, right."

"So, what you been up to lately?"

"Hustle, hustle. You know how it is. Bills to pay and mouths to feed. On that grind. It don't stop in Cabrini."

Darrion nodded. A long silence hung in the air until it made him well aware that Calvin and Angelique were looking back and forth between him and Ant. Waiting for something. Caught in his uncomfortable moment. Forced to bear it with him until the silence broke.

Ant broke it before he did. "Welp, man, let me get up out of here before I miss the bus." He checked his watch. "Last one runs at 1:00 in the a.m., so I got about ten minutes before I'm hoofin' it."

"The bus?" Angelique said sadly. "Oh no, it's the holidays. We'll take you."

"Yaw don't mind?" Calvin asked.

Darrion shook his head. "It's all good. As long as you don't mind squeezing in the back of a Firebird."

"You pushing a Firebird?"

"It's hers."

"Don't worry," Angelique said, "I can handle it. I promise."

"Alright then." Calvin reached for her boxes. "Let me carry these, then. And you just lead the way, Miss Lady Ma'am."

It took them less than five minutes to exit Bloomingdale's and make it across the parking lot. Ant cursed at the sight of her Firebird. Calvin wolf-whistled and walked around it twice—like a captivated man circling a woman's hypnotic physique. He stopped at the hood.

"What year is it?" he asked.

"Turbo, '81," she said, popping the trunk.

"V8?"

"Yes, Sir."

Calvin didn't seem to notice her taking the boxes from his hands. He walked around it one more time. Eyeing the colossal blower sticking up out of the hood. It all but decapitated the head off the Firebird's trademark golden bird.

"Stick or automatic?"

"Stick shift."

"Black paint, F-body, blown bird, white wall tires and bucket seats. Daaaaaamn."

"It's my father's," she said, waving off his excitement. She opened the driver's door and pulled the front seat forward. "After you."

They all piled in, she cranked the engine, and the Firebird came alive with an earth-shaking rumble.

♛

Stay in the car," Darrion said. "Keep the doors locked. I'll be back in a few minutes."

Darrion, Ant, and Punchy made their way to the front entrance of the highrise building and disappeared inside. Angelique hit the locks on the doors and looked up with a shudder at the graffiti-scarred structure. The building sat in the middle of its block, directly across the street from a dollar store and a gun shop. Twenty-two stories in all, every floor had several apartments with boarded up windows, burned out areas on the façade, and the entire height of the building's walkways stood enclosed behind steel fencing extending from the bottom floor to the height of its roof.

Instead of a green lawn, a large slab of pavement made the grounds which set the building back at least fifty paces from the street.

It looked like a prison.

Spending most of her childhood in the still, hushed city of Northbrook, Illinois couldn't keep the horror stories of the notorious housing project from reaching her ears. In Chicago, anyone with a pulse and a will to keep it knew about Cabrini Green. These low-income tenements sat located less than a mile from her own home on the Gold Coast.

Angelique knew her street knowledge stood lacking on which gang controlled which building. But with Darrion's ease of walking inside and his family history with gangs, she knew this high-rise must have belonged to the King Disciples.

She found it difficult to see well through the mesh of the terrace fencing, but on almost every floor a mass of thugs swarmed about the breezeways. Loitering in and out of doorways. Music blasting. Loud talking. Gathered in suspicious huddles. All of the commotion sent a nervous wrench through her stomach.

A few drunks stumbled about on the only small trash strewn lawn she saw. But the rest of the cracked concrete looked relatively abandoned save a few people moving about the side parking lot. Perhaps she had missed the midnight dope rush. Perhaps all the junkies were inside making sure the November winds didn't blow away their powder. Perhaps all of the bangers were out Christmas shopping or stealing cars. Perhaps their Christmas shopping was stealing cars.

Pondering nighttime extracurricular gangbanging activities was the last errant thought she entertained. Earsplitting screams rang out into the night followed by cries and shouts from somewhere up above. Angelique leaned forward, looked through the windshield, and froze.

Her eyes locked on an obscure, dark figure falling from the rooftop of the building. She gasped in horror as it hit the lawn with a loud, unmistakable meaty crack. For a split second, the world slowed to a jarring pause. If the appalling lucidity hit any harder she would've been hurled through the windshield of her car like a poltergeist.

What happened next she did not expect.

Training took hold.

Dr. James popped the trunk and unfastened her seat belt — cursing through the shock as she got out of the car.

"Oh my God. Christ!" She ran around to the trunk, shoved the presents out of the way, and snatched out her medical bag.

More shouts came from the rooftop. A man yelling threats over a woman's screams. "Now his debt is on your head! You got one week, bitch! One! And if you don't have my money, you catching free flyer miles with his ass!"

She blocked out the man's vulgar tirade and focused her vision on the twitching body in the grass. His full on seizure could be seen a mile away. Chancing the high heels on the cracked concrete almost guaranteed a twisted ankle or a fall or both. Her pencil skirt went down to her calves — which would make for a difficult sprint to the building. Hardly crisis ready. But, the thickness of the her coat would keep her from skinning her elbows if she took a tumble.

She slung the bag over her shoulder, dashed across the pavement to the grass, and the instant she knelt down on the bloody lawn, the man started seizing. His body was mangled. One of his legs lay bent in a direction no limb should go. His neck protruded in an unnatural bulge away from his shoulders. Both hands postured. Curling up into tight fists and with every spasm she heard gurgling deep in his throat. Then bright red blood came sputtering out of his mouth.

Angelique unzipped her bag, pulled out a C-collar, put a hand to his carotid to check for a pulse and put another hand on his chest to keep his body from shaking his broken neck.

A small crowd gathered near by.

Some looked as old as seventy and others looked to be as young as ten. All of them just stood there blinking. No one said a word. No one moved.

Medical instincts and her Hippocratic oath compelled what came out of her mouth. "Can someone help me hold him still please, I need to…" She paused, realizing people only came closer to see who he was, then they all started moving away from him as if avoiding the plague or they just stepped around him like he wasn't even there at all.

No one is going to help me, she thought. *No one is going to help him*. Pangs of alienated repression hit her and for just a split second, as if an ethereal door swung open from the other side of some deep abyss, Angelique caught a raw glimpse of cold detachment and self preservation in its darkest form.

For the first time in years, she could do nothing for a wounded stranger. She placed a gentle hand on his head to keep his skull steady and suddenly the seizing stopped. She remembered to breath when Anton's voice echoed out from the breezeway near the door. "Where the hell is all that screaming coming from?" he asked.

When the door swung open Ant and Punchy halted. Their surprise registered strange. They just blinked at her, seeming more taken aback with the spectacle in the bloody grass than the fact that she was knelt in it.

Ant dared a step closer and covered his whispered curses of shock with a fist. "Is that Jaliel?"

"Yup," Punchy nodded. "That's him."

Ant shook his head. "I guess he didn't pay up."

Angelique worked the C-collar on his bowed neck.

When she reached into her bag for a pupil light, his chest went still. He wasn't breathing. His entire body went limp and his eyes parted open in a lifeless, unseeing haze. She felt his carotid again. Still a heartbeat but no respiration. She cursed and snatched off her coat, laying it on top of his body, then reached into her bag for a pair of latex gloves and an intubation kit. She pulled the laryngoscope blade out, gloved up, and slowly worked it into his mouth. "I don't have a cell phone," she said to Anton. "I need one of you to call the police and an ambulance."

"Why?" Ant asked. "They won't come."

She slid the endotracheal tube down his throat.

"What do you mean they won't come? He just got thrown from a roof!" With swift hands, she attached the ambu bag, and started squeezing air back into his lungs.

Punchy shrugged. "So? That don't mean nothing. They still won't come."

She looked up at him. "Why not?"

"Disciples kept shooting at 'em," Ant said.

Punchy nodded in agreement. "Yeah, it was...um...about two weeks back." He pointed to a small patch of grass close to the parking lot near the side of the building. She hadn't seen it from the car. "Two po-po's got killed right over there on the other side of that fence. Ever since then, Chi-Town PD won't fuck wit' Cabrini no mo'."

"Well what about an ambulance if somebody's having a heart attack?"

"Nope," Punchy said dryly.

"They just keel over, I guess," Ant added.

"The coroner?"

"Nope," they both said.

"What about the fire department? Will they at least respond if we call?"

"Maybe," Punchy said with another cold shrug. "If we set his ass on fire."

"Yup," Ant said. "And even then they probably still won't come."

"Nope."

Angelique let out a frustrated puff of winter vapor. All she could do was keep squeezing that bag. But keeping his lungs working wouldn't last much longer if she didn't get him to a hospital. Night winds started in on her bones and both of her ears were starting to go numb. She could barely feel her fingers from the cold.

This isn't happening. This is not happening to me. Only one other option was yet to be exhausted. "What about family?"

"He got a grandma," Ant said. "But she in a old folks home."

"Mmm-hmm," Punchy added. "She ain't got no car."

"What about your ride?"

Angelique shook her head. "It's a Firebird. Too small. His entire spine is probably crushed, I'll kill him just by trying to cram him into the back seat."

"Oh yeah, true."

"They'll mete it out themselves, Angie," Darrion said.

She was so occupied with squeezing air into a doomed set of lungs she hadn't even noticed Darrion standing over her. Angelique looked up at him only to see a look of subtle pity staring back at her. Like she couldn't have possibly been more naive. Street ignorant. Blissfully oblivious.

This is Disciple turf. I get it. But I'm supposed to just let a man die at my feet without at least trying to save him? Really, Darrion?

"Yeah," Punchy agreed, "the last time Zane tossed somebody off the roof, he only laid there for like…a week."

"They finally scraped him up when they got sick of the smell," Ant chimed in.

Darrion pulled off his long coat and draped it around her shoulders then stood and held out his hand. "Come on, I'll take you home."

She kept squeezing the bag. "I'm a doctor, Darrion. I cannot just leave him here. This is a person lying here!"

She let go of the bag long enough to pull off one of her bloody gloves and reached up into his pants pocket for his cell phone. It was so bulky and heavy she wondered how it fit. She pulled the antenna out, flipped it open, and started dialing.

Kirkland Travis answered on the third ring.

"Who's this?"

"It's Dr. James, I need a favor. I need to borrow your truck."

As one of Scott Joplin's most astute new interns, Travis Kirkland had a very promising future in cardiothoracics and as his new attending in-charge, Dr. James felt it was her obligatory duty to make every second of his internship the dread of hell.

Now seemed like a good time to crack the whip.

"Do you mind if I ask why?"

"Do you mind if I can't answer that question?"

"Only if you don't mind listening to a dial tone."

"Okay," she said. "I'm in Cabrini Green where some drug lord threw a kid off of a roof, he is now smeared all over the lawn, and I am bagging him in the hopes that he will make it long enough for the trip to the hospital, and I need your truck so I can peel him up off the grass and take him to the nearest ER, so that his grandmother can possibly identify what used to be his face."

Kirkland went quiet for a long time.

Angelique thought he'd hung up. "Hello?"

"Jesus Christ, Dr. James what the hell are you doing down there?!"

Angelique could see his freckled forehead going up in shock through the phone. Those thick red eyebrows in an angry 'V', and that cornfed mouth hanging open in that shocked little 'O'.

She didn't have time for this.

"May I please have the truck?"

"Are you down there by yourself?"

"No."

"Who are you with?"

"Family."

"You have family in Cabrini?"

"You want in the double-ticker surgery, then get your ass down here pronto like!"

If that didn't make him cave, nothing would.

In just two weeks time, on Tuesday morning, Christmas Day, little Shawna Clark, a nine year old with cardio-myopathy, would be undergoing a surgery nearly unheard of in the western hemisphere. Dr. James would be grafting a donor heart onto Shawna's own weak heart to take over the arduous work of pumping blood so that her sick organ could rest until it was strong enough to beat on its own. Until her heart healed she would have two hearts instead of one. A double-ticker was the surgery of a lifetime for any intern. It was like finding shit from a rocking horse. It would never happen again. And he knew it.

"Okay, okay," Kirkland relented. "Just stay where you are and I'll be there in fifteen minutes."

Angelique looked down at the ambu bag and gave it another firm squeeze. "I'm not going anywhere, Kirk."

She hung up and waited.

♛

Jaliel had stolen five hundred fucking dollars. Five hundred to feed his habit. Even then Zane gave the crackhead a full week to pay it back. Not a soft move. A patient one. Jaliel was given the extension for one reason. He knew how to sell rock and he always brought back good money. Giving him a week notice plus interest seemed like the best decision to make at the time. Zane had given him until midnight on Thanksgiving. He didn't have the cash. He left the King of Kings no other choice. Now Jaliel's girl, Necee, had one week. Or she'd be tossed off the roof just the same.

Zane couldn't tolerate theft anymore than he could tolerate an informer. He would find another dealer that could make money just as fast as Jaliel. But that would take some time. He plopped down on the couch, put his feet up on the coffee table, and grabbed the remote. No sooner had he turned on the television, his walkie-talkie came alive. Whoever pressed the talk button didn't know he was listening.

"It's him."

"You sure?"

"I know what I'm looking at, man. I'm telling you it's him."

"Zane..."

He grabbed the walkie-talkie off the table. "What?"

"It's Q-Ball. I'm up on the roof with Lefty, walking perimeter. It looks like some doctor is on the ground in the Killing Fields. Working on Jaliel. Trying to save him or something. I sent Lefty down to check it out and you won't believe who's down there with her."

♛

Darrion watched the rusty, light blue pickup truck rumble to a stop. He mentally grimaced as a lanky, red-haired male — who must have been Kirk — cut off the engine and ran to the truck bed. At first glance he could have been no older than twenty plus six or twenty and seven.

He came running with a bright orange backboard in hand. White hospital jacket flapping against the cold winds, revealing light blue scrubs. He looked the part as one of the good doctor's established equals, but as he came closer, youthful features came into view and Darrion knew he would be carded at the liquor store for a long time to come.

He rushed to Angelique's side and the instant he laid the back-board on the grass. The twosome went back and forth, discussing the best way to get Jaliel onto the board without causing further damage.

What a waste.

Jaliel was dying slow.

With or without the rooftop helping him out.

If the fall hadn't done him in, the dope would have. Darrion stood there watching good hands — skilled hands — at work on a worthless two-bit junkie. If she wanted to save a life, couldn't she have saved the life of someone who wanted to live?

Darrion glanced over the small crowd still gathered at a distance. Some whispered or pointed. Most of them just stood there with blank empty faces. It made him wonder how long it must have been since a paramedic set foot in Cabrini.

Jaliel's broken body meant nothing more than another shattered remnant of an era long gone. Cabrini's gangland had become seventy acres of forgotten souls; the land hell had spat back out of its gaping maw.

"KD," Ant said.

Darrion blinked out of his grim thoughts to see Anton starring down the breezeway with his jaw clenched.

Zane Harris and his tyrannical brother Zeno came stalking down the breezeway. Darrion could tell by the obvious, cocky lurch in their steps this would be no pleasant reunion.

A mob of men followed close behind. Guns in hand. Several growling Rottweilers leashed on thick chains striding along side them. Curses and threats and angry muttering rose all around the men as they drew nearer. Most of the young new faces were

Disciples Darrion had never seen before, but Zane's smug face had not changed one flick over the past ten years.

He still stood shorter than his younger brother. With the dark eyes and hard, miserly features of a Harris. With every step, Zane carried the swaggered air of Napoleon's raging syndrome. Like a man obsessed with trying to knee and elbow his way up in the world. A thick gold rope chain swung against his black leather jacket as he walked. Blue denim jeans, white sneakers, and Darrion couldn't miss the Uzi in his hands.

As the mob trekked onto the lawn and came to a halt the ever-present malice on Zeno's face became all the more apparent.

Surrounding a missing eye an ugly scar slashed through the left side of his face from brow to cheek. Darrion knew the mark had to be anything but an accident. Yet it seemed a mutilation the gangster felt proud of. Instead of a red meaty hole or a sunken flap of skin for a shapeless eyelid Zeno embellished his marring with menacing style. In place of a standard matching glass prosthetic eye sat a polished white opal bejeweled by a sparkling black eagle. His long dreadlocks were pulled back into a ponytail and he stood swathed in low sagging black denim, clean black sneakers, and an outsized red leather coat.

Like his brother, Zeno came armed for conflict with an AK-47.

Darrion always kept two Colts in a twin holster for concealed carry strapped to the small of his back. But he doubted a .45 would save his life or the doctor's against the arsenal of Zane and his minions.

"Well, well, well," Zane scoffed. "The fallen prince. Slumming it from the Gold Coast to see the King, hmm?"

Darrion assumed by his referring to 'King', Zane meant himself. The Mad King was all the original Disciples called him behind his back and it was common knowledge in Cabrini that Pope ruled all Disciples from Stateville Penitentiary. But Darrion never dared underestimate a Harris' hunger for advancement.

"Zane," Darrion said in greeting and gave a nod to his brother. "Zeno."

"So what seems to be the problem here?"

"No problem. I just figured you wouldn't mind if we helped out with your exterior sanitation problem."

Zane cast a hard glare down at the doctor and her intern.

Somehow they'd managed to transfer Jaliel's broken body onto the backboard and Kirk had already fastened all of the belt straps and set to working on tightening the knee strap to immobilize the twisted leg.

"I do mind actually," Zane said, not lifting his shrewd glare from the duo. "Stop bagging him. Now."

For a moment the the good doctor was so shocked all she could do was blink up at him. Then she looked at Kirk and back down to the ambu bag. Zane's sharp tone seemed to seize her composure because Darrion could see the fear washing over her features. Kirk looked even more petrified than the good doctor. His face went whiter than his hospital coat. Angelique nervously blinked up at the Disciple leader again, then she gave one more squeeze to the bag and stopped. Jaliel's ribcage sank instantly, expelling its last lungful of air.

"This basehead owed me a debt," Zane said. "Until that debt gets paid in full by his girlfriend, he stays here to rot. And if she don't pay, she gets sent down here to meet him."

"How much does he owe?" Darrion asked.

"None of your fucking business how much he owe!" Zeno spat.

"Tsssss," Zane hissed and threw up a hand to silence his brother.

Darrion could see Zeno's cold glare from his peripheral. Giving Zane's brother the satisfaction of meeting that cruel, mutilated stare was something he would not do. Ignoring Zeno would snub that ego far worse than giving in to a verbal spat. So Darrion kept an intent eye on the Disciple leader instead of entertaining his brother's rudeness.

"Plus interest?" Darrion added to his previous question.

"Ten grand," Zane said. "Plus interest make it fifteen."

"He's got a grandmother. Same as you, Zane. And if anything happened to you, Muriel would want to know. As your grandmother, she has a right to know. She earned that right because she raised you. He owes you fifteen, I'll make it twenty to take him off your hands and make sure Ms. Loistene gets to bury him proper for the holidays."

For a long moment Zane said nothing. He sucked his teeth and looked down at the corpse, mulling it over. Contemplating. Darrion knew all to well how merciless a Harris could be. Even

Muriel was a wicked, bitter old crow. She didn't raise two grandsons to rule war torn highrise towers with kindness and kisses. That kind of reign came learned by the fist and the rod. Even still, Zane and Zeno adored Ms. Muriel. So, from one grandmother to another, Zane knew Darrion was right.

"You think you a real slick motherfucker, don't you?" Zane asked.

Darrion said nothing.

"You got the cash on you?"

Darrion pulled a money clip from the inside pocket of his suit jacket. "Fifteen now. I'm good for the other five." He pulled the folded mound of cash from the clip and handed it to Zane. "I'll get you the rest later on today before midnight."

Zane fanned through the cash and handed it to Zeno.

"Count it." He waited until his brother gave a nod, then he looked at Darrion. "We good then. If he *truly is* no longer among the living. See, I don't know what your Doc here did before I got here. So, before you take him, we'll be making sure he's real fucking dead." Zane cut his eyes to Angelique. "Take the tube out his mouth."

She kept her eyes on Jaliel's unmoving chest.

Darrion watched her whole body stiffen. Her spine, ramrod straight. Eyes, not one blink, but her hand gave a tremble. Darrion knew it had nothing to do with the cold. She tightened her grip on the ambu bag and gave a pull—disconnecting from the tube. Jaliel's misshapen neck gave an unnatural sinking motion as she slowly pulled the bloody tube from his throat.

"The collar," Zane commanded further. "Off."

Angelique just sat there on her knees. Staring in a detached daze at the red grass. Kirk blinked at her. Then at Zane. He willed his arms to do what she refused to and undid the Velcro strap from Jaliel's broken neck. Seconds later the collar was off.

"Tsssss," Zane hissed with a swift, sharp flick of his finger and popped his head in Darrion's direction. Her intern knew exactly what he meant. He rose promptly and moved aside. Angelique swallowed hard, slowly rose from the grass, and walked over to Darrion.

"Give him his halo," Zane said to his brother.

Zeno Harris stepped forward, aimed his AK, and opened fire on the corpse. Littering the ground with bullet casings. The crowd shrank back at the rifle thundering into the night air. Kirk dived to the grass and curled up into the fetal position, covering his head with his hands. Darrion threw an arm out to Angelique and pushed her behind him. She gave a wordless cry of terror and ducked down at his back, covering her ears. Ant threw an arm over his face. Shielding any stray bullets from finding his skull. Punchy stood slightly hunched over behind Ant with his head turned away.

Zeno emptied the entire magazine, sweeping his AK from side to side, spraying the corpse from skull to sneakers until the steel made that sharp metallic click of an empty chamber. A sadistic smile of true satisfaction spread over his scarred face as a wisp of smoke wafted out from the barrel.

Stunned silence hung in the air. No one moved.

With an eerie, professional detachment unlike anything Darrion had ever seen, Zeno leaned the rifle against his shoulder and coolly walked away. Whistling a tune as if he had just purchased the Sunday paper on a mid-summer's day.

"Merry Christmas, Doc," Zane said.

With that, he turned and sauntered back down the breezeway. His pack of loyal hoods and hounds following close behind. They laughed. Filled with a raucous as they disappeared around the corner.

♛

What in the hell is this?" Calvin Clyde asked with a frown.

"I need a favor," Darrion said.

"Looks to me like you need a miracle." Calvin looked at the corpse in the truck bed. His frown suggested a struggle to recognize what may have been a human being at some point in time.

Evergreen Mortuary had been handling bodies in the Near North for as long as Darrion could remember. Family owned since 1962, it was mostly supplemented by income from every Catholic Church in the area. The massive, three-story home bore a rough exterior of untreated brick creating stained horizontal lines along the façade from years of weather. But the parlor was a long-standing totem among friends and family who passed through its oak doors to say their last goodbyes to loved ones.

Darrion knew any time after midnight Mr. Andrew Clyde had gone. Leaving any nightly duties to his youngest son, Calvin. Other than the light Clyde skin, wide nose, and lanky build, father and son had very little in common when it came to running a legal parlor.

Mr. Clyde would never take a dime under the table to rid of an incriminating body. But, for the right price, Darrion could rely on Calvin to cremate or bury any unwanted evidence of a close encounter gone bad. Tonight, his mortician's skills were needed more than his discretion. Ms. Loistene deserved to see her grandson one last time without passing out from the sight of what thirty rounds could do to a body.

Darrion felt a wave of morbid curiosity tug at the better of him. Calvin had gifted hands when it came to handling the dead. Still, making a broken, bullet trodden man look like…a man again? Darrion had to see this.

Calvin let out a breath and scratched his head. "Do I want to ask what happened to it?"

"Got tossed from a roof and had a clip emptied into him from an AK. His grandmother is Loistene."

"Ms. Monroe?" Calvin asked, shocked.

Darrion nodded.

That took Calvin by surprise. He turned from the truck bed and looked at Darrion. His words came without poise. "Ms. Loistene? I worked on two of her sons last year. And two of her grandsons the year before that." He gave a glance back to the corpse. "Who is this?"

"Jaliel."

"She got anymore grandkids left?"

Darrion shook his head. "Not after tonight."

"I usually don't handle fragmented remains." Calvin tongued his cheek and shrugged. "He looks too tall for a smooth lay in a standard pine. Normally that would be a problem. But, often times me and my Pops, we get these bodies in that are so tall we can't get 'em in the casket. Then we have to break their ankles and fold 'em back just to get them to fit. So at least that won't be a problem here.

"We could just lay his legs on top of his chest and *voila*. But his skull…it's just caved in." Calvin shook his head in disgust. "I mean…damn. There was this one guy who got into a car accident and his head looked like a squashed beach ball. I just worked on rebuilding it with some cotton and plaster and Styrofoam. You know, reformed it from the inside out until his head fit his body. Then I…"

"Calvin," Darrion said, rubbing his tired eyes. "I've had a very violent, shitty week, man…Please just help me unload the corpse and get him inside."

Calvin shut his mouth and moved quickly.

He was a good kid.

Seventeen. Smart for his young years. But he always rambled on and on about little details of his work that not even the Son of Sam himself would care to know.

Darrion rapped on the truck with his knuckle. Kirk climbed out from behind the steering wheel of the old Chevy. He made his way around to the bed. Darrion could see some of the blood had returned to his pale face, but Zeno's madness still left him shaken and off-color.

Angelique got out of the Firebird and quietly stood by the back door of the mortuary. Watching in silence as the three men unloaded the backboard from the truck bed. Calvin told her to hold the door open as they moved past her with the body.

"Guess the reaper's never idle, huh?" Calvin asked the intern.

"Guess not," Kirk said dryly.

"Son of a bitch will never take me alive." He burst out laughing. "Get it? Alive?"

Darrion shook his head. "Christ, Calvin."

DEREK

Derek had never liked McCree's Pub.

He preferred to drink at home but, whenever his staff suggested he mingle with voters for the campaign trail, he never opposed. He had never seen the place more than half full before tonight and he preferred it that way. Crammed between downtown businesses, the pub sat on a block that ran a mile long and boasted plenty of TVs, cold beers on tap, and decent food. Die hard sports fans from all over the city came to watch a game here. Even the menu was pretty diverse. Anything from wraps and sandwiches to pasta, pizza, pork chops, or baked figs. They actually made their own hummus. For those who wanted a perfect bar to catch up with a friend without dressing up for the occasion, McCree's was the blue-collar dwelling. Which also made the establishment an electorate's paradise.

For the past two hours he'd been shaking hands with so many strangers wearing 'VOTE PORTER' pins, he was convinced hand to hand viral gastroenteritis would find him by morning. He hated shaking hands. A slight case of mysophobia was the last thing a political candidate needed to suffer through, but eventually the risk of avoidance forced him to take a quick bathroom break.

Derek came out of the bathroom stall, rolled up his sleeves, and washed his hands vigorously until the skin almost hurt. He checked his appearance in the mirror. As a result of all the mayoral activism, his reddish-brown complexion looked more pallid than ever today. His eyebrows had thinned and his moustache and goat-tee had threads of gray. A quick guestimate told a loss of at least ten pounds. But that was campaigning.

Pounding through the ceilings of promotion, contributions drew a total of $10 million from the Porter war chest so far. Even with the backing of the church, Duke, and Ugo Brassi, all of the stressors didn't seem to ease. Compared to Burns he was down in the polls by thirty percent. Against Caruso, he was down by nearly forty percent.

Derek made his way to the bar. Wendell sat nursing his third ginger ale next to Garrett and Prescott. Listening to their conversation as if he were trying to learn something imperative. But their voices were raised. Derek noticed now that his own staff didn't have a monopoly on the garish words. Everyone in the bar seemed in an uproar about something. Angelique reached past Wendell for the remote and aimed for the television.

Derek pressed against her and let the sweet scent of lavender hair fill his nostrils. When he moved his arms around her waist the smooth silk of her blouse slid along the palms of his hands.

"Did the Bears lose?" he asked with a wide grin.

Angelique held up a finger to her lips. "Shhhh. Listen."

She turned up the volume and a broadcaster's polished, breaking news voice drowned out every raised throat in the bar.

> *"…it was just two weeks ago when Mayor, Jayne Burns, moved into one of Cabrini's highrise buildings in an effort to control the brazen lawlessness of its residents. Around the clock she was flanked by police and bodyguards to ensure her safety. After the massive shootout between gangs and police, which left two officers dead, the Mayor was taking no chances during her stay. To increase her security, she went even further, having the back doors to the building welded shut. The fourteen days that followed were made of an uneasy, quiet peace, however. Not one shot was fired, not one drug deal was made.*
>
> *"Now that the Mayor has moved back*

*to her luxury condo, things seem to have gone
right back to the way they were, with one
exception. When Burns left, she didn't take
down the welded doors, which drug dealers are
now using to keep police out. What was once a
building authorities could enter, has now
become an impenetrable fort. Gang members are
now openly dealing drugs in front of the building,
even in broad daylight, and when police pull
up they simply walk back inside, lock the front
door, and walk away. There is nothing police can
do about it because they can't sneak up the back
to infiltrate the building.*

    *"Worsening matters, several other high
rises, which are also controlled by gangs, are
now copying what Burns did, welding their back
doors to keep authorities away. Occupants now
feel like hostages in their own homes, afraid to
let their children outside to play for fear of
gunfire. Those few Cabrini residents who are
employed are often unable to go to work. Several
elderly residents are unable to go to their
doctor's appointments. All of this has left some
Cabrini residents feeling that the Mayor's stay
was just a weak political ploy that has now
backfired against the same people she vowed to
protect…"*

Angelique put down the remote and called the bartender. "Marty, do you mind if we use your private barroom?"

"Sure, doll. Take it for as long as you need."

She tapped Derek on his backside, "Come on and bring the boys with you."

They convened in the wide, drafty secluded room. Marty brought extra drinks and a few side dishes of fries and hush puppies. He shut the door behind him, leaving them nothing but a private table booth, a wide bar, and a television.

"So what's cooking in that brain of yours," Garrett said to Angelique, smiling wide. His white teeth showed brilliantly against his dark skin. He scratched his goatee waiting to see what she had to say. Prescott was also watching her expectantly.

Derek, too — which must have given young Wendell the sneaky brass to reach for a bottle of Jack Daniels.

Derek didn't even look the kid's way. He just reached for the bottle, took it from him, and sat it out of his grasp. Out the corner of his eye Wendell's guilt-ridden, disappointed slump looked as sad as a punished puppy. Derek couldn't blame him for trying though.

Angelique grabbed the remote off the bar, turned it to the Channel 9 news coverage of Burns, and hit the mute button.

"This is perfect," she said. Her brown eyes narrowed with a wicked concentration. "You could really make a difference down there, Der. Think about it. Chicago's first black Mayor saves Cabrini Green. I could do gratis work. You know, house calls. Free shit like that. With my gratis work down there, it would be epic for this city, for your campaign. No cameras on the inside, just a few interviews and speeches about being proactive to make a change for the better. Except it wouldn't be just talk. What do you think?"

"I think you're insane," Derek said honestly.

"He's right," Prescott said. The dim lights above him gave a dull cast to his dark hair and pale skin and put deeps shadows in the blue of his eyes. He helped himself to a handful of fries. "Cabrini is World War III, Angie. Even the Mayor wouldn't go down there without a private army to protect her."

"That's because she knows what I know. No black resident of Cabrini wants some uppity white woman coming to their neighborhood, telling them how to live or how to behave. She wasn't wanted there. You heard it on the news, it was a sloppy campaign tactic, Prescott. And it blew up in her face." She looked at Derek. "But you...you have an advantage that she never did. Duke helped build Cabrini and his family grew up there. You spent summers there as a child. Cabrini was just as much your home as it is theirs."

Derek turned to study Garrett and Prescott. Tiny beads of sweat were dappling his forehead. What Angelique suggested was madness. But from the engrossed look on Garrett's face, it became obvious that some of what she said was ringing true. Prescott showed no signs of being bought and sold on the idea, but he showed no signs of protest either.

"You need this," she went on. "Voters need this. I'm serious. This mistake that dumb bitch made leaving that door welded, it's the end for her. Burns will never be reelected with the stunt she pulled. She's finished. Cabrini is your way in."

"She's right," Garrett agreed. "You can get into the hearts and minds of each person that lives there and every councilman in this city will be secretly thanking you for keeping the black problem out of their wards."

"They'd better be doing a little more than secretly thanking him," she said. "If you pitch our move on Cabrini to them, they can give their support where we need it most. Financing and patronage. With their muscle driving this campaign, you will skyrocket in the polls."

"The violence down there is not worth the risk, Angie." Derek said it a lot more calmly than his first response. He hoped that would ease some sense into her. It didn't.

"With the Councilman's soon to be wife there," she said, "they wouldn't even think about bringing any kind of heat on themselves by committing a crime, not with the whole city watching. This is it, Derek. This is what you need to win. Epic purpose."

Angelique turned abruptly towards the television but she didn't look up at the news. She wasn't looking at anything at all. Her eyes were wide with enthusiasm. Dream filled. Distant. Like someone who had just been hit with a jarring epiphany they couldn't keep to themselves. It was a look of seriousness Derek had never seen before.

"Epic purpose," she repeated. "Something that Caruso can't even compete with. Unless there's some Italian slum he can save from hell. And Burns? It's not enough to just live in the projects for two weeks until you can't stand the smell anymore. They don't want help from a rich woman who doesn't know dick about their problems. We can show the people that we're not afraid to get our hands dirty to fix what's broken. You can do what she couldn't. And you're going to use me to do it. You do the impossible and save Cabrini, you will crush her come February. And Caruso...He won't stand a chance in hell." She folded her arms and rubbed her chin, thinking. Then, "What do you guys think?"

"I thinks it's political suicide," Prescott said.

"I think it's literal suicide," Derek agreed.

"I think it's brilliant," Garrett said.

Prescott scoffed and shook his head.

"If we start down that road to redemption for those people," Wendell said, "they're going to expect us to come through on every promise made." He pushed up his glasses and shrugged lanky shoulders. "We have two months before the election. How are we going to win their trust in sixty days?"

"Even if we could pull this off," Prescott cut in, "Most of the thugs in Cabrini can't even read, let alone register to vote. We don't need faith from the damned. We need voters. And this may be a shit-dipped pill to swallow, and I'm sorry to say it, but we need the white vote more than the black's."

"This is the only way to get them," Garrett cut in. "But we do need every minority vote we can get. I agree with Brassi on that one. And he can take care of the media influence by running a few articles about it in the next issue of the *Sentinel*. That'll hit magazine stands in January. The news will be all over it, which will garner black votes from every southside neighborhood in Chicago and white votes from the north side and every barrio in between. Votes garnered for the same reason: Thank God a black man is finally stepping up to clean out the Devil's Mansion. Everybody loves a hero. And a black hero is as rare as white one. Only Superman will live a hell of a lot longer than Shaft. With the black votes plus the votes Brassi can pull in from the Italians on the west side we'll have all the ballots we need to defeat Caruso and Burns. We don't need just the white vote. We'll win the Mayoral election by a landslide."

"It's Monday," Angelique said. "Your next speech is scheduled in two days time. That's exactly two weeks from Christmas Day. I can have a medical plan in place with all the basic fundamentals ironed out by then. My hospital administrator would be all over it. The amount of patients I'd have pouring in to the ER and the OR would drive the hospital census through the roof."

"We need to set up a meeting with Brassi, Duke, and any other backers who might be willing to jump in on this one," Garrett said.

"Christ," Prescott groaned. "This speech on Wednesday night is going to make or break this campaign."

"Are we really talking about doing this?" Derek asked

"Yes," Angelique said.

"Yeah," Garrett agreed.

Derek looked at Prescott for the final stamp of approval. After a long moment, he finally gave a nod.

"Okay then. I guess I better toss the speech I had prepared out the window."

Angelique gasped and put a hand to his shoulder they way she did whenever she was struck with the bolt of an idea. "We'll start with this, 'Duke DeGrate once had a dream for this community. And I refuse to let that dream die...'"

RENFRO

A*nd I refuse to let that dream die…"*

Renfro turned up the volume on the television to hear Councilman Derek Porter's speech and put the phone back to his ear. "Yeah, I'm watching it now."

"I got a feeling shit's already rolling down hill on this one," Bishop said.

Renfro leaned back in his leather recliner chair. A loud pop reverberated off the walls of his living room when he cracked open an ice cold can of Michelob. He took a long swig and listened in on what the Councilman had to say. No doubt, it was an interesting one. No promises of tax reduction. No promises of jobs for the unemployed, yet the undercurrent of a political ploy from the Councilman was permeating through the television screen like ammonia through a piss soaked carpet.

> "…*Cabrini Green was once a place of beauty.*
> *A place of family connections, community,*
> *friendship, education, and respect. Today,*
> *these highrises are rife with poverty and*
> *absorbed by violence. Currently it saddens me*
> *to say that the Chicago Housing Authority's*
> *efforts have failed. This public housing did not*
> *reform delinquents; it simply replaced them.*
> *Now, it is time to take action against the*
> *crime-ridden slums it has come to be. These*

*lawbreakers can no longer assume that the
innocent residents and tax payers should have
to pay for their habits. No one should feel like
a captive in their own homes, especially the
weak and the ill who cannot receive the proper
medical care that they deserve. Therefore, in
an effort to aid this distressed and fragile
community, myself and Chicago Police
Superintendent Dan Whales, will be directly
involved in making sure that progress in
Cabrini becomes a reality.*

*"The Gang, Guns, and Narcotics Task
Force along with Scott Joplin Cook County
Hospital's new gratis faculty endeavor, Gratis
Health Program, will both be implemented
starting January the 1st. With the financial
backing of private investors.*

*"GHP is separate from the Medicaid
network. Insulated funding will be set aside
from state spending on medical programs to
ensure this endeavor begins without delays and
will therefore cost the state nothing. Set to be a
Cook County waiver medical program, it will
allow coverage for patients of the community
who meet eligibility requirements. Not only
will I be keeping my staff abreast on any and
all changes with the task force and GHP, I
will be holding weekly press conferences every
Monday to create more transparency with
Chicagoans about city operations and progress.
Here to speak on the medical details of this new
and innovative program is one of Chicago's
finest doctors, trauma surgeon and cardiothoracic specialist, Dr. Angelique James."*

Renfro felt his brow furrow as a slim brown skinned woman
with dark rimmed bifocals and a white medical coat took the
podium. She looked every bit a specialist. But he could not block
out the thought of how aberrant the sight of a black female
surgeon on television seemed. He noticed a glimmer of gold as

the light shown off her pupils. It came off as a stern flicker of intent as she spoke.

> *"Thank you, Councilman. Cabrini's GHP will help the community's poor overcome ailments worsened by financial lacking. It will be funded by private investors who are passionate about the plight of the sick and disadvantaged. GHP is designed to provide basic medical care such as checkups, immunizations for infants and children, and prenatal care for expectant mothers. Beginning just six days from now, on Monday, I will be making initial door to door house calls to begin basic medical screenings as well as both urgent and non-emergent treatments. These are the first steps that I will be taking to protect Cabrini Green's most fragile and vulnerable. Once GHP is in full swing, lack of care and medicinal neglect will no longer be balanced on the backs of the poor, on the backs of children, or the aged, blind, and disabled. I would personally like to thank the following individuals here with us today for their generous and selfless contributions. Walter Wheat of the Meridian Petroleum Corporation. Councilman Roderick Thomas, Councilman Howard Powell, Councilman Mick Chandler, and Cook Judicial Circuit Judge Ruby Garman…*

Bishop hmmphed. "Those are some big names she's dropping. Sounds like a hell of a swindle. You know how they all like making promises and suddenly get a quick case of amnesia once they're elected. You really think he's going to do all of that bullshit he just said?"

Renfro shrugged and took a long swig of his Michelob. "Don't know. But if that program is approved, it'll definitely look like he's not playing games."

"Well, he's already used his reach to touch the Deputy and the Superintendent. He and the Chief already had a meeting with him and his backers this morning at City Hall. Apparently we're lending whatever manpower the good doctor might need to get in and out of Cabrini with life and limbs in tact."

Renfro cursed.

"I know," Bishop grumbled. "And Delgado wants a meeting first thing in the morning, 7:30 sharp. Don't be late."

He hung up.

Renfro looked at the wall clock. It was 8:10 and darkness had fallen over Chicago long before. He'd been expecting his wife, Gwen, more than two hours ago. Their home...his home was in Wrigleyville on Bellmont Avenue. Aside from the drunkards and offbeat characters he would spot on occasion, there was low risk of encountering crime. Just to the east things would quickly shift and blur depending on the block. Some neighborhoods were well known as drug hubs and havens for prostitution and violence. Just for the last month of November alone the number of crimes in the city totaled more than 1,500, landing a spot among the nation's twenty-five most dangerous cities.

Headlights beamed through the window curtains. And the sound of a car engine revved up the driveway. It had to be Gwen.

Renfro jumped up from the sofa and rushed to the kitchen. He turned on the faucet and dumped the Michelob down the sink. She hated it when he drank. By the time he tossed the can into the trash, her key was in the door.

Perhaps the separation was a good idea. She looked better than the day they married and on that day she was beautiful. Color had rouged her skin once more. Eyes true blue. Raven hair shining. Cheekbones high. Thick curls flounced about her face as a gust of wind blew through the door. She shut it quickly, locked it, and adjusted the box tucked under her arm.

Gwen looked nervous to see him, but that was no surprise. Their last argument was so vicious; she had looked as if he was going to kill her. Renfro had half a mind to let her think it that night. He had drunk far more than usual. Infidelities seemed to bring out the worst in people. Not once had he ever thought Gwen was capable of such a thing. Now he knew.

Put nothing past no one. Even my own wife.

"I can't stay long," she said, brushing past him. "I just came to get some more clothes."

He watched her head towards their bedroom. His bedroom. He followed and leaned against the doorway. She pulled out a drawer from the dresser and stuffed a handful of underwear in the box.

"If you need some furniture, take whatever you need."

"I'm fine."

"I'm gonna need the key after you leave."

"That's fine."

"Look, I don't know how long this separation thing is supposed to last. I don't know how this goes. Usually I just wait for the divorce papers to show up in the mail."

She turned around and cast a hard glare at him. "What the fuck are you talking about, Sam? You put me out, remember?"

His eyes lowered to the floor. "Yeah, I know."

"I can't say I'm sorry any more than I already have. I don't have enough tears left to do it."

Renfro shrugged. "That would be enough, if I knew exactly what the hell it was that you were sorry about. Like, if I have to explain to some angry and brokenhearted mother why I shot her twelve year old kid dead in the chest, I would say what I'm supposed to say. I would say that I'm sorry she's gutted. I would say that I'm sorry for what I took away and that her life would never be the same. But I wouldn't be sorry that some drug dealing punk who pulled a Glock got dead before he could do it to me."

"For the past six years you've been floating through my life like a ghost," she spat. "I'm not proud of what I did. But at least I can admit to your face that we got nothing good left for each other. But you'll deal with something being shit for the rest of your life as long as no body cops to the smell."

"So my brother's shit must smell like potpourri, then?"

Gwen stood there wordless. Tears welled in her eyes. Just as she opened her mouth to snap back the phone rang.

Renfro went back into the living room and grabbed the phone before the answering machine clicked on.

"Hello?"

"Hellooooo, detective."

It was a voice he didn't know. Male. Adult. Most likely white. His voice came thick. Gravel like. His hello stretched out in an unnerving eerie tone.

"Who is this?"

"Your new friend. I'm going to help one of my pure soul brethren rise in the ranks of the Chicago PD as I shall soon rise in the ranks amongst my kin. How will we rise together, you might be asking? Well, as of recently, you and I have a common stone in our path. Hindering our way forward."

He paused as if he was waiting for Renfro to bite the bait.

"Who would that be?"

"Darrion DeGrate. Former black prince of Cabrini."

That last name was familiar. But Duke and Dutch DeGrate came to the forefront of his mind with Cabrini. "And why would he be of any interest to me?"

"You're gettin' promoted tomorrow, detective, to a joint gang task force. You'll be spearheading that little doctor lady's gratis work in the slums. You might run across a little pharmaceutical commerce while you're there. You'll make a few arrests if those bangers are sloppy enough to get pinched. Some of your own blue bloods might not like that too much. Might interfere with their...surplus dividends. So if I were you, I wouldn't be expecting to stay on that task force for too long before you've worn out your welcome. Unless you do a little homework on the side to make your stay worth while."

"And that would be?"

"Slay the beast that shares our garden. If you having a hard time with hunting that game, here's a little spur to help you pick up his scent. A month ago almost to the day, there was a bank robbery up in Northbrook. Still unsolved. I do believe your new promotion will give you a hell of a reach. I suggest you look into it."

He hung up.

Renfro just stood there. Blinking with an earful of droning dial tone.

He snapped out of his daze and looked up when he heard the front door slam. A gust of perfume and orange blossom assaulted his nostrils. Gwen was gone. Her house key was on the kitchen counter.

Renfro cursed and hung up the phone.

♕

Buon Compleanno!" the crowd shouted. "Buon Compleanno!"

Forks and knives clinked against raised champagne glasses as the ballroom exploded into applause. All of them had dressed to paint the night a party. All of them filled with laughter and celebration and the good capo regime's finest liquor. Come to the Waldorf Astoria to wish Zosa a happy nameday.

So have I, Darrion thought. *So have I.*

He had been waiting patiently for nearly an hour. Unnoticed. Watching the sea of formal evening wear. White ties, tails. Elegant gowns. Flowered hair. Their diamonds alight. Dancing the night away under soft lights of coffered ceilings and crystal chandeliers. All the while the courses came and went. A thick lobster soup. Salads of leafy greens topped with grilled salmon or orange roughy. Escargot in a sweet plum and honey sauce. While some dined, others danced. While others danced, some drank their wines and watched the merriments.

It was a night made for the movies.

Zosa took no pains in hiding his love for celebrating in style. But it would all soon be undone. Darrion DeGrate could hardly wait until the arrogant Mafioso laid eyes on his cake. Just the anticipation of all that delight turning to dread sent a morbid tingle of pleasure up his spine.

Like a rock split a river, a massive serving tray was carefully brought out on a rolling table through the mass of guests. They all stepped aside, eyeing the glimmering silver. Cheering on as it was wheeled to the center of the floor. Zosa stepped forward, ever the soul of courtesy. Giving a slight bow. Smiling that gallant smile. A strong breeze swept through the room just then. A cold breeze. It seemed such a timely omen, Darrion felt a crooked smile come to his lips. He stepped forward and slid his hands in the pockets of his wolf's fur coat and waited for it.

The server began singing happy birthday and the rest of the room joined in. At the song's end, applause exploded once more. Darrion felt compelled to clap along with everyone else and so he did. With a slight bow, the server lifted the silver top, exposing a beautiful, white iced, five-tier cake. Topped with all the ripe comings of Christmas. Fondant silver bows, red poinsettias, glittering baubles, sprinkled sugar snowflakes…and a festering, rotted wolf's head.

Zosa's smile abruptly faded and he stood there, frozen. His face as hard as cold steel. The Mafioso blinked at the severed head as if trying to register whether or not he was truly seeing what he was seeing. Gasps sounded out like shockwaves through the ballroom. Applause abruptly traded for screams. A few wine glasses went crashing to the floor.

But Darrion didn't end his ovation. He just willed his hands to firm, slow claps that sounded out so loud and hard and cynical everyone heard him.

Heads turned, wide eyes looked his way, and Zosa followed their stunned gaze until his eyes fell on him. After a few more claps to seal the moment, Darrion relaxed his hands into his pockets and waited to see what the Mafioso would do next.

Without an order given to do so, the appalled server immediately covered the tray and took the cake away. Another man in a dark suit sauntered quickly onto the floor. Waving his hand in a furious flutter at the band. Strings, percussions, and piano keys sparked to life. Playing something. Anything for distraction. But Darrion didn't recognize the composition. An upbeat tune. A desperate attempt to warm the icy tension. But the damage to Zosa's perfect night had already been done, for no one danced to the sprightly timbre.

Zosa walked toward him and so did several of his men. They approached with hard faces and cruel eyes. But Darrion knew they wouldn't dare harm him here. Not before the eyes of the capo regime's prestigious guests.

"Are you out of your fucking mind?" Zosa spat through clenched teeth. "Do you know who I am? Who I work for? What I could do to you and your entire family for what you just did?"

Darrion didn't flinch. "Yeah, I know who you are and I know who you work for. And I know what you already did to my entire family. And if I were as cruel as I could be, I would have waited for *your* Christmas vacation and *your* holiday dinner with all of *your* family and then paid *you* a visit. That would be justice, the way I know the word. But being the man that I am, if my problem is with you, Zosa, then I keep it with you. That being said, you and I, we have two choices here. We can have a little sit down in the back of the room and discuss it like men. Or we can settle up right here and right now like a raw nigga and a WOP enforcer. The choice is yours."

One of his men put a hand on the capo regime's shoulder and mumbled something in his ear. Then Zosa's face transformed. His eyes flicked in three directions and his jaw clenched. Darrion knew Taran's unmovable bulk had just been spotted at the far corner by the entrance doors. T-Bone dreads had just been seen by one of the back dining tables. Lunch was a hard miss at the champagne table—easily pinned as the only black man in the room with blonde dyed hair.

Darrion watched the realization settle on Zosa's face.

Did you really think I'd come alone, idiot?

"Watching authority turn into careful pause," Darrion said, "it borders on humorous. It's almost like watching a fat kid realize all the cake is gone."

Zosa motioned towards one of the back tables. "After you."

The host had the attention of the party patrons and he had successfully taken their focus back to the festivities. Some left in disgust, brushing past Taran, through the double doors with twisted, queasy faces. A few eyes were still watching when Darrion turned and made for a table.

He chose an empty one not far from T-Bone. Lunch moved closer. Taran stayed at the double doors with a keen eye on Zosa's underlings.

Both men took a seat across from each other.

Neither spoke for a long moment.

Despite the upbeat jazz resonating off the walls, the uneasy atmosphere still hung in the air when Zosa finally spoke. "You got balls the size of Texas. I'll give you that. Gargantuan colossal fucking balls coming at me like this."

"I don't do the passive aggressive thing. Not my style."

"I'd really like to know how you got past my security."

"We just snuck in."

Zosa grimaced at Darrion's fur coat and dark denim jeans. "Yeah, well you dressed for it."

Darrion's brow lifted. "Did I?"

Zosa suggested he looked like a hooligan thug and the irritated look on his face all but said it. "Unfortunately this establishment requires a suit and tie. Perhaps you monkeys misremembered that since the last time I saw you. But I will say that's quite a coat. Is it real?"

"Canus Lupus," Darrion answered. "Gray wolf. Courtesy of Brookfield Zoo. You like it?"

Darrion threw that at him to see how he would take it. Zosa gave no hint of being slighted by it. He just nodded with a cynical smirk, then reached in his suit jacket and pulled a cigar. He took his time lighting it. A thick cloud of smoke wafted the heavy, sweet scent of tobacco into the air before he spoke again. "From what I hear, your father's turned a new leaf. I guess you're leaf's on a different branch. I wonder what he would have to say about your little birthday present. Considering how I like to deliver presents back, I doubt this was a sanctioned move."

"From what I hear, neither was yours," Darrion said. He leaned forward and folded his hands on the table. "But don't worry, I won't be running to your boss...telling him that his underling's lust for advancement is about to start a war. Because I'm sure after this little pow-wow, you're gonna fall back in line, stay in your lane, and do what you're told like a good bulldog is supposed to."

"There's a flip side to that coin, DeGrate," Zosa spat back. "I know Duke DeGrate. I've known him since he was your age. I was doing business with your father back when you were just a million to one odds in his nut sack. Someone sends him a message, he's old school. He knows how to send a message back. But a move like this on my nameday? Not his style. So this little act of bravado, with the church backing your daddy's real estate investments, and with everything he's got riding on Porter's campaign, I think he'd be pissed off to learn that his son is stamping out his only shot at legitimacy and starting fires." Zosa shook his head. "Not that I'm complaining. I got no problem with you niggers chopping each other's heads off. But he might. If violating you gets him one step closer to public legitimacy, don't be surprised if he does just that."

Darrion rubbed his chin and looked out over the party. Nearly all of guests had taken their attention back to the celebration. He found it amazing how a little music and enough wine could make a room full of social climbers forget almost anything.

He let out a breath and looked at Zosa long and hard before he spoke. "Violation. Now that's a term I haven't heard in a long time. My gangbanging days are done."

Zosa's brow lifted and he scoffed at Darrion with a look of derision twisting his face. "You sure about that, DeGrate?" He cast a quick glance up at T-Bone and Taran. "For someone who's clearly in denial, looks to me like you got no problems making moves like one. You're a hothead and a threat to your father's political advancement. Whether you realize it or not, it's in your nature to destroy your own. You deny it, that demon will just keep eating at you. Do yourself a favor, young blood, let it in." Zosa ran a hand through his graying hair and leaned back in his seat. "This move you made, I respect it. It's the way of all things. Young lion versus old lion. But there's a consequence for that law of the jungle. It's when the old lion is near his end that he's at his most fierce." Darrion felt a swell of rage in his chest. Just for a moment, he wondered how a steak knife from the table would look in Zosa's eye. The man certainly liked to hear himself speak. Darrion calmly folded his hands on the table and let him keep talking. "You do realize this can't be undone?" Zosa went on. There is no making amends at this point. And any further action from your Family had better bring about my demise. Because if I survive it, I will bring a wrath you never knew existed to your doorstep."

"First of all," Darrion said, "I've never been violated before a day in my life as a means of discipline, so I don't even know why you brought that up. Second...I'm not a threat to my father's advancement. You are. And lastly, when word gets back to Duke about this little visit...as far as my punishment goes, him cussing me out will be about the extent of it." He gave a blasé shrug. "Believe me, when it comes to *bringing about demise*, my father's cussed me out on many a moon." Darrion slid his chair back and stood from the table. "Happy nameday, captain. You enjoy that cake."

With that, Darrion DeGrate left the ballroom whistling a tune.

VIOLA

Viola left her showroom office at 9:00 Thursday morning.

She drove to North Lakeview Avenue to view the progress on a client's home, thankful and relieved the highrise condominium was less than a mile from her boutique. Viola didn't like leaving Lincoln Park to conduct business. With ice on the roads and intermittent flurries, driving wore on her anxieties.

During this time of year, Chateau Decor had its longest list of clients. David and Linda Kozak had two Christmas dinners to host along with a formal party to give. The primary goal was impressing every corporate guest and socialite on the invitation list. Their condo was one of her favorites. After approval of her sketches, they put money into fixing up the bathroom and the kitchen area and allowed her team of designers to come in and knock down a few walls.

The result was a wider foyer by doing away with the front sitting room. But the open space also yielded more attraction to the winding stair case. She had also put in custom granite flooring, lighting, and cabinetry throughout. Their air jet whirlpool was not her idea but it certainly added a swanky touch of living. But the most beautiful areas were the two balconies belonging to the main living room and the master bedroom. Both gave wide views of the lake below, the park, and city. Not a bad abode for $6,000 a month. The Kozak project was her most gratifying development to date. She stayed busy, it was a marvel to look at, and it kept her mind off of Duke's ailing health.

Viola hit the alarm to her Range Rover and walked up to the highrise building. She took the elevator to the 15th floor, walked the short distance to the front door, slid the key in, and took off the alarm as she stepped inside to an empty quiet. As expected, the Kozaks were away on business and wouldn't be returning until two days before their Christmas party, which was now just twelve days away. Her primary visit was to make sure all was on schedule. Her team often alerted her of any problems or setbacks, but she still liked to drop in on their work from time to time and look for herself.

She stepped through the foyer and into the living room.

Instantly she felt the morning heat coming in through the windows. *Hopefully the curtains I ordered will be in by tomorrow or at the latest next week.* She looked around with a silent nod of approval. It was impeccably neat.

Minus the curtains Viola had chosen, everything the Kozaks procured now adorned their home. Their Christmas tree all but touched the vaulted ceiling, spritely enhancing the room with silken silver ribbons and wide royal blue bows. Every bulb and glass ornament glowed and shimmered. Atop the highest branch sat the North Star. The Kozaks had chosen it because it represented the only star in the sky that remained a constant unwavering light.

Viola skimmed over the rest of the room. Her eyes fell on the Rickety tables snatched from a Paris flea market. The Kozaks never would have wanted them had they not read in the paper about the market's owner who put a pistol in his mouth over a mountain of debt to the IRS. To Viola the rugs were ghastly. Their being Parisian was their only redeeming quality. Old brick had been traded up for rare strains of marble that now made up their fireplace. That rare marble came from the home of a notorious mob hit man who asphyxiated his victims and then slashed their throats to be sure they were dead. $20,000, and the Kozaks had one gruesome story to entertain their guests with. Black lacquered artisan chairs stood well spaced around the coffee table. The Kozaks dropped $10,000 when they found out the chairs belonged to a member of the Manson family.

Even their lush black and gold home theater was snatched out of a mansion tied to scandal and murder. $250,000 for that bit of gore and while enjoying a feature in the Kozak's home, one would never think the it came from the estate of a demented Dutchman who strangled his wife while Casablanca played on the screen. Every fixture and every finish that graced a Viola DeGrate decorated home owned a seedy tale or came with a dark adventure attached. That was how she made her name in the world of interior design. Scandal and scarlet sin. She was good at it and her clients lived for it.

Viola walked through the living room then moved on to the home theater. The only modification necessary was to replace the fixed screen with a rolling retractable. She took off her white long coat and laid it on the couch, then removed her scarf. She searched for the remote until her eyes fell on the end table by one of the sofas.

She studied it carefully, searching for the right button and pressed 'SCREEN UP'. With a near silent whir, the screen slowly rose. Viola felt abruptly astounded by how far and advanced the new 80's were from the 70's and 60's she knew.

Phones ringing without cords now.

Macintosh phasing out manual jobs.

Remote controlled everything.

Home theaters with roll-up screens and…blood?

Viola blinked at the wall. Watching the screen rise, revealing a collage of pictures splattered with red.

Without warning, her lungs weren't working right and it felt like her heart had stopped beating in her chest. Both knees went slack. Then a surge of fear knotted in her stomach when she realized the pictures were of her. Of Duke. Of DaVita and Devin. Her family. All of them black and white candid shots, wet with red. Duke leaving the house. Duke getting in his car. DaVita leaving the library with a friend. Devin leaving school. Devin leaving the house.

Viola wanted to vomit when she spotted the pictures of herself. Several were taken of her leaving the Kozak's building. Two of which she was in the same white long coat and red scarf she was wearing now.

Her bottom lip trembled. She didn't even notice the remote had slipped until it hit the end table with a hard thud. Gooseflesh rose on her forearms and everything began to move and sway in a stomach-churning spell of vertigo.

Fear is a logical emotion, she told herself. *No one can hurt me from a wall.* Viola let out a slow, controlled breath. Calling Duke wasn't an option. His heart was bad enough. Viola knew alarming him would only make his health worse. Even if she could call her husband, Darrion would wind up cleaning it all up anyway.

As she saw it, she had two choices. She could either bolt for the front door and drive straight to Darrion's place. Or she could find the nearest phone in the Kozak's place and call him.

She ran into the living room, snatched the phone off of the receiver, and called her son.

♛

"You beckoned, your highness?" Darrion exhaled a puff of vapor and shut the back door to the sedan. He looked at Derek and motioned to himself. "Here it is, your grace."

Unaffected by the cynical greeting, Derek laid the morning paper on his lap and gave a nod to the driver. "Take us for one around the block. This'll only take a minute."

The driver nodded and pulled away from the curb of City Hall. Darrion didn't like car meetings. But for now he was pleased to be out of the cold. It had snowed massively the night before, leaving mounds of snow pushed up into curb-side piles by the road ploughs. Grime-blackened ice patches lined the waysides of every street. Salts littered the highways and boulevards, leaving dusty white imprints of tire tracks on every travel way.

Still, Chicago winters were adaptable. Brutal. But adaptable nonetheless. Most Chicagoans acclimated because they had no other choice. With the Windy City sitting on the coast of Lake Michigan, no winter would ever be a light one. Until March arrived, wear a thick coat, keep gloved hands, and learn to love a hot cup of java. Regardless of his address, Darrion knew he was a spring, summer, fall man.

Darrion unsnapped the collar of his leather coat and glanced out of the rear windshield. Another black sedan followed close behind, affecting an air of stylish assurance and assertion. Councilman Porter still used men from his private security company. Darrion couldn't fault the man's caution. Given the past few weeks, any man in his position would have acted with equal vigilance. If not more.

Today, the Councilman looked strident for business. A black long coat draped with a red scarf. A nice contrast to his dark blue suit. Gray tie. Cuff links. He had even taken the attention to fashion a red ruby tiepin instead of a loud, metallic clip. Darrion had to acknowledge, this was his world. Downtown Chicago. Where municipals cut throats, lackeys slipped on the blood, and the political sharks came to feed on the remains.

Darrion hated politics. Almost as much as he loathed the politicians who flourished from their deeds.

When the car was in traffic, Derek spoke. "I'm sure you're well aware of this new project Angie's starting at Cabrini."

Darrion nodded and looked out the window. "I am."

"I'll only allow it if she has security."

"Hire more men from Executive Protection." Darrion could tell by the short silence that followed Derek didn't like his response. Short silences between them always revealed a familiar cold distance instead of brotherly love. "If I recall, you own it. Every hired gun on your pay-roll will stand guard if you tell them to."

"If that were the answer," Derek said bluntly, "why would I have called you?"

"Because you think I'm the answer." Darrion looked at his half-brother. "I'm not." Now he remembered all of the things that separated them as men. He understood why Derek wanted his intervention at Cabrini. But what the Councilman didn't seem to grasp was how much things had changed over the years in that project. After watching his campaign speech on the news, Darrion thought the political spectacle was the dumbest idea he had ever heard of. Taran laughed. T-Bone called Derek an ass and Lunch just shook his head. Cabrini Green was no place to garner votes. Darrion felt obligated to inform him of that fact. "You're not using my old ties to open a door that's already been closed and bolted shut. You step in the middle of a cesspool, Derek, you're the only one that's going to get infected. Pope runs Cabrini now. Zane Harris is one of his top regents. Bringing outsiders into their organization...that won't be welcomed."

"She's not going down there to be cheered, applauded, and greeted," Derek said calmly. "People who need help the most are going to get it. And throwing a monkey wrench in Pope's criminal activity is exactly what this city needs. His blatant disregard for law and order and his underground economy needs to come to a screeching halt. If this is a small step in that direction, then I'm all for it."

Darrion regarded the Councilman for a moment, wondering how long he practiced that one in the mirror. *I honestly believe you would eat your young,* he thought. But he said, "This is not a move to make because you need the black vote. You're about to disrupt a multi-million dollar drug ring. A business built on greed and blood. Disrupting Pope's operation won't go unanswered. You want the support of your soul brethren, grow a Jerry curl, hit the southside, and give a speech at Ford City."

"This is a chance to change things, Darrion. I believe in this city. The hell and the heaven of it. Maybe you've given up on the poor, maybe you've washed your hands of the unfortunate, but I haven't. Neither has Angie."

"You want to help the poor? Open up a med clinic. Start a treatment center somewhere. Cabrini is not the place for unwelcomed encroachment. And the good doctor she may mean well, but that doesn't mean her help will be appreciated. The Disciples are in the middle of a building war. One highrise against another. With all that greed and ambition, a fifteen year old kid will kill her for a stripe and a reputation."

"Not if you're there," Derek said with stern conviction. "You have history with the Disciples and you have Pope's respect. That's more than enough street cred to help his thugs see the bigger picture."

Darrion shrugged, unaware of what the Councilman meant by that other than party-political gain. "And the bigger picture would be...what?"

"Being able to function instead of just surviving." Derek pulled a manila folder from the passenger door storage pocket and handed it to him. "The opportunity to live like human beings instead of monkeys in a shit throwing fight at the zoo."

Darrion opened the envelope and pulled two folders. Both had trademarked logos. Crown Petroleum and Meridian Electric. He unfastened Crown Petroleum first and pulled out a thick stack of documents. The first page was a work order invoice. He skimmed over it quickly. Every section for work to be done, materials, and labor were left blank. The signature at the bottom read Walter Wheat. Darrion looked up at the Councilman and took note of the knowing expression on his face. "Walter Wheat?" he asked. "The oil tycoon?"

"The one and only," Derek nodded. "Wheat doesn't just own the Crown Petroleum Corporation. He also owns Crown Petroleum Plumbing and Heating." He nodded at the second folder and said, "Howard Powell is the owner of Meridian Electric. Within two month's time, we can have every busted piping system along with every electrical problem in Cabrini repaired and in working order. That is, if Pope is willing to cooperate and give little resistance to our efforts."

Darrion opened the Meridian folder and looked over the documents. Several were detailed blueprints of the electrical wiring for every building in the housing project and an invoice, also yet to be filled out. Darrion spotted Powell's signature at the bottom. Fixing two of the most central problems to Cabrini's living conditions was certainly a way to get Pope's attention. But getting the kingpin's ear and keeping it were two completely different monsters. Especially when that ear was being pulled away from millions of dollars in drug profits. Darrion wondered what Duke had to say about this.

"My advice," Derek added, "call a meeting. Have a sit down with Pope. Make sure he understands that this is far too public to make waves and his cooperation won't go overlooked."

"And Walter Wheat's cooperation? Powell's? Will their generosity go overlooked?"

"In my world, if a man want to progress, he has to make alliances."

Darrion didn't know if that was an honest attempt at evading an answer or if he just said that to explain his intentions. Knowing the half-sibling he knew, both were probably intended. Nevertheless, Darrion's loathing of politics didn't mean sheer ignorance of the tactics used to sway advantage. "True," he said, "and well put by the way. But that two step only works with the ladies on the dance floor. You didn't answer my question. Then again you don't have to. If I were a man in your position, looking to secure the Mayoral seat of this city, I would need to secure the backing of every affluent muscle willing to weather the storm of putting a minority in office. Anybody that eager to weather such a storm must have one hell of an umbrella."

Derek said nothing. He kept his bearings in tact as always. But Darrion had grown up with Mr. Porter. What he read now was a firm stance of silence with a hint of underlying animosity. So he kept going. "Supremacist pigs like Powell and Wheat don't power up with a brother, especially publically, unless you have something they want. Because they definitely don't want your black ass in office. So let me see...what would be the one thing they would stab their mother in the heart with a fucking ice pick for? I believe I'm gonna have to go with you giving up Class A shares of O'Meravingi." Derek still said nothing. So Darrion just kept on going. "Not enough shares to lose your voting power on the board of trustees, of course. But just enough to seat the big dogs at your table right where you want them. Well-tossed poker chip. I hope you have a nice stack of them left to play. Seeing as you have yet to secure the shares from the church, you're gonna need 'em. And while we're on the subject of poker chips, nobody in this family plays one without Duke's sanction." He cut his eyes to the window and shook his head in disgust. "So I see you two have been discussing my new babysitting detail behind my fucking back."

Derek exhaled and both men sat in silence. "If it makes you feel any better," he finally said, "he's no more thrilled about this move on Cabrini than you are. But unlike you, Duke does see every acre of the forest for the trees and he knows the ends will outlive the means for years to come. For our children and their children after them. If you're not with us on this, Darrion, everything we set in motion is going to crumble."

Darrion's hand tightened to a fist on his knee.

He relaxed it.

As it was, if Duke had already consented, he had no choice in the matter — which caused him to wonder why he was even being asked. But, he found some comfort in the agreement. Doubtless in part that his father was against the idea and he probably gave Derek a firm talking to about obligating the Family without going through him first. *Then again, what was father to do once the Councilman and his staff ran a mile with it in front of cameras and microphones?*

"In or out," Derek pressed. "What's your answer?"

Darrion grimaced and kept his gaze out the window. *Damned if I do, damn us all if I don't.* "What's up with Five-O? If they get anywhere near that building, snipers will shoot 'em dead before they throw their squad cars in reverse."

"I just came from a meeting with the Superintendent and the Chief of Police. They'll be providing a mobile incursion of sixteen officers on Monday morning to escort Angie and one of her interns to the area."

Darrion gave Derek a terse look. "A mobile incursion to the *area?*"

"No officers will go anywhere near the buildings after that last shoot out got two cops killed. But they will escort her to the intersection of Cleveland Ave. and Hobbie Street. Near Jenner Elementary."

"And you expect me to go Lone Ranger the rest of the way where a sniper can easily pick me off from a hundred feet away?"

Derek shook his head. "No, not just you. You and several newly employed members of my private security company. Look in the envelope and you'll find several blank applications."

Darrion pulled out the applications. He counted four of them and an application for a concealed carry license. Suddenly, he did not like where this was going and he took no pains in hiding the scowl on his face. "So, not only do I work for you now against my consent...may I ask who are these other four lunatics you slapped on your payroll at the last minute?"

"With Casper, Turkell, and Taran with you, Darrion, at least you'll have solids you can trust watching your back and Angie has as much protection as possible."

Darrion cursed and shoved the applications back in the envelope.

"If I do this, I go in my own way. I don't want Five-O anywhere near me."

"The Chief of Police feels it's best that—"

"I don't give a shit what that bloated bastard thinks," Darrion said, cutting him off. "He'll be watching it on television while I'm catching a bullet right between the eyes. If I'm going in with the doctor, I'm bringing her in my way. You can tell the cops to stay the hell back. They don't even have to make their bumpers seen. If you want me to reach out to Pope and keep his jets cool with what we're about to do, me getting in bed with the CPD will negate that worse than you talking to him your damn self." He paused and rubbed his chin. "Just…I'll handle it."

"Alright," Derek agreed amiably. "Now, as private security employees, you'll all be cleared to carry a concealed weapon in public as well as in federal buildings. So if anything should transpire in Cabrini, and you have to use deadly force, it's justifiable homicide. You'll moonwalk right out of court. So, just fill out the applications as soon as possible and get it to my head of security. He'll get you approved in less than 48 hours.

"Angie worked out her schedule so it won't interfere with her time at the hospital. Her gratis work begins at 8:00 in the morning. But by sundown, I want her out of there. As far as security goes, between the four of you, I suggest either a two-man or a four-man shift. Either is up to you."

Darrion feigned his best antebellum slave voice, "Anythang else I's can do fo' ya massa?"

"There is actually," the Councilman answered without hesitation. "When you can get information from the residents, find out where the worst of the damages are coming from, make a list of all the needed repairs for the highrises and get it back to me as soon as possible."

Darrion sighed and his eyes narrowed. There was no hiding the meaning behind that request. What the Councilman really meant was:

Once you're knee deep in the slum's shit, find out how much of that shit needs to be scooped, shoveled, and heaped. Oh, dear brother…if you think I'm itching to turn rat for you and this new accord you made with the Chief of Police, you're sick with fever.

"Anything else?"

"Yes," the Councilman answered. "I'm trusting you to keep her from harm. Protect her with your life."

DARRION

Darrion answered his car phone. "Hello?"

"Were the hell have you been?!" Viola screamed. "I have been calling you for a half hour!"

Her tone alarmed him. Darrion hadn't heard his mother snap at him like that since the night he and Lunch took her Cadillac for a joy ride and ran into a utility pole. Lunch tried to take the blame, but Duke saw through the lie. Most of his childhood memories of adults in the family were clouded with a terse word or two. An argument here or there. But his mother's anger was ever clear. When she raged, everyone in the house found a room with a locked door. Her wrath didn't happen often. But during those rare, ill-fated times Darrion knew the devil made flesh. He was fifteen then. Now, the sound of her anger threatened to make him swill in a glass of scotch, and it wasn't even noon yet.

Strangely, her voice carried something he never heard before. An undercurrent of panic. Of anxiety and fear. That wasn't like his mother.

"I was in a meeting, Mom. What's wrong?"

"I just came from a client's house. I find a wall full of blood-splattered on pictures of Duke, me, DaVita, and Devin. Whoever put that there, knew exactly when I was going to walk through the door, so I'm pretty sure I'm still being watched."

Darrion's stomach lurched.

"Where are you?"

"I'm at Simone's Café. The coffee shop across the street from the apartment building."

"Stay where you are, I'll be right there."

Darrion drove from City Hall to Simone's Café in less than twenty minutes. Viola was standing in the window waiting for him, dressed in a long white coat, matching slacks, and a red scarf. She stepped out onto the sidewalk to meet him before he made it to the door.

"Are you okay," he asked.

"Not really."

Viola studied him intently. It was a searching look. Like she was trying to pry something out of him without saying a word.

"Did you hear anything when you walked in?"

"No."

"Nothing was out of place?"

Viola looked up at the highrise building. "Not that I noticed."

Darrion glanced up and down the block, skimming over every building within view. No windows looked occupied. Nothing seemed suspicious. "I called T-Bone, Taran, and Lunch from my car phone. They're on the way. When they get here, we'll go back inside and sweep the place. I doubt anybody's close enough to get noticed."

"I run a very reputable business, Darrion," Viola said. "Do you know what this could do to me if the Kozaks find out about this? The world of interior design is a small one."

He turned back to Viola. "We'll clean it up. I promise your client will never know."

Less than thirty minutes later, Darrion was standing in the Kozaks' private movie theater staring at the work of a sick screw. Only one sick screw came to mind.

Kincaid.

Since the botched robbery, they put every free minute into finding out where he was hiding. Mount Greenwood wasn't a large area, but there were plenty of houses for a supremacist on the run to hide out in. Now with their time being split for guard duty at Cabrini, it would soon become even more difficult to hunt for the psycho.

Worse over, if Kincaid watched the news, he would have no problem keeping tabs on their whereabouts. This collage of blood on the wall was meant to deliver a message. *I know where you are, where your family is, and I know where they're going to be. Anytime. Anywhere.*

Darrion wondered who betrayed him to give up that much information on his family's whereabouts. Maybe he hired one of his own neo-Nazi comrades to keep tabs? One thing was for certain…He wasn't working alone. Kincaid wasn't smart enough to pull off something that methodical unaided.

Now came the thorns. Lying to Viola sometimes came back to bite him when he least expected it. He went back to the living room to find Lunch staring in that awkward way he had at a painting on the wall. He had removed his black sweater and stood dressed in his wetwork uniform. Knee high booties, cleaning gloves, a butcher's smock, and protective eye goggles.

Taran and T-Bone wore the same to guard their shirts from taking on red stains. While Taran kept himself and Viola entertained in the kitchen with the espresso machine, T-Bone was in the master bath mixing the cleaning solution. It was a simple mix of table salt, hydrogen peroxide, hot water, and Murphy's Oil. Just enough to remove the blood from the naked eye without damaging the paint. Hopefully a black light never swept the wall or the Kozaks would find themselves standing in a room brighter than a thousand suns.

"What kind of painting is this?" Lunch asked.

Darrion shrugged. "Hell if I know. Ask Moms."

"Aunt V," Lunch called out.

Viola walked into the living room and he pointed at the massive canvas. "What kind of painting is this?"

"A Karr Zandinski."

"A real one?"

She nodded.

"How much?"

"About 2.5, I think."

His brow lifted. "Million?"

She nodded.

Lunch studied the musical instrument on the canvas. "This looks like…"

"A violin perhaps? Or a woman?" Viola mused, stepping closer. "Actually, it's both. This painting is one of his finest. *The Violoniste.*"

"French?"

"Mmm-hmm."

"Gothic?"

"Renaissance."

"Seventeenth century?"

"Fifteenth."

"Hmm," Lunch said.

"I think I remember reading about him once in the paper," Darrion chimed in.

"I studied him some in my art class," Lunch added.

"Karr is one of my favorite painters," Viola said to Lunch. "Would you like to know why?"

He nodded.

"He was a cruel man. Harsh and unforgiving of his enemies. But he was all about family. He treasured his children. And he adored his wife. In her youth, she was a very timid, shy thing. She lived under a drunkard, abusive father who was obsessed with music. And whenever she played the violin, if she missed one note, he would beat her senseless. Karr was her music teacher. She was his finest student. One night, after her father nearly beat her into a coma, Karr drug him from his home and beat him in the street. Using her violin to crack his skull in front of every watchful neighbor. Then he took him to a small cabin by a river, skinned him alive, and sold his corpse to a school of medicine for $100. He used the money to buy her a new violin. And he never loved another more. Every night she played for him. Every day he painted for her. They even died on the same day, of natural causes. Like all of the great ones long dead, he never valued his work. He once regarded his artistic legacy as *'a trivial thing of infinitesimal significance.'* During his thirty year long span as an artist, he produced nearly 2,000 paintings and more than 5,000 works on paper."

"Where was he taught?"

"Nowhere. Karr was self-taught."

Lunch seemed locked in a trance staring at that canvas. Darrion wondered if he took his meds today. The room fell to a strange silence until T-Bone emerged from the master bedroom popping the rubber of his gloves. "We're ready to work."

"Did you take pictures of everything?" Darrion asked.

T-Bone nodded. "I can get 'em developed tonight. Your smock and goggles are in the back. Gloves and booties too."

"I can get the primer and paint if you need it," Viola said to T-Bone. "I have the color pallet on file back at the office."

T-Bone stared at her for a long moment before he answered her. Turkell often did that. But he was smartly enough to never let his eye rove in front of Duke. "Yes, Ma'am," he said like a good little boy. "I'll let you know if we do."

For her age, Viola was a beautiful woman. But Darrion's mind assaulted with images of T-Bone bedding his mother was a torment far worse than Chinese water torture.

"Christ," he spat with disgust, rolling his eyes. "Let's get to work."

♛

Viola stood quietly in the movie theater, watching Taran and Lunch carefully cover the couches and end tables with plastic while T-Bone slathered cleaning solution on the wall. Darrion thumbed through the bloodied candid photos, looking for anything that might give him a clue as to how Kincaid had gotten to him. Once T-Bone had the roll of film developed maybe he'd notice something. For now he had nothing.

Viola turned and looked up at him. "Who is this sick twist?" she whispered. "What the hell do they want from this family?"

Darrion shook his head. "I don't know."

"Oh, I think you do." Her eyes narrowed. "I've been staring at walls and the canvases mounted on them all my life. And the one thing I've learned about art is it's not what's there that tells the tale. It's what's missing that spills the secrets. Out of everyone on that wall, only one DeGrate is missing."

Darrion just looked at her, wordless.

"Now either you're divinely favored," she pressed on, "or massively despised. I'm going with the latter. And there's three more missing from that wall as well." She gave a quick glance to Lunch, T-Bone, and Taran. "Do they know?"

Darrion hated it when Viola did that. Just picked through his lies like a prosecutor flaying a culprit. She would've been a hell of a lawyer if only she decided to go for a judicial life instead of a well-cultivated one.

"We're taking care of it," he heard himself say. "Right now he's in hiding. But I promise you we are going to find him."

"Who the hell is he?"

"I can't tell you that."

Viola's brow tented and her eyes went dark.

That warning glare. Even under comfort of the warmest sheets in the warmest bed, when her eyes went cold, nothing could make you feel warm.

When she spoke, she kept her voice low. "Is it the same one who came after us at the cabin?"

"No."

"Then who?"

Darrion said nothing. He couldn't think of a lie fast enough so he kept his mouth shut. He could tell it infuriated her. But Viola kept her composure.

"Now is not the time to be hiding shit under the table," she harped. "With everything that's happening with the church and Cabrini, your father's heart, Derek's campaign. If there's a threat to this family, it needs to be put down before it hurts us all."

"I know," Darrion said a little more loudly than he intended. Lunch stopped and looked up at them for a few seconds then went back to cleaning. "And because of everything that's going on keeping it under the table is what we have to do."

"What if this asshole decides to make some serious noise? Right now the warning is in the condo of a client who conveniently happens to be out of town on business. Right now we can keep it quiet. What about next time? What happens when this bastard tries to hurt us?"

"That won't happen. We will get to him first and we will put him in the ground."

Viola drew back and gave him a searching look.

Darrion knew she cautioned in believing him. Fear often did that to a person. Especially one recently attacked by wolves. "This twist is not going to hurt us," he assured her. "I promise. From now on, Fang goes everywhere you go. Even if it's to the grocery store to buy a pack of squares. I mean it."

Viola nodded and went back to watching the men clean.

An hour later everything was spotless. Left as it was before. All of the supplies brought with them were neatly put away in several large duffle bags. Taran and T-Bone hauled them down to their cars. Darrion held the door open for his mother and Lunch.

Viola made for the door and Lunch followed close behind. Then he stopped at the Zandinski.

"Aunt V," he said.

She turned in the doorway and looked at him. "Yes?"

"Zandinski, who was his wife?"

"Madelisa Michelete." Viola tied her red scarf in an eloquent loose knot around her neck and smiled at him. "She was his cousin."

DUKE

Duke looked up when the steel door buzzard sounded.

Pope was escorted into the visitation room by three guards. Duke knew what that meant. Two guards were normally assigned to common hoods who just got caught on the wrong day pulling the wrong crime. Three guards to shepherd were only reserved for the most volatile of inmates.

He lifted the phone off the hook as Pope sat in the visitation booth opposite of the dividing glass. Stateville prison food must have been enough to thrive on. Xavier Marquis Pope — for it was undoubtedly his old friend — looked well fed for a man locked in a five by nine cell with nothing but three hots and a cot for the last eight years. Still broad shouldered. Tall and sinewy. Heavy eyes set in dark skin that reminded Duke of tempered pelts. Cured in the sun until it was steel tough. His hair was so low trimmed, the tinge of gray on his black head stood out like the shadow of a sliver crown. More than ten years had passed since they had spoken and the pull towards nostalgia was so intense and vivid, he had to stop himself from starting up a conversation about old times. Duke knew Xavier didn't want to waste a visitation day crowing about way back when.

"Finally got your weight back up I see," he said. "You look good, man."

"You know I don't go down easy," Pope grinned. "A knife in the ribs ain't enough to keep me down."

Duke studied him intently for a moment. "You and me, we go way back from the war to the revolution. I have to ask…why did you turn down the transfer? I know the move would compromise your status. But at Moline, it's level 6, corruption is low, nobody riots."

"Time is time," Pope said flatly. "Whether I'm serving it here or elsewhere. At least here I know the lions from the lambs. So why move to another jungle?"

Duke nodded and waited. Knowing Xavier couldn't abide a long silence when there was business to discuss. Just then he saw a flash of distaste in his eyes and out it came. "This limelight you're putting on Cabrini, under different circumstances, Duke, you'd be on my permanent shit side. You gave up your crown, you walked away. And I respected that. But, in light of recent events, I'm inclined to use this untimely transgression to my advantage."

"How so?"

"A blade parting my flesh is an intimacy I'm familiar with. But, I'm quite fond of that blade coming at my chest. Not at my back."

Disloyalty is a foreseeable ruse when you give the loyals a reason to be so, Duke thought. But he said, "Betrayed by one of yours, I'm sorry to hear it. And I know what you will ask of me." Xavier was more readable than a child's favored fable. Someone in Cabrini tried to murder him and they had a reach far enough inside the prison to set it in motion. Duke respected his anger about that. Any man living in his world of violence would want retaliation. Nevertheless, Darrion was not in Pope's world. His need to get righteous would burn anyone he ensnared. "I won't allow my son to be involved in any blood grudge you're tied to on the streets. His being back in Cabrini, I'm against it. Period. I didn't want him there. I don't want the Councilman's fiancé there either. But, while they are there, I need a guarantee that no harm will befall them. Out of respect for what we once were, from you to your senior regents, to your lieutenants on down to your foot soldiers, I'm asking you to do me this kindness."

♛

"Are you ready?" Darrion asked.

"If I'm not," Angelique said, "I hope you are."

Darrion exhaled a gust of frigid air, looked around the grounds of the highrise building — known in the projects as Head Quarters — and wondered what insane impulse or resurfaced grudges he provoked from old enemies by accepting Derek's forced invitation to hell.

Cabrini was silent today. Most of the people walking around at 0830 in the morning were walking to and from Jenner Elementary. Taking their children to school. Only a few lingered around the grounds or the parking lot to get an up close view of the doctor's arrival. Darrion knew a 006 code for silence went out to the beepers of every foot soldier walking the buildings and every lookout in the windows and on the rooftops. That sent a dominant message of authority. Disciples controlled the building and nearly every building in the projects. Darrion imagined the 006 went out well over a mile.

Just as he spotted a van extolled with Channel 5 and another belonging to Channel 9, a third van for Channel 7 pulled up. Beyond the vans the media swarmed, ready to capture the classic image of good facing off with evil. Though they would fail to give the public a glimpse of Dr. James entering the building, Chicagoans sitting in front of their televisions would probably hear she was a young promising surgeon, risking her career to make a difference. They'd also get an upshot glimpse of the highrise and mentally dissect all of the lewdness and vehemence inside its red brick walls. But whatever assumptions the reporters fed them would stay that way. Zane would make sure no resident hiding inside, who valued their lives, talked to the media.

Darrion fixed his eyes on the doctor. She looked almost sick with fear, but he knew she would never admit it.

"Fear is normal," he said. "It's one of the most primal human emotions. A reaction induced by a perceived threat to make you aware of danger and prepare you to deal with it. Because it's a reaction, fear is a choice."

Angelique blinked up at him then nodded acquiescence.

"Block it out. In Cabrini Green, fear won't buy you kindness and it damned sure won't buy you mercy. You're about to walk into a house uninvited. So, don't be surprised if the welcome is as warm as the weather. Look past it. You're not here to make friends, shake hands, and kiss babies. You've got a job to do and they'll respect that as long as you don't give them a reason to disrespect it. And remember, Zane and his soldiers won't be dealing with you directly; they'll be dealing with me. Okay?"

She nodded, this time with a certainty that seemed sure enough, but he had to be convinced. He reached into his pants pocket for her car keys and popped the trunk. "Recite the layout back to me."

"Okay," she said, clearing her throat. "Cabrini Green is divided into three territories. The Whites, the Lows, and the Reds—"

"How do you know the difference?" he interrupted.

"The Lows are the lowrises, the Whites are the concrete highrises, and the Reds are the brick highrises."

Darrion reached in the trunk, pulled out his twin gun holster, and strapped it to the small of his back. "Where are we?"

"We're in the Wilds," she said. "The Reds on Hudson Avenue. Locust is the cross street south. Oak is the cross street north. Durso Park, also known as Hell's Back Yard, is southeast. Jenner Elementary is northwest. Disciple territory is from Chicago Ave. to Division Street and from Sedgwick to Larrabee."

Darrion nodded. *So far so good.*

He checked both of his pistols, making sure they were loaded. Colt M1911's were reliable steel. They held a manageable kick, smooth cocking, and they chambered .45 ACP rounds. But just in case his Colts ran empty, he kept a spare pistol strapped inside his Kevlar. "And what buildings are those?" he asked.

Angelique blinked skyward, thinking. Then said, "The Rock, the Castle, Bank Roll, 61 Macs, Deuce One, the Boulevard, Hudson Mob, Camp Ball, 2 Bill, and 41 Deuce."

"What building are we going in?"

"The one building gridlocked in mutiny. Disciple Head Quarters."

He glanced at the building. "What's the territory split inside?"

Angelique paused. Thinking. "Okay, the north towers belong to the King Disciples and the south towers belong to Sampson's crew, the Almighty Renegade Disciples. The revolt ignited on extortion from Pope. Sampson's rebelling against his street tax."

"Good," Darrion said.

She let out a breath, swallowed hard, then pulled her medical coat closed over her sweater. When a strong gust of icy wind blew a short silence drew out between them. When she spoke again there was sincerity in her eyes. An earnestness that made him question why in all of hell had he agreed to this proposition.

"I just wanted to say thank you for agreeing to do this," she said. Her hands tensed to fists at her sides then she relaxed them and looked off toward the building. "Derek told me that you and Duke have some bad history here and I know coming back is the last thing you want to do. I'm sorry to be the cause of that." She looked up at Darrion and her voice went solemn. "I never told Derek about what happened…the other night. The body. The morgue. None of it."

"Didn't think you would," Darrion said.

Of course you didn't. If you had, none us would be standing here right now.

Derek was as self-serving of a politician as any other bureaucrat he ever met. But even Councilman Porter wasn't capable of serving up his own fiancé for the taste of victory. Derek adored her. That was his one redeeming quality. That much about the man Darrion knew. But he was also learning quickly about Angelique.

A meeting with Zane was a meeting not easily forgotten. For her to have witnessed his wrath and still have the brass to come back, there was more than a need to help the poor set to her will. Darrion detected a profound need for reprisal. Some deep-rooted drive to validate and enforce whatever part of her Hippocratic oath she thought Zane had shattered. Her rationale was absurd. Brave, but absurd. He had a nagging suspicion she'd find that out the hard way.

Darrion reached into the trunk and pulled out a small sized Kevlar. "I need you to put this on."

♛

If you want your son out of my war, then pull him out of my projects," Pope spat. "Because right now, he's walking right in it while I'm facing a mutiny in my Head Quarters."

Duke's brow lifted. "A mutiny?"

He blinked through the dividing glass at his old friend, visibly unsettled. That came as a surprise. Pope ruled Cabrini with an iron fist and a steel boot. No one questioned his authority. Those who did often came up missing. Things were worse in those projects than he feared. Now his apprehension morphed into foreboding.

"May I ask what sparked the revolt?" he heard himself ask.

"One of my former regents, Sampson, decided he's no longer obligated to pay taxes up the chain. All efforts of negotiation to bring him and his renegade crew back into the fold have failed. Slowly but surely he's taking over the HQ. If he owns that highrise, he has everything. The sunshine, the seeds, and the rain to keep 'em growing."

Duke hadn't heard those words in a long time. Suddenly he was aware the phones could have been wire tapped. So, the slang was necessary. Pope couldn't exactly say Sampson was holding the dope, the money, and every weapon the building had in its arsenal, now could he?

Pope's eyes darkened and his voice hardened. "And that's not the worst of it. A month back, the King Cobras were the last hold out in the Reds. They were muscled out of The Rock and pushed across Division Street to the Whites — which means they formed an alliance with the Black Dragons. It won't be long before they retaliate and when they hit back, they're going to hit back hard. Right now, your son is in the middle of a building war." Pope let out a breath. "You do understand that as of now I have no governance over Sampson and his crew? I can bring my men to heel. That can be done with one phone call. But I can't guarantee the same for a rebel and his Renegades. Pope checked his watch. "Right now it's a quarter 'til nine which means your son and the Doc are already there. Waiting for a call from you to cross the Killing Fields. And my eagles already have them in their sights so it's too late to go back now. How they cross is up to you."

Here it comes, Duke thought. *The ultimatum.*

"Are they walking the lawn as moving targets," Pope threatened, "or aides-de-camp?"

Duke didn't flinch.

Rage swelled in his chest until a flash of pain burned under his sternum. His weakened heart beating a warning. He ignored it.

"You're asking me to tell my son to step in the middle of an insurrection?"

"I'm asking for Switzerland," Pope said, correcting him. "I need a neutral entity. Someone who can see from both sides of the frontline, yet gives no aid to one side or the other. That's how you put down sedition. An impartial force unaffiliated to either camp — who holds no loyalties to Zane or Sampson. Darrion will only answer to my governor, Caesar Black — who only takes orders from me. I will make Zane well aware of that and he will honor it or he'll have to deal with me."

Duke went quiet. He studied Xavier intently. This Sampson had brass. It was a smart move. If there was no more money to extort, the junkies wouldn't score, the families would starve, and the soldiers couldn't pay the rent or Pope's street tax. Not that he gave a damn about them. They could all burn. He couldn't have cared less. But their plight now tied in to Darrion and the doctor responsible for his new heart. If she died before her time, so would Duke.

Some wars stood for profit in the aftermath. Others crumbled economies and crippled entire organizations. Xavier Pope had no intention on suffering the latter. He made that crystal clear.

Duke lowered the phone to his chin.

♛

This is madness, Darrion thought.

Bringing her here was lunacy.

Who in all of hell brings a rose to a war?

Because of Sampson's revolt, Hudson Avenue wasn't the safest street to be on. But it was safer than being on a street lined with cops. If favor was on his side, the squad cars on Cleveland Avenue would provide enough target practice to keep the lookouts occupied and entertained. He wondered what was taking so long for his cell phone to ring. Sometime before Christmas he expected to hear from his father.

Darrion looked past Angelique to the dreadful sight of a rusty, light blue, paint-faded Buick Electra pulling up to the curb. Its wide bodied frame stretching 225 inches from head lights to tail pipe had earned it the moniker 'Deuce and a Quarter'. Its frayed hardtop flapped in the wind. One busted side view mirror hung by a wire, clanking against the driver's door as it backfired to a stop.

Turkell was behind the wheel.

His dreadlocks and dark sunglasses fading fast behind the black cloud of exhaust as smoke engulfed the car. Hopefully the snipers didn't mistake the backfire for gunfire. It was loud enough to rival thunder. Darrion looked up at the highrise and spotted a few snipers in the windows of several top apartments. They were looking down on the Buick. No one fired a shot, but he saw a few of them laughing. No point in killing a car that sat a sputter away from death. Darrion entertained the thought of firing a shot into the engine block just to put it out of it's misery.

To look at Turkell's rattletrap made him instantly regret driving Angelique's Firebird. He was against the doctor driving at all and even more so against using her car. She insisted it would be a greater loss for his Mercedes to get assaulted with bullets than her father's Firebird, so he relented.

That was the last compromise Darrion intended to give.

He waved off the pungent smell of exhaust. Through the dusty windshield, he spotted Lunch in the passenger seat and Taran in the back. Their doors creaked open and the trunk popped up.

T-Bone walked up to the Firebird, spoke a hello to Dr. James, and gave Darrion a nod and a one-armed hug. He looked into the back window and lowered his glasses for a better look at the white boy sitting frozen in the back seat.

Darrion had almost forgotten the intern was there.

He tapped on the window. "Get out of the car."

Kirk hesitantly stepped out onto the street and looked around. His blue eyes darting in all directions like a petrified rabbit in a wolf's den.

T-Bone looked Kirkland up and down from wool coat to fancy loafers. "Who's this?"

"Ricky Schroeder," Darrion answered handing the intern a Kevlar.

T-Bone laughed. "No shit!"

"Schroeder," Darrion said to Kirk, "this is T-Bone. He's my brother."

"Hey," Kirk said, slipping on the bullet proof vest. "Nice to meet you."

His southern accent came so thick Turkell's eyebrow arched under his shades. "Where the hell are you from?"

"Kentucky."

"You about as white as Wonder bread, ain't you?"

Kirkland shrugged. "You don't miss much."

"He's my intern," Angelique cut in. She still had her eyes on the building. "He's also a registered nurse. So I need him."

T-Bone nodded and watched him shaking like a leaf.

"You shoulda brought some Nike's and a thick pair of denim, man. Chi-Town weather ain't no joke."

"I got my sneakers in the car," Kirk said.

"Well, you best put 'em on, cause we about to rock and roll very shortly. And you ain't running from shit in them loafers."

Kirk reached in the back seat and grabbed his sneakers. Lunch tapped T-Bone on the shoulder and handed him a Kevlar. "You and Taran locked and loaded back there?" Darrion asked him.

Lunch nodded. "Just about."

"How does that work anyway?" T-Bone asked Dr. James as he pulled off his coat and slid his Kevlar over his head. "I mean, if you want to you can just stop doing surgeries and come to Cabrini anytime you feel like it?"

"Not exactly," she said. "Scott Joplin has been trying to get a gratis faculty program started for years. County facilities are always hurting budget wise. As you can imagine no surgeon worth their scalpel is going to kiss off a multi-million dollar career just to help the community. Especially if most of their time is going to be spent kissing it off with newbie interns and amateur residents. No offense, Kirkland."

Kirk waved it off, unfazed. "None taken, Dr. James."

"So...when I mentioned it to the hospital administrator last week, she practically snatched me out of the chair and hugged me she was so thrilled."

"Wait a minute," T-Bone said. "I don't mean to get in your personal business, but how are you getting paid at all? You gotta get paid sometime, right?"

"I still have surgical privileges at Northbrook Heart. That's where I'll be doing Duke's surgery. And I'll be fine financially until I can open up a cardiac clinic of my own. That'll take about a year or so."

T-Bone slicked the Velcro straps of his Kevlar with his hand. "Sounds like you got everything all mapped out."

"So what exactly are we doing today?" Darrion asked her.

She took her eyes off the building and looked at him. "Basically Kirkland and I will be going from door to door, asking general questions about health and any medical history. Then once we have a solid list of who needs medical attention, we can start providing that medical attention in the order of urgency. Maybe we can start with the Reds and work our way to the Lows and the Whites? If that's okay?"

Darrion nodded. "I hope you don't expect us to hit every door in one day?"

"I hope you don't expect us to hit 'em all in a week."

"I don't know if my Maserati here is gonna last that long," T-Bone said.

Darrion looked at the beat up Buick.

A loud cocking sound came from the trunk. Taran was loading whatever munitions he saw fit to bring. "Where in all of hell did you get that death trap?" Darrion asked.

"From a hype on Ashland."

"The Kings might just blow it up to see if their guns work."

T-Bone shrugged, pulled a rubber band from his denim, and slipped his dreads into a ponytail. "They can blow this piece of shit back to the cluck-head it came from for all I care, but they ain't shooting up my Benz."

"How much did you pay for it?"

"Fifty."

Lunch laughed. "Fifty dollars? That's it? I need to start swapping off of junkies."

Taran handed three Mossberg 12-gauge shotguns to Darrion, Lunch, and T-Bone. Then went to the trunk and came back with two loaded Browning pistols for Lunch and T-Bone's holsters. He locked the trunk, laid his shotgun on top of it, slipped off his coat and pulled on his Kevlar.

"Do we really need all of that just to walk in the building?" Angelique asked Darrion.

"Walking in won't be the problem, Doc," T-Bone said. "Getting out is why we brought 'em."

Darrion scowled at T-Bone's remark.

He could have kept that one to himself. She was scared enough already. "Nothing is going to happen to you unless it happens to me first," Darrion assured her.

She looked up at the building. "Am I staring at snipers in those windows?"

No point in lying about it. He nodded. "Usually they're a bit more furtive, but...Yeah."

"What's keeping the bullets from flying our way?"

"My father's working on that as we speak."

"What if Pope won't allow it?"

"Duke is a very persuasive man. They have history. Don't worry."

♛

I mean to stay in power," Pope said. "And it's that same power that's going to keep your son alive in Cabrini. Now, I'm not suggesting that KD goes stomping around terrifying every soldier in the projects. The less noise he makes on this, the less they'll suspect. Darrion has a sharp ear for lies and 20/20 vision for treachery. Just the fact that I'm still breathing has somebody a little pissed off about that. And that somebody will slip and try to make moves to finish the job. When they do, all he has to do is report back to Ceasar or to me." After a moment of staring at Duke through the glass, he said, "Out of respect for what we once were...*you* do *me* this small kindness, and I'll make sure Zane stays in his lane. One phone call from me and every sniper walking the Reds will stand down. Not only will they stand down, they'll walk Darrion and the Doc through and provide cover fire against the Renegades."

Duke stayed quiet, using the time to think. He knew to deal with Xavier very carefully if he wanted to keep their agreement from reaching the ears of the church. If any affiliations with a criminal faction got back to Archbishop Courdenay, he and Derek's accord with Saint Victor Catholic would be refuted. "I need some diplomacy that's not in your nature, X. Any communication between you and I has to be kept undisclosed at all costs."

Xavier Pope nodded and a devilish smile warped his features from wise to wicked. "Ahhh, and the Duke schemes a ruse to become Emperor. But he must first become Archduke before he takes the throne. And to do that, he will need the muscle of the Marquis."

ANGELIQUE

Hello?" Darrion said.

Angelique stood quietly, waiting. Her heart sank when his brick phone rang. Inwardly she hoped the answer was a no go.

A strong gust of wind whipped her face and she was grateful for the sweater keeping her chest warm. When the breeze settled she could hear Duke's commanding voice coming through the receiver. She glanced down at her Nike's, then up at the building. Then up at the light sky. No matter where she looked, time didn't hasten. It just slowed even more. She crossed her arms over her medical coat and waited, trying to make out some of the words. All she caught was "Negotiate" and "Sniper."

Darrion nodded once. A few seconds later he said, "Yes, sir." Then he was silent for a long time before he hung up.

He looked at Turkell. "Let's go."

♛

Lefty took aim through a hole cut the cardboard he used to cover the window. DeGrate's head was perfectly centered in his crosshairs. He slid a finger to the trigger and waited. Behind him the door opened. Then a rustle of denim and a scrape of sneakers neared his back. Lefty didn't pull his eye from the riflescope to see who it was. The only man coming up behind him in the abandoned apartment had to be Zane.

"You still got him in your sights?"

Lefty gave a slight nod and put his eye back to the scope. "Yup."

Zane's brick phone rang. He pulled it from his coat. "Hello?"

After nearly a minute of silence, he hung up. "Send out a 13-23."

That pulled Lefty's eye from the riflescope.

He was expecting to see a 13-4-4 on his pager instead. Unless he miscounted the letters of the alphabet, 23 always stood for 'R', which meant 'Renegades'. Every time a 13 went out to the soldiers, 'M' for murder was the message. So, instead of seeing a beautiful 13 and two 4's on his pager — for 'D D' — he was being told to shoot at the Renegades? All morning long he was waiting for the order to Murder Darrion DeGrate. Lefty was outdone. "What?" he said in disbelief.

"When the Renegades start letting off, we're walking in our uninvited guests."

"What?" Lefty said again.

"Are you fucking deaf?" Zane spat. "The order came down from Pope. So stand down and do it. Take your ass up to the ninth floor. And when the Renegades start it, you end it. Go!"

Lefty stood from his post and left the apartment, sulking all the way up to the ninth floor.

♛

Kirkland grabbed a black medical bag. Darrion locked the Firebird, and they all moved in a steady pace towards the building, being careful to avoid the news cameras.

When they stepped onto the lawn, the massive crack of a high-powered weapon thundered in the air and glass shattered. More shots came in rapid fire from all directions. They all dropped to a crouch, grass exploding all around. Bullets ripped through the lawn.

Without warning, Darrion threw a hand to Angelique's chest, knocked her to the ground, and fired his 12-gauge.

The buckshot struck a foot soldier in the chest, twisting his entire body around. He lay face down, unmoving. A few more soldiers came shooting wildly from the front of the building. Turkell, Taran, and Lunch fired their Mossbergs and with every shot the whole world drowned into roaring, explosive blasts. Angelique's ears were ringing so loudly from the barrage of bullets, she couldn't think. She covered her ears, tucked her head between her knees, and tried to focus her sudden blurred vision on the blades of grass. Instead of green, she saw Darrion's discharged red slug rolled between her Nikes still smoking. A pungent stench of gunpowder assaulted her nostrils and abruptly, she was laboring to breathe. Her chest burning from oxygen deprivation.

A firm hand clamped down on her arm, snatching her up.

"Move!" Darrion yelled.

Closing in fast on the front entrance, she could see a few unit doors were open through the steel mesh that ran the entire height of the structure. Every boarded up window had soldiers in them, firing automatic weapons, their muzzles flashing through cut out holes. All of the windows that weren't sealed off or boarded up were vacant, black spaces.

They dashed across the lawn, dodging more bloody bodies than she dared to slow and count. Darrion threw up a hand to pause when they reached the corner of the building. Sirens sounded from two blocks away. Undoubtedly responding to the salvo of shots.

Angelique glanced behind her and saw Taran aimed in the opposite direction. T-Bone cursed, aiming upward at any threat he could see.

Lunch was reloading fast while Kirkland was making inventive promises to God under his breath.

More shots rang out from inside the building. For nearly a minute, no one else fired down at them. As if suddenly, the gangsters decided to start killing off each other. That didn't escape T-Bone's attention.

"What the fuck is going on?" he spat. "Why aren't they firing at us?"

"The Kings are giving cover fire against the Renegades," Darrion shouted above the gunfire. "As soon as it's clear, break for the entrance." When the gunfire ceased, Darrion peered around the corner, then motioned forward with his fist. "Let's go!"

They dashed through the entrance and two foot soldiers shut the door behind them. Inside the lobby, men were running and shouting, dashing for cover. Taking off up the stairs before Angelique could make out anything other than coats, white sneakers, denim, assault rifles aimed skyward. Darrion slammed her back against the wall, knocking the wind from her lungs. With shocking speed, he aimed down the main hall and fired two slugs. She couldn't see who fell, but she saw blood splatter against the opposite wall.

Screams and shouts echoed down from above. Shots were still exploding on the upper floors. Everywhere she looked, mayhem and murder invaded her vision. Turkell was right. If she ever wanted to see her warm bed again, they'd have to shoot their way out.

"We're taking you up to Zane," one of the soldiers said. Dressed in a black pullover sweater and dark blue denim, he looked like a taller, lighter-skinned T-Bone, with shorter dreadlocks. Angelique didn't recognize him from the first night she met with Zane.

She wasn't looking forward to a second meeting.

"Q-Ball, this is Dr. James," Darrion said, "and this is Kirkland, one of her interns."

"What's up," Q-Ball said. He nodded at the stairwell. "This way."

For a brief moment the gunshots ceased.

Maybe every soldier in the building had to reload at the same time, Angelique thought. Doubtful. But maybe.

They all followed Q-Ball. Passing dead bodies and the instant they reached the stairwell, Angelique was nearly knocked backward by the rancid smell of urine, trash, and insecticide. Lunch cursed and drew back. T-Bone cursed even louder and coughed.

Taran leaned his Mossberg against the wall, pulled a bandana from his back pocket, and tied it around his nose. Darrion did the same. Angelique tried not to gag, but the sound of Kirk's gag reflex made her stomach wrench. She shut her eyes tight and swallowed down gastric juice. Something wet was shoved in her face. She opened her eyes to gauze pressed against her nose. "Hold this," Kirk said. He reached in the black bag and wet another one for himself.

"Let's move," Q-Ball said, starting up the stairs.

They made their way past an elevator and moved up to the ninth floor. Every wall along the way was littered with graffiti. Smeared with blood both old and new. It looked like a war zone. Q-Ball made a left and led them to a door halfway down the hall.

He gave a firm knock. "Open up, Lefty."

The door flew open. "Quick, get in," a voice said, "and stay away from the windows."

They all stepped inside and Angelique froze. A chill shot through her as she laid eyes on Zane.

Sitting in a black leather chair with an appraising look in his dark eyes, the Disciple leader was impeccably dressed in the latest fashion. A black fur coat, black leather gloves, his denim the blackest black. His hair was so low trimmed, tiny waves curved around his head in neat rows. Blue diamond earrings adorned his lobes.

Angelique wondered if the gems were real. Given his profession, they probably were.

No visible sign of Zeno made her pulse drop out of the red zone. The last thing she needed to see was that dark, lurking stare and that false, fucked up eye.

On instinct, she moved behind Darrion and took in all of the room within seconds. Two foot soldiers were standing in the far corner by a busted out window. The walls were cracking paint, the floor was grimy, and the air carried an overpowering mix of tobacco and metal. When she exhaled and saw her breath, she realized it was no warmer inside than outdoors. Other than the chair Zane sat in, only a few metal chairs were pushed back against the wall and a glass coffee table sat inches from him. A lit cigar wafted smoke from an ashtray.

The Disciple regent looked at Angelique. "Next time, ditch the white lab coat," he spat. "You're a walking bull's eye in it."

She kept her mouth shut and blinked at him.

Zane stood from the chair and looked at his men. "Take their wam wams and pat 'em down."

Darrion aimed his Mossberg at the first soldier who neared him. "I don't think so." Guns rose in a flash and every barrel marked a skull.

Zane stared at him, unblinking.

Kirkland dropped to the floor and covered his head with the medical bag.

Angelique felt her bowels liquefy.

"I appreciate the cover fire," Darrion said, keeping his eyes on the soldier.

"I was on orders," Zane said, coldly.

"Appreciated nonetheless. But if you think I'm walking Cabrini unarmed, you must be doing more dope than you sell."

Silence sat in the room as everyone stood deadlocked in the standoff. Angelique could tell Zane was pissed off at Darrion's defiance. His foot soldiers aimed with their merciless glares. All of them itching to pull triggers.

"You're out numbered, DeGrate," Zane spat. "Five on four doesn't leave room for you to call the shots in my project. Now lower the fucking metal before you get smeared."

"Pity for you that Pope and Caesar Black disagree," Darrion said. "That makes six on five and the last time I checked, Pope rules the Reds in Cabrini, which means his word supersedes your rank. So you tell *your* men to lower the fucking metal. I'll be keeping mine."

"I second that," Taran seethed through his bandana.

"And I third it, bitch," T-Bone spat.

Lunch laughed, but he kept his aim steady.

Zane sniffed casually and plied at his leather gloves. Another cold draft wafted through the window frame, but he didn't seem to notice. He kept his eyes on Darrion.

"I tell my men to let off, you all drop like dice, and who knows…we are in the Wilds. Accidents happen. I'm sure Pope would understand."

"Yeah," Darrion said. "So would your grandmother. Then again, I'm sure Muriel's well aware that there'll be no such thing as an accident when you get a wop. You let off…we let off right back. The whole room gets smeared and we're all missing Christmas. Doesn't that sound lovely?"

"Oh, my dick is busting concrete just thinking about it," T-Bone said.

Zane glared at Darrion for a long moment. Then he glanced at Q-Ball. "Gentlemen, lower the metal."

No one moved at first. Then slowly, one by one the men lowered their weapons. Angelique let out a breath of relief, but she wasn't fool enough to feel safe. After witnessing what Zeno could do to a body at Zane's command, no doubt his soldiers could do the same carnage to her.

"Let's step in the back for a few ticks," Zane said.

♛

Q-Ball closed the door behind them, leaving the two men alone to converse. "I understand this is putting a monkey wrench in your operation," Darrion began. "It shouldn't take more than a couple of weeks to see all of the residents in the Reds who might need care. After that we'll give you a list of everyone that needs to be treated and you can set up the doctor and her intern anywhere you see fit to administer their treatment. They'll barely be seen and seldom heard, I give you my word."

"I don't need your word," Zane said. "Guarantees will do me just fine."

Darrion quickly scanned the room but nothing stood out to him. One chair sat near the door and a few cockroaches scuttled in an out of a massive crack fissured up the wall. He noticed the muzzle hole carefully carved in the boarded up window. He kept his Mossberg aimed to the ground, but his grip firm.

"Most wars, we profit from. This one, if we don't take out Sampson, will break us all."

Darrion shrugged. "So kill him. Why tell me? I'm not in your drug war."

Zane's eyes flashed but he kept calm. "Not in it? The second you crossed the Killing Fields you were all up it, through it, around it, and in it."

"I'm here to keep the doctor safe and negotiate a truce, Zane. Not stack up bodies."

Zane glanced at the window. "Oh you mean like the twelve Renegade soldiers you and your crew just shot down in the courtyard? Bodies like those?"

"They let off first." It sounded childish, but it was no less true. He was supposed to just let them kill him? Darrion was certain that would have given Zane the best day of his homicidal life. It was disturbing. Standing in a room next to a man who cared nothing for the value of mortality. Then again, his ruthless ways were the sole reason why he rose in the ranks so quickly after Zander Harris died...Yet there was a flip side to that coin. He only rose in the ranks so far. Even Pope knew better than to let that beast out of his cage. For that reason, Zane Harris would never rise above the rank of regent. And he knew it.

Darrion had half a mind to speculate he was responsible for the hit on Pope in Stateville. Which caused him to further surmise that a man like Pope was no simpleton. He must have known Zane had a hand in it. He just couldn't prove it.

Now it made sense. Pope didn't need Darrion to find out *who* ordered the hit. He needed a confession that no member of his street board or his prison board could dispute. Zane made money. A lot of money. Ending his life would damage profits. Profits that Pope and all of his generals had come to depend on for their own financial security. Both the prison board and the street board would have to have a unanimous decision to green light his demise. So getting a confession out of Zane — with witnesses — was Darrion's true aim.

"They let off first," Zane repeated. "Yeah, and it won't be the last. I can promise you that, DeGrate."

More shots rang out somewhere off in the distance. Darrion couldn't tell exactly which building it came from. Hudson Mob or Bank Roll. Maybe the cops.

"Now," Zane went on, "Pope passed word down to me, that we're to set up a meeting by the end of the week. Discuss a ceasefire. I really don't see how that's set to fix a damn thing. Even if Sampson and his wild bunch come back into the fold, we would still be on the verge of war with the Whites. The Black Dragons, the King Cobras and the Vice Stones formed an alliance. And they plan to strike hard and soon. So unless you're God almighty, I don't see how your presence is turning shit to sugar."

"Put brains before bullets for a millisecond," Darrion said, "and maybe you would see it."

Zane cast a cold glare at him, but he didn't reply.

"All it takes to make a ceasefire possible in a war is for both sides to feel like they won the war. Which means both sides have to give up what's wanted to gain what's needed. And what's needed for the Whites and the Lows, more than money, power, and dope, is running water and electricity. The wants they have to give up are overthrowing the Kings and seeing you get your halo. What's needed for the Reds is pulling the Renegades back in, becoming a unit once more, and regaining control of the product and the weapons to protect it. The wants you have to give up are settling up with every slight to your fragile sensibilities."

"Okay, Confucius," Zane spat. "That would be worth a go if Sampson wanted amenities and voltage. But what he wants nobody can accommodate."

Darrion exhaled. "How much is the street tax?"

"Seventy percent."

His breath froze in his lungs. That larceny led to wonder how in all of hell they were even surviving. Now Darrion understood Sampson's rebellion. "Seventy?! I would've pulled a Beirut a long time ago behind that extortion. How the fuck is anybody around here eating?"

Zane's eyes lit up as if Darrion had just said something intriguing. "Ah," he said, "speaking of eating...It's time to feed the herd."

He walked over to the closet and pulled out a sniper rifle, then went over to the window and took down the boards.

"What are you doing?" Darrion asked.

"There are three things my herd needs to continue to thrive." Zane propped the rifle on the window frame, but he didn't take aim. He slipped his gloved hands in the pockets of his coat, pulled out a silencer, screwed it onto the muzzle, and watched the courtyard. "Food, fear, and pharmacological sustenance. And not necessarily in that order."

Sounds of ruckus below drew Darrion to the window. Dozens of addicts and bums crowded the courtyard. Absently scratching themselves. Oblivious of the dead bodies laid out around them. Apparently this gathering was routine.

Soldiers brought out tables full of food and sat them down in the middle of the lawn. None of the junkies or bums moved toward the tables until the soldiers went back inside the building and shut the door. Then, like a surge of ravenous fiends, they all rushed the table. All of the stronger and faster beggars were pushing and shoving the old and the weak out of the way.

Snatching up food and running off like a bomb was strapped to the tables.

"See that hype, right there?" Zane said, pointing at the farthest end of the courtyard. The gray haired old man was barely visible. Tucked into the edge of the courtyard, he stood hidden by a thick of trees. If Zane meant to shoot him, a clear line of sight was impossible.

"He won't move," Zane said, taking aim. "Not yet. That one, he's still water." He pulled the trigger and the bullet struck a woman in the back of the head. She fell gracelessly. Her head spraying blood on the grass. She was the farthest back from the tables and none of the others fighting for food seemed to notice. Darrion suspected that was the reason for the silencer.

"I feed my herd every morning on Mondays," Zane said with an unnatural calm to his voice. "On the first Monday, I kill one. On the second Monday, I kill two. On the third Monday, three go down. And of course on the fourth Monday the body count's the highest. Since there are only four weeks in a month, obviously I never kill more than four." He took aim again and fired. A man at the back of the crowd fell fast, the bullet tearing through his chest. Still no one noticed.

"The old man by the trees...he knows," Zane said with a hint of amusement inflecting his voice. "I don't know how he figured it out. But he knows." He took aim again and hit a man at the table dead center in the back of his skull. Blood sprayed the food as he fell forward and hit the ground. They all scattered like seeds. Breaking in all directions. Undoubtedly, every reporter with a camera and a microphone was getting the story of their lives. The courtyard cleared in seconds.

Then the old man limped forward. Slowly stepping over the bodies. In no hurry as he reached the table and carefully picked around the bloodied food, taking his fill.

Zane lowered his rifle. "It's the third Monday of December. So, he knows there won't be a fourth. Not today."

Zane was a sick twist. Yet, for some reason, Darrion just couldn't tear his eyes away from the carnage. He never did have qualms with looking down on a corpse. As long as it wasn't someone he knew. Two years in Vietnam taught him to step over a body like a rock in the road. So if Zane was trying to intimidate him, the regent was failing miserably.

"He's known my pattern of killing for months." He turned and looked at Darrion. "So why doesn't he say anything?"

Darrion knew the answer to that, but since Zane seemed pleased with the sound of his own voice, he let him ramble on.

"As long as he keeps the secret to himself, I won't be forced to change my routine. As long as he stays in his lane, I won't kill him. It's a silent tacit agreement between he and I. And we've never even met. Yet, our unspoken accord still stands unbroken. Guarantees, DeGrate. Guarantees are all I need. With that old head down there, we have an understanding where words don't mean shit. So, tell me, do you and I have an understanding?"

I understand more than you know you crazy fuck. "We do."

Darrion knew that wasn't a threat against him alone. It was a threat against Angelique as well, if not more so. He could have easily glazed the wall with Zane's brains just then. But killing him wasn't an option. Not today. Not tomorrow. He'd kill him later if he had to. For now, there was no showing abhorrence. No matter how much he wanted to shove his Mossberg in the man's mouth, knock his teeth out, and pull the trigger, Darrion would have to wait.

"I hope you can bring the Doc to a similar understanding." Zane said.

"Like I said," Darrion said, losing patience, "she won't be a problem."

"I want her out of my projects no later than 8:00 p.m.," Zane ordered. "The white boy too."

"Understood. Anything else?"

Zane shook his head. "That's it. For now."

He'd have to work on Angelique's fear of Zane. First things first, he would give her a pager in case anything went wrong, then he'd purchase that tracking device Taran was always rambling about. They were worn like watches and when activated, they signaled distance between the two wearers in kilometers. He'd also have to give her a side-arm similar to the one she carried during the hunt in Galena. If she could take down a wolf in the woods, she could take down any animal in Cabrini if she had to.

Zane was an animal.

And all animals sense fear.

DARRION

Darrion spent over an hour showing Angelique and Kirk through and around the buildings. Avoiding the news cameras whenever possible, but a few persistent reporters got in a few snap shots as several coroners loaded corpses from the Killing Fields into their vans.

Fourteen buildings made the Reds. Most of the elevators in them were non-functional and had been turned into makeshift quarters by the homeless. In one building they actually saw a man urinating openly in the elevator without a care of who passed him by. However, inside Head Quarters and Hudson Mob the elevators worked nonstop.

Angelique found quickly that she had to be careful where she stepped. Down every hallway, around every corner, up every stairwell, her Nike's either trudged on or just missed some form of filth. Rats the size of beavers ran freely through the lobbies and halls. Using gaping clefts in the bricks as thruways. Roaches owned the walls and the rancid stench was so intolerable she often had to fight off spells of nausea and vertigo. Kirk ran outside twice to throw up.

Darrion left him outdoors with Taran and Lunch the second time to collect himself and walked Angelique back to Head Quarters.

T-Bone followed, singing an old Isley Brothers tune as if he had no care or concern in the world.

When they neared the stairwell, Angelique paused.

"Where are we going?"

"To the tenth floor," Darrion said.

"What's on the tenth floor?"

"You'll see."

By the time she reached the fifth floor, she complained about her legs burning with exhaustion. Darrion told her to breath through it. He assumed she had to inhale so deeply the rancid stench left her completely nose-deaf by the time she reached the tenth floor because she didn't complain about the smell. Darrion opened the door to an apartment and motioned for her to step inside.

Angelique did so hesitantly. Her jaw dropped at what she saw. Every wall of the apartment had massive holes in them large enough to summersault through. None of them were neatly created. Frayed and ragged, the holes looked knocked out with a forceful tool. A sledge-hammer had likely made them. Every floor was littered with trash and debris and fragments of drywall. Except for the front door, every doorway she saw was voided space with bare hinges.

"On the top floors of every building in the Reds there's the Maze," Darrion explained. "The Kings put man-sized holes in the walls of every apartment on this floor. None of them are occupied and the only door you'll ever see is the one you just walked through."

Angelique stepped forward, eyeing the Maze in awe.

"Where does it go?"

"Everywhere. If you know where you're going."

"And nowhere if you don't," T-Bone added.

It was an elaborate tunneling system. Every hole led to another room and every room led to another hall and every hall led to another apartment. Darrion could easily see an unsuspecting fool getting lost in that catacomb for hours. Any unsuspecting fools were the police.

It must have dawned on the good doctor because she said, "So, if I were a cop, a raid would be a complete waste of my time, right? I mean, by the time I ran from the bottom floor all the way up to the tenth floor, I'd be lucky if I found my way out alive, let alone make an arrest."

"Exactly so," Darrion said. "What you're standing in is an impenetrable nest. And thanks to the Mayor welding the back door, it's the perfect place to commit a crime."

"Well, what good does this do me if cops can't even find the gangsters in here?"

"That door swings both ways, Angie. If Five-O can't find the thugs up here, the thugs can't find each other when they're on the run. Which means they can't find you."

Angelique stepped through a manhole to her right and found herself facing three more. She chose the one on the left and stood before two more holes in the next room. Both men followed.

When she paused Darrion said, "If anything happens to me —"

"That's not going to happen," she said, cutting him off.

"Anything happens to me," he repeated, "you get here. However you have to. I don't care what you have to do or who you have to put down to do it...just get here." He leaned his Mossberg against the wall, opened the front of his Kevlar and pulled out a pistol. "This is similar to the twins I keep strapped to my back. This is a Colt. It carries .45 ACP rounds. Seven, plus one in the chamber. The only difference is, mine are registered. This one's not. The serial's filed off and the grip is a skin resistant TEC-KOTE finish. It won't hold a finger print. If you have to use it, the cops can't trace it back to you." He handed it to her. "I'll get you a shoulder strap tomorrow. I want you wear it at all times. For now, use the back of your denim."

Angelique stared at the gun, feeling the weight of it. To Darrion, it was not heavy, but weighted enough to ease the recoil.

She looked up at him. "Thanks."

He nodded. "Don't hesitate to use it if you have to. And aim true. Because if you miss, they won't."

"I'm a good shot. I can handle myself." She turned left and took the next manhole like she knew where she was going.

Darrion smiled at her brazen confidence as he and T-Bone followed close behind.

"Yeah, I noticed," he said.

♛

Hello?" T-Bone said.

"Who's this?" a man's voice asked.

T-Bone scowled at the brick phone. "Who the fuck is this?"

"Derek."

"Aw," he said flatly. "Well what's up, man?"

"Where's Darrion?"

He tapped Darrion on the shoulder and handed him the phone. "It's *Councilman Porter*. For you."

Darrion put the brick to his ear. "Yeah?"

"I've been trying to call you for over a fucking hour!" Derek screamed.

"Well we get bad reception in some of the towers."

"That shoot out was all over the news! Is she alright?"

"Yeah, it was just cover fire. The Disciples walked us through the courtyard. Once we were inside everything was —"

"Put her on the phone, now!"

Darrion rolled his eyes, pulled the brick from his ear and handed it off to Angelique. "It's his liege for you, madam."

She smirked at him. "Stop it, be nice."

"He started it."

"Oh what are you twelve?" She slid the Colt in the back of her denim and put the brick to her ear. "I'm fine I promise."

"Are you sure?" Derek asked.

"Yes, I'm fine."

"If you don't feel safe, we can call this off right now."

"No, they're taking care of everything. I feel totally safe. T-Bone and Darrion are with me. Lunch and Taran are with Kirk. We're good here. I'm not backing out. Everything's fine. I mean it, so stop worrying."

Darrion exhaled. Then he heard the Councilman's voice through the phone.

"Please be careful."

"I will."

"I love you, Angie."

"I love you too."

She hung up.

♛

They stopped in the next room and surveyed four more manholes.

"Now which way do I go?" Angelique asked.

"Oddly enough," T-Bone said, "you're going the right way. To get from the door to the main elevator is right, left, left, right, left, right."

She repeated it to herself, then walked through the holes, made the last right and found herself facing the elevator.

"To get to the next stairwell and come down in the other building," Darrion said, "is right, right, left, left, right, left, left. Not from here. Back at the door where we started."

Angelique blinked at him, confused.

"How many outs are there?"

"The last time I checked, I think like...fifteen."

That registered with shock. "How many dead ends are there?"

"Twice as many," T-Bone said. "I hope you got a good memory, Doc."

She blinked at both men and swallowed hard.

Leaving the Maze, stepping out of Head Quarters onto the lawn was like walking into a nightmare in broad daylight, but she couldn't wake. She didn't dare imagine the hell Cabrini transformed into at night. The only way she forced her mind to deal with it was the fact that she wasn't there alone. Oddly enough, being guarded by four men who weren't afraid to do murder was comforting. Still, she had to ask herself, how people lived like that everyday?

While walking from building to building, most of the people she saw passed them by without a word spoken or just stood there staring. Angelique was surprised at how many residents knew Darrion, Casper, and Turkell. Anyone who knew them often spoke with respect, giving warm welcomes and polite nods of acknowledgement. Taran Carter, Dr. James had found out, didn't grow-up-Cabrini, as Darrion put it. Nor did he grow up a Chicagoan either. He met Darrion in the Army and fought by his side for two years during the Vietnam War. When the war was over, he had no family left in his hometown of Brooklyn, except an elderly uncle and a distant brother didn't see much. So, Darrion claimed him as family and invited him to stay.

Nightfall came faster than expected and she couldn't wait to take a shower. By the time Darrion dropped her off at Duke and Viola's, she was so mentally frayed all she could do was shower, slip into a nightgown, slide under the sheets, and close her eyes. It didn't even matter that Derek had another late one and his side of the bed was cold and empty.

She was fast asleep before she could begin to feel one way or the other about it.

♕

By Tuesday, the media was less frantic and every hour gone by seemed to mold some kind of routine. Lunch and Taran knew the territory well enough to branch off with Kirk. Darrion and T-Bone stayed with Dr. James. They all agreed splitting into two groups of three would cover twice as many apartments in half the time.

Until the week was over, Angelique accepted she would be spending nearly every day from 8:00 in the morning until 8:00 at night with Darrion and T-Bone.

Door to door. Stepping inside filthy apartments. Surveying the health of every resident.

When they broke for lunch she was barely hungry and at dinner, she ate at Duke and Viola's in the guest room. She barely saw her charmer, who was busy blazing his campaign trail with public appearances and speeches. Within days, he was catapulted in the polls. Not only was Burns lagging behind by more thirty percent, the Councilman was running neck and neck with Caruso.

More than ever she wished he was there. Guiding her with a sure hand on the small of her back, leading her into every room like he'd done so many times before whenever they were at a gathering or business dinner.

I started this mess, she told herself. *There's no going back now.*

Her life became Cabrini Green and for the sake of her fiancé's campaign and her career, every deprived resident's plight was her mission. She handed out medical questionnaires to be collected at the end of the week and listened to the tenants complain about their poor circulation or arthritis, while Darrion and Turkell handled quick inspections of the amenities and listened to the gripes and moans from the residents about their living conditions.

Darrion was the model of courtesy and politeness, treating everyone he saw with far more respect and dignity than Zane and Zeno's henchmen, but he never let his guard down. Neither did Turkell. Keeping their Kevlars on and their Mossbergs close at all times. Ready for anything.

Some highrise units were well kept by lonely elderly tenants who found safety in their homes behind bolted doors. Or single mothers doing the best they could manage, kept their living conditions as up to par as possible. Other units were left to neglect and decay by addicts and prostitutes. Dried vomit, empty liquor bottles, and hypodermic needles littered the floors. Broken mirrors dangled on grimy walls. Filth encrusted, scarcely used furniture sat worn and frayed.

The Lows were no better. In one of the lowrise apartments Angelique spotted a strange small glass cylinder. Cloudy at one end, it had an unusual burnt residue at the other.

She held it up for a closer inspection and looked at Darrion. "What's this?"

He looked as mystified as she was.

"I don't know," he answered. "Some kind of pipe."

He took it from her and held it up to his nose. A quick sniff warped his face in disgust. "But it smells like burnt ass." He tossed it away, shattering glass all over the floor. "Let's go."

Angelique held up the clipboard. "Don't you want to inspect this one for repairs?"

Darrion shook his head and tightened his grip on the Mossberg. "Naw, just mark this one as '*unoccupied unit*' and check off '*derelict*' in the unit condition box." He stepped back out into the sun, repulsion still locked on his dark brown features. "Let's get the fuck out of here please."

Regardless of the apartments they went in, every unit they surveyed had the same communal concerns. Cracked ceilings, molding bathroom walls, poor electricity, and insufficient plumbing.

What Angelique noticed in most residents was a sickly cough as if they all had a cold or symptoms of the flu. She assumed Kirk had noticed the same, but if a few home remedies and some cough syrup was all she had to recommend, she considered herself lucky.

By Friday, she was exhausted, mentally and physically.

Just when she thought she was beginning to numb to it all, the threesome hit Bank Roll — one of the largest buildings in the Reds — and when they reached the first occupied apartment on the fourth floor, a familiar face opened the door.

♛

What's up, KD," Anton said. "I was wondering when you would be hitting Bank Roll. What's up, T-Bone?"

Both men spoke back then Darrion re-introduced Angelique. "You remember Dr. James, right?"

"Oh absolutely," he said, nodding politely. "We had a night to remember the first time we met."

Dr. James nodded politely. "Hello, Ant."

"Hello, Ma'am. Come on in." He stepped aside, waved them into the living room, and shut the door.

Angelique took in the thick smells of baking bread and pasta sauce. She didn't realize how hungry she was until her stomach gave a growl. Sounds of a tiny infant voice drew her attention to a beautiful young woman sitting on a worn sofa, holding an adorable baby boy. He was all cheeks. Pure brown eyes covering nearly half his face. Cooing away at the chew toy in his mouth. Completely unaware of their presence.

"KD, you remember Taniesha, right?" Ant said.

Darrion's composure seemed to change with a flicker of surprise in his eyes when he looked at her.

"You're a mommy now, hmm?" he asked. "How've you been?"

She blinked up at him, but she didn't give him the same excited welcome Ant did. She looked uncomfortable with Darrion being there. It wasn't a rude uncomfortable, just a standoffish one.

"I've been good."

With flawless skin and a voluptuous figure that was the epitome of youth, Taniesha couldn't have been more than twenty plus five — give or take a few years. Even though she was a strikingly attractive woman there was something about her that caught Angelique's attention. Eyes shining brown and beautiful, yet bare and sad.

Taniesha and Darrion both looked at each other in silence for a long moment, until T-Bone cleared his throat, obviously aware of the awkward silence between them and excused himself to inspect the plumbing in the bathroom. In that moment Angelique knew. These two had history. But that history was none of her business. She stepped forward like the professional surgeon she was and cut the silence, extending her hand to Taniesha.

They said hello and shook hands.

"I'm Dr. James. It's nice to meet you. I'm here to hand you a quick medical questionnaire and ask you a few questions about your health and the health of your baby."

"Grandma!" Ant called out. "The doctor's here."

Then he left and went into one of the back rooms.

Just as Dr. James began asking Taniesha questions, the baby coughed unhealthily. She removed the stethoscope from around her neck and asked Taniesha for permission to check his breathing. With a nod from his mother, she pressed the cold steel to his chest, listened, and pressed the steel to his back.

"He's adorable," she said. "What's his name?"

"Amari," Taniesha answered.

"How old is little Amari?"

"Eleven months."

"Almost a year, hmm?" Dr. James drew back when a tiny cockroach crawled out of his ear. She didn't panic. She didn't let her face betray the shock. She quietly stood up, pulled a pair of latex gloves from her pocket, knocked the roach onto the floor and stomped on it.

"Wow," she said. "I'm surprised it was able to crawl back out. Probably because it was a small one. If it had been any bigger, it most likely never would have came out."

"How do you know that?" Taniesha asked, with a glance to dead roach on the floor.

"Well, roaches can't crawl backwards and the ear canal of a human adult is a small one. Let alone a baby's. So if anything gets in there, normally they don't have much room to turn around." She pulled a form from her clipboard and handed it to

Taniesha. "Okay, Mom," she said, forcing a smile. "Just fill this out and I'll collect it later on tonight."

"What time tonight?" Taniesha asked. "I have appointments."

Appointments? Dr. James didn't know what that meant, but, "Just after sundown, but definitely before nine."

They all looked down the hall when the back door opened. An elderly woman in a floral pullover dress shuffled into the kitchen on swollen ankles. She spoke a hello and checked a pot on the stove. When she removed the lid, steam wafted up to the stove light overhead. So much steam, there should have been a reaction from the heat. There wasn't.

Dr. James didn't cook much. Her profession rarely afforded the luxury. Yet she knew steam that hot should have caused her to draw her arm back. But she just held it there over the pot as she reached for a stirring spoon. She looked the classic diabetic. Obese, sluggish, and her legs looked reddened and tender. Neuropathy was normal in most diabetics who neglected their health and her legs were beginning to display the warning signs of skin blisters. She pulled at the silver wig on her head, straightening it, and stirred the contents of the pot. Then she reached across the counter for a cigarette.

Dr. James didn't know Ant was back in the living room until he spoke. "This is Grandma Ida," he said. "But everybody around here just call her Grandma."

"Ms. Ida will do just fine, young lady," Ida said with a nod to Dr. James. "She came around the kitchen counter and let out an aching moan as she slowly took a seat at the dining table.

Angelique didn't need to ask, but she needed Ms. Ida to be forthcoming about her health. "Ms. Ida, are you a diabetic?"

"Yup," Ant said before his grandmother could answer.

"If you knew just by looking at me," Ms. Ida said, "why you ask?"

"Because there's a difference between a diabetic who's taking care of themselves and a diabetic who is not." Dr. James gave a quick glance to the pot on the stove. "I'm pretty sure you just burned your arm over that stove. Mind if I take a look?"

Ms. Ida just looked at her, so Angelique took that as a 'if you want, makes no difference to me' glare. She went to the table and gently turned over her arm. It was red and already starting to swell. "You didn't feel that at all?" she asked.

"She won't take care of her blood sugar," Ant complained. "The doctor told her, but she won't listen."

"Who's your doctor?" she asked Ms. Ida.

"Dr. Loos, down at the clinic."

Angelique knelt down. Inspecting her legs and ankles. "What kind of medications does he have you on?"

"Insulin, metformin and…uh…he got me on that uh, what's the name of it? Starts with a N. It's for pain relief. Supposed to be an anti-depressant."

"Norpramin?"

She nodded. "That's the one. But I don't like it cause it makes me too sleepy and I can't go to the bathroom with it."

"You haven't been taking your meds?"

"No!" Ant cut in.

"Neuropathy can be very aggressive if it goes untreated," Dr. James said to Ms. Ida. "You need to take your medications."

"She don't care," Taniesha cut in. "She still won't take it."

"Shut up, Taniesha," Ms. Ida spat.

"Okay." Dr. James slid off one of her house shoes. As expected, her foot was in decay. All five toes were blackened of severe necrosis. If Ms. Ida wanted to keep half of her foot, the toes would have to be amputated. She let out a breath and stood. "I would like for you to be checked in at Scott Joplin. You need to be seen through the ER."

Ms. Ida frowned and shook her head. "I ain't going to no damn hospital. I know I'm overweight, but I done lost almost twenty pounds in three weeks."

"That rapid weight loss is glucose related. That's not a good thing. And that foot, your legs, and that arm need to be treated. Tonight. And I am willing to bet my salary that your sugar is sky high as we speak. You're very sick. Ignoring it and living in denial won't make it go away."

"Well, I'll start taking my pills then."

"Ms. Ida, it's medicine…not magic. And at this point, the necrosis has gone too far for medication alone to do any good."

"You're going, Grandma," Ant said.

Ms. Ida looked at him like she wanted to slap the teeth, tongue, and tonsils from his mouth. But she said nothing.

Ant looked at Darrion. "You wanna stay for dinner, there's plenty?"

"I would, but I got this meeting to go to tonight."

"I know. Everybody know. I'mma be there too."

Darrion blinked at him. "Oh yeah?"

Ant nodded.

Dr. James glanced out of the living room window and checked her watch. It was just past 7:00 and the sun was all but gone from the sky.

She looked at Darrion. "We should get going. Since the meeting's at 8:00, if we leave now and take them to the hospital, we can be back by then."

T-Bone came into the living room. "I got this unit checked off. The plumbing's not too bad in this building." He handed off the clipboard to Darrion, looked at Ms. Ida, and smiled a mouth full of gold. "Grandma Ida!" He smothered her in a long hug and kissed her cheek.

To Dr. James' surprise, they started speaking in fluid French and fell into a conversation everyone else clearly wasn't invited in on, so Dr. James made sure Ant and Taniesha had everything they needed before they left.

"Ant, you should take some of that food for her and when you pack an overnight bag, make sure all of her medications are in a separate bag so they know what she's taking and bring any form of ID...Driver's license, Social Security Card, and any insurance cards. Bring a pillow, because sometimes the ER is out of them and make sure you bring any toiletries she might need. Toothpaste, toothbrush, comb, underwear, etcetera etcetera. Also make sure she has comfortable pajamas with no metal buttons on them in case the attending wants a CAT scan or X-rays."

"You sound like you gonna be there for a week or something," Taniesha said.

"Maybe longer," Dr. James said. "She really is sick. I can tell you now, she's going to be admitted. She's not coming home tonight."

Ant and Taniesha busied themselves packing food and an overnight bag for Ms. Ida. Then everyone left and Darrion drove to Scott Joplin Cook County Hospital.

♛

Surprisingly, the ER was slow for a Friday night. Angelique expected the waiting room to be packed and Ms. Ida's wait to be hours before she was seen. Instead, she was immediately registered, taken back to bed 3, and the nurse had her finger pricked and glucose checked in less than ten minutes. As suspected, her sugar was 400 plus.

Dr. James informed the nurse of Amari's cough and convinced Taniesha to have him checked in and seen as well. Having his blood drawn was a nightmare. He kicked and screamed until the needle was out, but it was worth it. Thirty minutes later, his lab results came back positive for roach poisoning, streptococcus faecalis, a mild ear infection, and asthma. Taniesha was given several prescriptions for home treatment and Amari was discharged. Ant seemed to take the news well when the attending ER doctor informed him that Ms. Ida would be admitted to treat her foot and get her diabetes under control.

Ant promised his grandmother he would come back to check on her in a few hours. Then he kissed her forehead and walked Taniesha and the baby back out to the car.

The four mile drive back to Cabrini was a quiet one. Marvin Gay and Otis Redding serenaded them through traffic. By the time they made it back to the highrises, it was five minutes to 8:00. As Darrion pulled into the parking lot of Bank Roll it seemed like they all had been teleported to the Twilight Zone.

No news crews were walking about the lawns. No hype heads roamed about the lot. No prostitutes loitered in the breezeways. It was quiet. Too quiet. Angelique was the first one to speak on it. "Where the hell is everybody?"

Darrion pulled the key from the ignition. "I'm sure they found a new spot for their nocturnal deeds."

"All the news vans probably scared 'em off," T-Bone said.

In the lobby it was so quiet they all stopped and looked around. Usually by sundown, every building was mayhem. But it was so vacant the icy wind blew a hollowed shrill of air off the walls and down the main hall. It looked like no one had lived there for eons.

Taniesha shuddered and pulled her baby close. "What the hell?"

"This is some creepy shit, man," Ant said. "Even when the Mayor was here, it wasn't this bad."He pulled a set of keys from his pocket. "I'm gonna get Taniesha and little man up stairs."

Darrion looked around and overhead, then down at Anton. "Me and T-Bone will meet you at the meeting. We'll find out what the hell is going on."

"I'm not supposed to be here past 8:00," Angelique reminded him.

Darrion waved it off with his hand. "That's just Zane proving how big his dick is. If you're with me, he'll give you a pass. The meeting starts in less than five minutes and we don't have time to take you back to Duke's, so he's going to have to make an exception."

"Pretty much," T-Bone added.

She was in no position to argue, nor did she want to. She trusted them so she just shook her head. "Okay."When Taniesha and Anton were out of earshot, she said, "Darrion, things are worse than I thought here."

Darrion gave her a concerned look. "What do you mean?"

"Amari's just the start of it. I thought everyone had just caught a virus that was going around. But I am willing to bet my salary no one is coughing around here because they have a cold. They all have roach poisoning. I'm sure of it."

He blinked at her, shocked. "Shit...So what now?"

"Everyone who's sick needs a massive round of antibiotics. And soon."

"At the hospital?"

She shook her head. "No, it can come in pill form. But they need it. Putting it off until Monday is not an option. So, you're going to have to mention to Zane that I'll need a pass for this weekend."

"I don't know if he's gon' let that happen," T-Bone said. "Saturday and Sunday is when he makes his longest green serving up customers."

"Basically," Darrion agreed. Then he thought on it. "But, with this stand off Sampson's got going on, Zane's supply is running low anyway. I'll talk to him. We'll figure something out."

ZANE

Darrion was waiting for the blood to spill.

Sampson and Zane on the same roof was like a tank full of ether next to a blow torch. As soon as things heated up enough, anyone near the blast would die bloody.

Both men decided Head Quarters was no place to hold an indoor meeting. With snipers perched in windows of adjacent buildings, there was nothing to stop a Renegade from picking off Zane, and nothing to stop a Disciple from picking off Sampson. So they both settled on the one spot that no sniper could target. The roof.

But neither came alone. Sampson had more than ten of his men with him. Zane had his younger brother Zeno and all of his henchmen present for the discussion. In fairness no weapons were allowed on the roof, so when Darrion was satisfied that every Disciple and Renegade had relinquished their weapons at the door, he left his Mossberg and twin Colts with T-Bone.

Turkell volunteered to keep watch over Angelique and remain outside of Zane's top floor apartment. They waited in the hallway with Q-Ball inside the door, standing guard. On the roof, Ant stood quietly behind Zane and Darrion watched the two self-proclaimed kings go at it in forty-degree weather for nearly a half hour. By the time Darrion cut into the conversation, his nose was starting to run and his ears had gone numb.

"Gentlemen," he cut in, "we can stand out here in the cold all night going back and forth about haves and have nots and it's not going to get you anywhere. Why don't we start with what you can have instead? After all of the buildings have been inspected and all of the sick residents have been treated, Meridian Electric and Crown Plumbing will restore water and electricity to every highrise suffering without it.

"But they won't come if they're going to get sniped before they hit the grass. The only way every man out here is living better is if you all come to a truce. Bank Roll seems to be one of the few buildings unaffected by the shortage. But the rest of you are boned and more than half of you out here have families of your own to raise. You want to be able to cook meals for your children and shower with the lights on for a change, a ceasefire has to happen first."

"A ceasefire ain't gon' happen with this motherfucker holding my bricks," Zane spat at Sampson.

"And I'm gonna keep holding up until Pope lowers his bullshit street tax," Sampson said.

He was a tall and handsome youth of no more than nineteen, with long cornrowed braids, dark even set eyes, and a frame as thin as a knife. At first glance, Sampson looked too young to rule his motley crew. He was king. But he was a young king. In a clash of thrones all kings must keep good council. Darrion hoped Sampson's men had advised him well.

"Seventy percent," one of Sampson's men said, "man, that's straight up theft. We not gon' stand for nobody extorting us no more. If we shut down his profits in Cabrini, when that deficit starts pinching his pockets and the pockets of his generals and senior regents, then maybe he'll start seeing shit our way."

"Look at how long you been a regent, Zane," Sampson said. "That selfish bastard ain't never gone let you climb the ladder. No way. Not with the history between him and your Pops. Rising in the ranks ain't gonna happen for you. Me either as long as he's holding power."

"He might be holding power," Zane said, reaching in the breast pocket of his leather coat, "but he ain't holding this." He held up a wide, short glass vial filled with what looked like little pieces of yellow tinged chalk.

"What the hell is that?" Ant asked.

"This is the future," Zane said. "No more heroin. No more blow. This right here is going to change the game forever. And it starts right here in Cabrini."

"But what is it?" one of Sampson's men asked.

Zane looked at every man on the roof. "Crack."

"Crack?" Ant repeated. "It look like broke off bits of candy."

"And how is that gone change the game?" Sampson asked. "Don't nothing hit harder than heroin."

"Over half the fiends in the Lows would call you a liar, Sampson. Every single hype in the lowrises who took a hit of this been getting higher than the Sears tower and coming back like they never even left."

"You expect me to believe that a little white rock is supposed to have the game in a choke hold?"

"With my recipe, the cost to make it is 70 percent cheaper than what it takes to cut up powder, but it's twice as potent."

"What's the recipe?" Sampson asked.

"As long you got the bricks I need to make it, you don't get that answer."

Sampson did not look pleased. He folded his lanky arms across his chest and let out a deep breath. Both men said nothing for a long moment. They only regarded each other with cold, unyielding stares until Zane broke the silence.

"Everybody in this room wants to get paid. And not just paid, but rich. The only way that's going to happen is if I get the keys back, we start cooking up product, and I cut out Pope and cut you in on a percentage."

Sampson scowled at the offer. "How much of a percentage?"

"Ten percent."

"Fuck you! Man, that's twenty percent less than what we was making from Pope."

"But I'll be selling twice as fast as anybody in the Whites or the Robert Taylor projects. So let's just say Lefty here is making $5,000 a day and —"

One of Sampson's men scoffed. "Five G's a day? You out of your mind, man. No way."

"Oh it's very possible, cause last week, I was pulling $6,000 a day. Of that, if I were under Pope's thumb for the crack, I'd have to fork over $4,200 to the man. But if every soldier in this room was making $6,000 a day," he looked back at all of his men. "Multiply six times ten of my Disciples, that's $60,000. A day. Ten percent of that is what I was making just last week. And that's not including every King serving in the Reds. You take a hundred soldiers serving and multiply that times $6,000 a day. Do the math, and you're ten percent cut is a take home of $60,000 a day total. And you don't even have to hit the block to sell a rock."

Several men wolf whistled like his enthused proposal was the smoothest plan they'd ever heard. Darrion wasn't buying it. All that added up to was Zane collecting ninety percent and Sampson stuck with ten just for stepping down. It was like trading one fist up the ass for another one twice as big and he was still being extorted.

"Fifty percent," Sampson countered.

So the Renegade king was no dummy. Darrion was pleasantly surprised. So much so he had to smother the grin threatening to show.

Zane's eyes flashed fury, but he held his tongue.

"You don't take the percentage we're offering," Lefty said, "you keep the bricks and keep spending our money, soon, they'll be no more cash left to spend. And you'll have to hit the block and start serving up those keys. Only you'll find it hard to make a dollar when we just start sniping all the hypes before they reach your door."

Zane smirked triumph. "No hypes, no sale. No sale, no profits. No profits and nobody's eating. And believe me, nigga, if I ain't eating, everybody up in Cabrini is gonna be starving with his belly in his back. You feel me?"

This was getting nowhere. Darrion rubbed his temples to sooth the headache that was threatening. This wasn't his war, but he had to end this. "What about split territory?" All heads looked his way. "Among the Reds and the Lows. That's an even split. Seven towers to the Renegades, seven to the Kings. There's fifty-four lowrises which also makes an even split. That's twenty-seven to the Renegades and 27 to the Kings. You change the territory, you change the economic system. Which means there can be no more locked market. If two factions are operating within a mile of each other private enterprise has got to go. It has to be free enterprise.

"That means no more production, distribution, and profit solely belongs to one man. That means, when the coordinator shows to re-up your supply, you two men cut it up and cook it as you see fit. If somebody washed their dope to make more money and they start losing customers because their product is bunk, that's on you. No whining. No bitching. No moaning. And no war. If somebody's product is better they're gonna get the sale. So if one territory is making more green than the other, take that one on the chin and charge it to the game."

"What about Pope?" Sampson asked.

"When word gets back to him about this new product and the profits, he'll start seeing things your way. For now, free enterprise could be one hundred percent profit, until Pope comes down off the street tax."

"And you really think he's gonna go for that shit, huh?" Zane asked.

"Like you said, no product and nobody's eating. That includes Pope. Sooner or later, he'll realize that and come to a bargain. Until then, cut him out. You got no choice. Sampson is right. Seventy percent is bullshit, man."

"And what about when Pope sends his enforcers to take what he thinks is his?" one of Sampson's men asked.

"Last time I checked, eight of his henchmen can't take on all of Cabrini. And the Whites can't stand him...If you really want to make him play nice, strike a truce with the King Cobras, the Black Dragons, and the Vice Stones, cut them in on the product, and Pope will have no choice but to relent."

"What guarantee do I have that Zane will make good on it?" Sampson looked at Zane with nothing shy of contempt on his face. "I know how you get down, motherfucker. You get slighted in the least, or even think you got slighted, that ceasefire will vanish like a fart in a fan."

"Well I guess your men better stay in their lane then," Zane said.

Sampson cut his eyes to Darrion. "I want a guarantee. And until I get one, no deal."

"Alright," Darrion said, "how about this...you agree to the truce and split up the keys evenly amongst both gangs, and I'll see to it that the electric and the plumbing gets fixed in your towers first."

All of Zane's men began to protest. A few curses flew in the air and the scowl on Zeno's scarred face was priceless.

"Fuck that," Lefty said. "Come again, DeGrate. Cause that ain't happening."

Darrion's jaw clenched. This was going to take all night. Everyone was starting to argue again. One voice loud talking another until the roof was engulfed in anger and dispute. He wasn't the only one that was starting to tire. He watched Ant slip away without being noticed by anyone else. Before left the rooftop to step back inside, he held up a cigarette for Darrion to see, letting him know that he was leaving for a smoke break.

♛

Angelique heard the flicker of a lighter down the hallway. Out of curiosity and boredom she told T-Bone she was going for some fresh air. She walked towards the open breezeway and found Anton at the steel mesh fencing lighting a Marlboro.

"You smoke?"

Ant nodded. "Stress."

Angelique looked out onto the night through the steel mesh. The sky was gunmetal gray. Tonight, a dark moon loomed over the tall northern buildings of the city. It was an eerie feeling being able to see the affluent life from the slums she stood in. By now, all of the prosperous families were home in their luxury apartments. Dining well. Soon to be sleeping peacefully. For a fleeting moment she felt the isolation and rejection everyone in Cabrini must have felt. Trapped. Angry inside. Looking out on a world that had passed them by.

"What are you doing out here?" she asked. "It's freezing. You'd be warmer inside."

"Zane and Zeno's grandma, Muriel. She got a bad heart. She on oxygen and shit. She'll skin me alive if I light a square in front of her."

"Smoking," she said, "it'll kill you."

He shrugged. "Liquor kills faster. I used to drink. Had to give it up. Too many bad dreams."

"I thought the nightmare started around here when you wake?"

"It does. Can't have the nightmares both sleep and awake. That's why I quit drinking."

She nodded understanding. "How's it going in there?"

Anton shook his head. "Not good. Even with a promise of the water and heat being fixed, and the offer of shared territory, Sampson won't fold and Zane won't give up his clientele."

"What's the worst that'll happen if they can't come to a truce?"

He took a pull from his Marlboro. "A building war and they kill each other off."

"And the best if they do strike an accord?"

"A building war…and they kill each other off."

She looked at the cynicism on his face. For a moment, she pitied him. A sick grandmother, a sick nephew, and they probably all slept in the bathtub just to avoid stray gunfire. She couldn't think of anything to say to that. So she just turned her head back to the skyline.

"No truce lasts forever, Doc," Anton said. "Every war in history should've taught you that."

♛

Angelique left Anton alone with his thoughts and went back to the hallway. T-Bone was leaned against the door throwing a field knife at another short blade stuck the wall. As the knife missiled to the brick steel struck steel and the dislodged short blade flew right to his hand. He threw the short blade. Steel struck steel. The short blade jammed into the brick and the field knife flew to his hand.

It was a fascinating feat to see. If not a deadly one. She hoped he'd trained first with pastic untensils for that little trick. For a short while, Angelique just stood there. Watching him barter blades until she remembered what she had to say.

"I need to speak to Zane," she said.

He caught a knife and paused. "Okay?"

"But I need to see his grandmother first."

He looked at her like he didn't know what to make of her request.

"Okay."

"Well, if I go…we go."

"Yeah, that's the way this goes, Doc."

"Okay then," she said.

"Okay then."

She knocked on Zane's door. It opened immediately.

"Hello," Q-Ball said.

Dr. James blinked up at him. "Hello, I'm—"

"I know who you are."

How he cut her off wasn't rude but there was a get-to-the-point undertone to it.

"I'm here to see Zane, please."

"He's in a meeting right now."

She forced herself to smile. "I'm aware that he's in a meeting. I'm here to examine his grandmother's health and make him a truce offer. That is if he'll speak with a woman. Or is that not allowed?"

His dark eyes narrowed and he looked past her to Turkell. "You can come in, but he stays in the hallway."

Turkell wasn't in the least bit offended. "No problem, Lefty. As long as you realize bullets do go through walls. Especially the moist, fleshy kind."

Q-Ball opened the door. "Fuck you."

Angelique stepped inside and as the door shut behind her, every thought in her head froze with shock. All of the other apartments she had visited before—water damage, roaches, rats, it was jarring. But this…she was nearly traumatized.

Zane lived like a king. Plush carpets, the walls were immaculately clean. Tall onyx vases, ivory white leather couches sat on a marbled black and white rug. Light sconces bathed the living room in soft white light. Zane owned a television that covered the entire main wall and a massive sound system that could drown a jet. His living room was large enough to park a Buick. She was so awestruck, she barely noticed Anita Baker blaring through the speakers until her smooth crooning was abruptly cut off. Angelique whipped around at the sound of a harsh rasping voice at her back.

"Who the hell are you?"

"I…I'm Dr. James," she said, nervously. "I've been making some house calls to some of the residents here."

Old eyes stared back at her with a hard glare that the disease of the spinal cord gives the bitter, bed-ridden.

Muriel Harris. Zane and Zeno Harris' grandmother. It was an easy recognition of resemblance. Zane's same dark brown stark eyes. Zeno's same cruel brow. But instead of the arrogant stance her grandsons carried, her sagging frame was hunched over. One arthritic hand clutching the handle of an O2 tank. Angelique couldn't tell if she had Zane's cruel mouth. Nose to chin was covered with an oxygen mask.

"So you that woman on the TV, huh?"

"Yes…I…um." She was wavering and hesitant. She stopped it. "Q-Ball let me in."

The old woman looked her up and down with ridicule. Like she didn't quite know how to take her unexpected presence — knowing now who she was.

"Where the hell are you from?"

Dr. James' didn't answer. Her eyes flicked to the kitchen. Several pill bottles littered the counter. She was far worse than Anton let on.

"Are you sick?"

Muriel squinted. "Naw, I just like taking twelve pills a day cause it keeps me humble."

"May I?" she asked, nodding to the medications.

"Help yourself." Muriel shuffled over to the dining table and slowly sat down in a chair.

Dr. James went over to the kitchen counter, picked up several prescriptions, and skimmed over the labels.

"Doctor say I have…um…goddammit, I can never pronounce it right. Mitro-something or other.

Just by looking at the pill bottles, it was obvious. "Mitro valve regurgitation."

Muriel nodded. "That's it."

"Mitral insufficiency. Blood flows backwards through the valve when the heart contracts, reducing the amount of blood pumped through the body. Your doc's got you on all the right stuff to maintain. Lisinopril for hypertension. Coumadin for blood clots. Hydralazine as a vasodilator. That relieves the pulmonary edema." Dr. James put the pill bottles back and looked at Muriel's oxygen tank. "It doesn't look like the shortness of breath is getting any better."

"No shit," Muriel spat.

"M.R. That's very serious. It carries a sixty to eighty percent mortality rate. And that's with surgical intervention."

"Does it look like I'm unaware?"

"May I ask why you haven't had it repaired?"

"May I ask if you got a hundred and fifty grand lying around?"

♛

Darrion watched Angelique shoulder through several of Sampson's men. Five Disciples broke off from their discussion suddenly. "What the hell is she doing out here?" Zane asked, his voice thick with disgust.

"I have a solution," she said.

"And that would be?" Sampson asked.

She looked at Zane. "With your grandmother's heart condition, she'll be dead in a year. If you both agree to a truce tonight, I will do your grandmother's surgery free of charge. Pre-op expenses, her valve repair, post-op, all of it."

Zane looked at her like she was a monkey who had just done an interesting trick, then glanced at Darrion. "Is she fucking serious?"

Darrion looked equally shocked. "If she offered, I believe she is."

"Every dime," Dr. James said, "paid in full. If you end the war today."

Darrion watched the slumlord's face transcend from loathing to contemplation to distrust then scrutiny.

If his love for Muriel didn't make him bend, nothing shy of killing him twice would.

"I want all of her medications covered too."

"Okay."

"And she's supposed to see a physical therapist twice a week but due to our war-time situation, that bastard ain't been coming around here. You'll find me a new one. PT certified. IDFPR official."

That sounded much too edjucated coming from a hood like Zane Harris. But okay. She gave a nod. "Alright."

"And I want guaranteed protection every time she leaves for any follow up appointments that you can't make it here for."

"I'll agree to those terms on one condition, I need a pass for this weekend. A lot of the tenants are very sick. So, they need antibiotics. It can't wait."

Zane's brow arched. "Daylight hours only, Doc. Tonight was an exception that won't happen again."

"Well, luckily for your grandmother exceptions save lives."

Zane gave her a sharp look. Mr. Harris didn't like being talked back to.

She ignored his glare. "Do we have an agreement, gentlemen?"

"As long as the Renegades get the AC, plumbing, and electric fixed first for the south towers," Sampson said, "oh yeah, we definitely got a deal. From my end anyway."

The room fell starkly silent for a long moment.

Then, "It's all on you, Zane," Darrion said. "What's it gonna be?"

RENFRO

Looks like he's been keeping tabs on our boy," Bishop said.

He skimmed over the front page of the *Daily Eagle*.

Renfro stepped closer to the window and watched as Track and Field Coach Charles Nokes laid into one of his athletes. The kid looked to be of good stock. Tall. Lean muscled. His thighs didn't have the bulk of a sprinter. But he looked born for speed. He'd done something the coach didn't like. Nokes was balder, shorter, far stockier, and probably twice as slow as the young buck, yet even from where Renfro stood the man's authority was irrefutable. He was yelling and pointing his clipboard at the kid's chest, waving his free hand at the track like the kid made the mistake of running it backwards.

If memory served, today was Sunday, December 23rd, at four o'clock in the morning. Nokes was having his athletes train just three days before Christmas out in twenty degree Chicago weather. Renfro got the gut feeling he was standing in the office of a formidable man. That kind of hard driving was unheard of. Then again, so were his accolades.

Over the past ten years, Near North High School athletes had won dozens of league championships. Three state titles— from the 100 meter all the way up to 3000 meters, on the track; his cross country team was currently holding standings as being perennially among the best in the country.

Renfro turned from the window and looked at Bishop. He couldn't make out the headline from where he stood. "Keeping tabs, hmm? How's that?"

Bishop turned the newspaper around for him to see it clearly. Renfro was so stunned all he could do was blink at it in disbelief:

WAR IN CABRINI GREEN OVER!
Five Major Gangs Strike
Citywide Truce!

A truce was good for the city. A truce was good for the politicians of that city. A truce was never good for a cop.

Ever.

When gangs stopped warring against each other, they just joined forces in warring against police. Now, collaborating their efforts in trafficking drugs and humans in the projects was about to become twice as lucrative. Their new push for peace wouldn't prevent them from using violence against their victims, only against each other. For state and city police, a truce only made the task of ending criminal activities more laborious and exhausting than ever before.

For the first time in his career, Renfro wanted to put in a two-week notice and tell everybody from Mayor Burns on down to Commander Van Zant to go fuck themselves.

"Why hasn't my pager gone off?" he asked.

Bishop shrugged and unfolded the paper to read the full article. "Don't know. Probably because the Chief hasn't rolled his fat ass out of bed to get the paper from his drive-way yet. And I know the Superintendent doesn't know and the Deputy doesn't know. So if they don't know, the Commander and the Captain don't know. And if Delgado doesn't know…"

"We don't know," Renfro said, finishing his sentence.

"I'd like to play dumb long enough to enjoy a cup of coffee and a decent breakfast before we get hauled into his office on a Sunday."

"Agreed." Renfro looked at his watch. It was 4:55 in the morning. "What time should we call him?"

"We don't. On Sundays, Delgado is always up by 6:00 and he's always at mass by 11:00, like clockwork, so that means we'll get a page just after sun up and we'll be in his office no later than 7:00, bet on it."

Renfro shrugged. "Or we'll be in his office by noon because he'll be busy catching hell from Van Zant all morning who probably just got through catching hell from the Deputy."

"Shit is about to hit the fan."

Renfro turned back to the window. "And when it does we'll be stuck cleaning the walls."

"So, if we want a stomach full of food while the Captain is bitching and moaning, we should probably wrap this up with the coach in ten minutes or less?"

"Or less," Bishop said, nodding his approval.

"Truvy's?"

"Nathan's."

"I don't like their coffee."

"Cheddar's?"

That pulled Bishop's eyes from the newspaper. "Hell yes."

The office door opened and Coach Nokes walked in.

Renfro watched him take a seat behind his desk and lay his clipboard on top of a stack of papers. His eyes flicked to the paper Bishop was still holding.

"Oh, I just spotted the headline and couldn't help myself," Bishop said. He promptly put it back on the coach's desk where he found it. "Apologies."

Nokes motioned them to take a seat and shook his head. "No problem. You can keep it if you like. I can just grab another one from the teacher's lounge."

Renfro adjusted his posture in his seat and loosened his suit jacket to shift his holster. Coach Nokes had the kind of wood chairs where the arms were just high enough to press his gun right up against his ribs. He really hated that. "So there are other teachers in this early in the morning besides you?" he asked.

"No. Just the janitor. He always brings in the paper. He knows I like to read the sports section and he knows he can find me where the coffee's hot."

"Do you always train your athletes like this? In the middle of winter?"

Nokes nodded. "Always. Winter is a good time to build an anaerobic threshold. Weight training and tempo work. Plyometric work. Agility drills. Awakening new neurological pathways and shocking muscles not ordinarily used in distance training. It's all used to address weaknesses in a relaxed block of time when competition isn't looming."

Renfro forced a kind nod of understanding. Then, "You're probably confused on who's who. We only spoke over the phone. I'm Detective Sam Renfro and this is Detective Brian Bishop."

"There was no confusion," Nokes said bluntly. "I know what a white man sounds like on the telephone."

Renfro smiled and gave a quick glance to Bishop then looked back at Nokes. "And how does a white man sound?"

"Not like a black one."

Renfro didn't know quite what to say about that so he just sat there.

Bishop laughed.

Nokes didn't.

"You came in quite early to see me this morning," he said. "It must be important. What can I do for you gentlemen?"

"Were with the Gangs, Guns, and Narcotics Task Force and I just wanted to —"

"If this is about drugs," Nokes interrupted, "you two have come to the wrong place. All of my athletes are tested regularly and at random. They're all clean."

"Oh no, sir. It's none of your athletes that we're here about. We came to ask you about a former athlete. Does the name Darrion DeGrate ring a bell?"

"That name is always ringing bells in these halls," Nokes said, motioning to the doorway. "And out there on the field. But why am I suddenly aware you two already knew that?"

"Well, we know he attended Near North High all four years, but we thought you might be able to tell us how you came to know him. From what I understand, he was quite the voice in Cabrini Green during his father's…influence there."

"His *influence*?" Nokes repeated the word as if he was aware of the unlawful connotation underneath Renfro's choice of words. Apparently this wasn't his first unofficial interview with a cop in his office about the DeGrates. Renfro knew he couldn't flat out label a surname as being synonymous with organized crime, but the coach caught it nonetheless. With him eyeing Bishop reading the paper, Nokes had to be blind not to think Darrion DeGrate had a direct hand in the sudden gang truce.

Which also meant he had to be well aware the Task Force was watching his former athlete.

"Duke DeGrate was once a member of the Chicago Housing Authority," Bishop said. "He helped build the Frances Cabrini Homes and he had a hand in building the Cabrini extensions as well as the William Green homes that were added to the projects. So, the DeGrate name sort of holds as an eminent status down here."

"I'm aware, Detective. I was there when they cut the bow in the courtyard."

"And what year was that exactly, if you don't mind me asking?"

"More than 40 years ago, 1942. I had just turned twenty. And Duke was twenty-one."

"From what I hear, you were an original gangster. One of the first King Disciples."

Nokes shook his head. "I wasn't one of the Five Founding Fathers, no. But I was an original member."

"Not anymore, though?"

"If anybody put my name in the same sentence with a Disciple today, it would be the last words they ever spoke without a twitch and a stutter."

"I take it you're a little crestfallen with the Kings of today?"

"More than somewhat, yes."

"Would you care to elaborate on that?"

"Back then the Disciples were there to protect the weak from the corrupt. We didn't see ourselves as a gang. We just came together to do what was necessary to form unity. For our mothers, for our children, for our elderly. So they could walk to the store and make it back home at night without being spit on by the police. Back then, we were the guard dogs who protected our sheep from the wolves stalking in the trees."

"And almost fifteen years lather, when the riots struck after Martin Luther King's assassination, what were the Kings to the community then?"

"Back in '68 the riots struck every black urban area except Cab-rini Green. From West Madison all the way to Lawndale and Austin. The Westside got hit hard with destruction and chaos. Yet Cabrini was as quiet as a dead bell. The Founding Fathers got together and held a meeting with every senior regent of every zone in the Near North and they put the word out on the street that no establishment or business protected by the Disciples was to be touched by looters. We handed out stickers that were crowns about the size of a fist. Store owners put them up in their front windows. And anybody who came to that establishment looking for trouble knew that store was protected by the Disciples. Looters knew not to even try to burn up Cabrini." Nokes cast a glare at Renfro. "Police knew as well."

"And two years later," Renfro said, "after the riots, two Patrolmen were shot and one killed by gang members while walking across the Cabrini Green baseball field. And I don't think they were spitting on anybody when they were gunned down like a rabid dog with a kid in its mouth."

Both men sat there in silence, looking at each other. *Hard-nosed prick*, Renfro thought. *Christ, what does he think? I'm every white cop who ever wore a fucking badge?*

A small tent of irritation appeared on Nokes' brow.

Bishop cleared his throat and switched tact.

"I understand, as rumor has it, that Duke was not okay with that. And that's what sparked his decision to give up his crown four years later. Supposedly there was quite a dispute amongst the Five Fathers on which way to go with the Kings. Duke wanted peace, Zander wanted war. Then Casper and Xavier were emulating Switzerland and Troy found God. What made you walk away?"

Nokes didn't answer him right away. He had a discerning look about him as if he was carefully contemplating what to say next. "Pastor Troy gave our brotherhood its name," he said finally. "Did you know that?"

Bishop shook his head. "No I didn't."

"The original name was spelled K-I-N-G-apostrophe-S," Nokes explained. "We never called ourselves 'King' you see. We only referred to ourselves as Disciples because our one true king was God. And we were all his humble believers. And the name of our brotherhood was supposed to represent that there was no one man above the Family except God almighty himself. We were all in our maker's image. We were all his greatest creations. His students. His Disciples.

"What's out on theses streets today is not the Disciples we were meant to be. Slowly, but surely, in spite of everything done to stop the monster we unleashed out into the world, it was inevitable, see...We became a modern day Frankenstein story. Where the creation kills the creator. After Casper was slain Duke left, Pope got sent down the river, and everything just crumbled. Our mission statement became a mockery. All of the power and prestige became too lavish to resist and too plentiful for one man to control. And our men became the exact same demons that we were trying to put down. So what made me walk away? There was nothing left of what we built to make me stay.

"And after ten years," Bishop said, "after all this time, why would DeGrate go back? Why now?"

"Other than his obvious ties to Councilman Porter," Renfro added, "what's he after. I mean if Cabrini's such a lost cause."

Nokes motioned to the window. "Well the projects are just right across the way there, Detective. Why don't you mosie on over to those highrises, flash your badge, and ask him?"

Renfro gave him a strident look. "Oh, I don't think I'd be as welcome as you." He motioned to the trophy case at his right. "That trophy case tells me you two were very close once. Obviously he was a gifted runner."

"Darrion DeGrate was and is my greatest athlete."

"You make it sound like he'll never be beaten." Renfro smirked. "Other than his speed, what makes him so astounding? He's what...28 years old now? In a couple of years he'll peak and tank like all the others. I mean, as fast as you are there's always somebody faster out there waiting to take the gold from you."

Noke's brow lifted. He spun around in his chair and reached for a life-sized replica of the human heart. He placed it on the table and turned it backwards for the men to see. "Notice anything...*astounding*?"

Both men looked at it. Then at each other. When it became apparent they were drawing a blank, the Coach gave them a push.

"This is an actual model of Darrion DeGrate's heart."
He picked up a ballpoint pen. "What you're looking at here..." He motioned with the pen. "Is a true fifth chamber."

They both still looked bewildered.

"So, how many chambers does a heart have?" Bishop asked.
"Only four."
"Is a fifth chamber normal?" Renfro asked.

"Never."

"You mean like ever in medical history?"

"Never," Nokes repeated.

"So, what does a fifth chamber do that the other four don't?" Bishop asked.

Nokes smiled broadly. "I thought you'd never ask." He stood from his desk holding DeGrate's heart in his hand. "Follow me."

Bishop and Renfro followed him into a viewing room. The coach pulled out a sealed box from the closet, broke the tape, and took out several old film reels. Then Nokes shut the door, cut the lights, and flipped on the projector.

For the next thirty minutes Renfro found himself watching old track and field films in silence.

Nokes had recorded every track meet DeGrate ever ran. Even at eighteen, his physique was bulked up for massive speed. Nokes talked the whole time. His weight lifting regiment, the rigorous running drills, the stringent diet he had his track star on. Everything.

What Renfro found to be most bizarre and interesting was the wind sprints Nokes made him do. Turning an industrial sized fan on full blast, strapping a parachute to his back, and making him run towards a marked strip of tape on the gymnasium floor as fast as he could at the fan until exhaustion.

As insane as the training sounded, stellar results were seen on every reel. On the 100, 300, and 400-meter dash footage it was easy to see how he dominated the track. When the gun went off his opponents never stood a chance. He blew past them like it was nothing. One of his 400-meter films was so cut throat, Renfro found it hard not to shake his head. Just 50 meters after his spikes left the starting blocks, his fist was in the air in a conquering salute. Long before his chest broke the tape at the finish line, he knew it was over. Cocky wasn't even the word for it. DeGrate was as self-possessed and arrogant as they came. His vanity on the 800-meter films were the most shocking.

Like a die-hard Bears fan reciting the best football plays he'd ever seen, Nokes commentated every long stride. "Right...there!" Nokes enthused. "Just when his opponents think they're gaining on him, he takes off! Like hell just scorched his back!"

DeGrate was rude, unsportsmanlike, and mocking as hell. But it looked like the whole city flooded the bleachers just to watch him bolt and they all went crazy every time he crossed the finish line.

Nokes cut off the last reel, opened the door, and motioned for the men to step out.

Bishop stood and straightened his suit jacket. "That was quite a show."

Both men sat back down in the office chairs. Renfro watched the coach place DeGrate's heart on the desk with the gentle care a father shows to a baby's fontanelle.

"I understand that he's seen as a local celebrity and probably a luminary figure in the Near North," Renfro said. "But after all of that bad history, him returning just to help the good doctor, I find that a little hard to believe."

Nokes adjusted his haughty frame in the chair. "If you want answers about his glory days on the track, I'm your man. But if you want to know about Darrion DeGrate and what's going on inside of Cabrini Green, you've come to the wrong one."

Bishop stood and buttoned his suit jacket.

"We appreciate the tapes."

"I thank you for your time, Coach Nokes." Renfro followed his partner to the door and paused when he laid eyes the trophy case again. "Wow. This really is quite a trophy case."

"That's just a replica. The prominent case is out in the main hall."

Renfro studied each one. He counted fifteen. Every one was polished to a high gleam. He couldn't spot one speck of dust on the bronze or one smear of a fingerprint on the glass that kept them protected. Nearly every trophy carried the name of Darrion DeGrate, save two. Each sat placed in order by year from 1970 to 1974.

The largest trophy was placed in front. It read:

1974
STATE CHAMPION
DARRION DEGRATE
100 METER DASH
TIME: 9.77

Renfro wolf whistled and turned from the trophy case to look at Nokes. "That man was a bullet. Does he still hold the record for the 100 and the 400 meter?"

Nokes leaned back in his chair, interlaced his thick fingers, and laid them on his stomach. "And the 800 meter."

"In the state?"

"In the country. The National trophies are in the prominent display."

With that, Renfro quietly nodded and left. Yet, he couldn't help but notice the triumphant gleam in the coach's eye on the way out the door.

♛

Renfro was dead on about Delgado. By noon, he and Bishop were sitting the Captain's office, watching his face turn several interesting shades of red while he vented for more than a half hour on what every cop in the city already knew.

He ranted about the celebratory commentary from the clueless American media. Shady Councilman Porter shaking hands on the news with gangsters to reap votes. Then the crux of what Renfro was waiting for came spilling out of the Captain's mouth. Every crooked cop on Pope's payroll would concentrate their evils elsewhere, making it twice as difficult to find the mole in the department.

"I want you to find this son of a bitch!" Delgado screamed. "He's here! Right here on the other side of that fucking glass! Making an ass out of you, me, and every badge in this unit!" He stormed over to the door, snatched it open, and yelled out at every uniform and plain-clothes cop he saw. "You hear me? You Benedict Arnold motherfucker! I know you're in here somewhere, and when I find out who you are, I'm gonna see to it personally that you wind up in Menard or Stateville screaming ass rape for the rest of your sodomized, pillow-biting, shit-stabbing life!" Delgado slammed the door and stalked back to his desk.

Renfro smartly waited until his face dropped out of the red zone before he spoke. "Captain, how do you expect us to find who Pope's street scout is?"

"Yeah," Bishop added. "When we don't even know where to start. Whoever they are, they're well protected. So, they know how we're coming at 'em. Every time."

Delgado let out a long, tiresome breath. "You're new promotion ain't just going to be roses without the thorns. From now on, my OC is gonna be reporting to the both of you."

Renfro and Bishop exchanged a surprised look.

"You got an undercover working it?" Bishop said.

"How?" Renfro said.

"A few weeks ago, somebody tried to assassinate Pope in Stateville. The hit got botched obviously, because he's still a relevant pain in my brown ass."

"The OC told you that?"

Delgado nodded. "Now with this truce, word is, they cut Pope out. He's no longer a factor. Which means I'll be lucky if I get a trickle of information on him now. Let alone enough to wet my mouth for solid surveillance on his Colombian connect."

"Well, the Disciples are getting their bricks from somewhere."

"The only reason there even is a truce is because they aren't getting paid," Bishop added. "That's it. That's what it all boils down to. The attention from the media, the Mayor, the crackdown from the Councilman, and the incursion from that doctor. Everybody heard about Sampson's Renegade crew. So that truce is about one thing and one thing only...making money."

Renfro went quiet.

Now the Captain's rant about the truce in Cabrini Green really made sense. It was expected to see him pissed off about several gangs turning up the heat on local and state PD. It was expected to see him equally pissed off about not finding the mole fast enough, but his rant was far more furious than usual. There was only one reason why.

"If this truce is a direct threat to your pipeline of information on Pope's connect...your OC is inside the projects," Renfro heard himself say. "Jesus Christ. You got somebody in deep enough to infiltrate Cabrini." He went quiet again and rubbed his eyes. They were starting to burn for some reason. "Did you by any chance, get word from your OC about our new Task Force being leaked out to the streets before we made the announcement to the press on Friday?"

Delgado shook his head. "Why?"

"Just after the news broke about the doctor passing out Band-Aids at the highrises, I got a phone call from some hick sounding piece of white trash. He tells me that I'm about to get promoted to the Task Force, then he puts me on to Darrion DeGrate about a bank robbery that happened up in Northbrook about a month ago."

Delgado just blinked at him, stunned. "A robbery?"

Renfro and Bishop nodded.

"With DeGrate's name on it?"

They nodded again.

"Think you can work it?"

Renfro shrugged. "Trying to. But my point is, no way is that kind of clandestine information about a new Task Force just floating out to the streets, before we even get the promotions, by the same Benedict that's diming us out to Pope. No way. Every cop that's working this unit is on Xavier's radar. And if he knew about the Task Force being put together, it would have gotten back to Cabrini, and it would have gotten flushed back out to you through your OC. It didn't. Somebody else updated the hick on current events. So there's not just one mole in this unit, Captain. There's two. At least."

Delgado calmly folded his hands on the desk. "Find them. Flush 'em out any way you can. I can only keep the Deputy off my ass for so long. If we don't find them soon, all of our careers are as dead as the Mayor's. And if Burns thinks I'm going down with her, she's dumber than all of America knows she is."

DARRION

Here," Darrion said, holding up a red jewelry box.

Dr. James shuffled the package of antibiotics under her arm, opened the red box, and gasped. It was a beautiful gold Movado watch. Swiss bold shine. Firm clasp. Black dial in a round case with a lone diamond for the 12th hour. It was a feminine classic timepiece of a silhouette. Darrion took it from the box frame, slipped it on her wrist, and pinched the clasp closed. She stared at it in silence for a long moment then looked up at him.

"A little early for presents don't you think?" she said. "You're two days off. Christmas isn't until Tuesday."

"Don't flatter yourself, Doc. It keeps time like a watch. It looks like a watch...It's not a watch."

She looked at it with curious scrutiny. "What is it?"

"A tracking device. If anything goes wrong, just pull out the side button like you're trying to change the time and it sends a signal to mine." Darrion held up a similar watch on his wrist. It was wider, thicker. Masculine sized. He lifted the doctor's wrist and flipped the open. "The face flips up like this and there's a reading in distance from me to you in feet and kilometers. This way I can find you anywhere in the projects. And keep this beeper." He pulled a black pager from his pocket and pushed the power button. When it buzzed to life he pushed another button and loud beeping rang out, echoing off the brick walls. "If the watch fails, my beeper is your back up. Dial my number and put in 911. And if I ever page you, call back."

"Well, what if I'm busy with a patient?"

"If I don't hear from you, I'm coming to get you. I'm not kidding. And if I think something happened to you, by the time I find you this little truce will probably be blown all to hell."

She looked off at nothing in particular. He could tell by her expression, she didn't like the new rules.

Too bad, Doc. Suck it up.

"You really think I need all this?" she asked.

"You're starting to get a little too comfortable in these breezeways."

"There's a truce. The war's over. And besides, since the exterminators got here I haven't seen one rat in two days." A mischievous smirk came to her lips. "Maybe we got them demoralized."

Darrion shook his head in disagreement and started down the breezeway. "Doubtful."

Dr. James called after him. "Where are you going?"

"I'll be in a meeting for a while. Taran will keep you company."

"And how do you have something like this?"

He started up the stairwell. "I don't. Neither do you."

"Ah...okay." She called after him again. "Speaking of Christmas, I need to finish my shopping today."

"Yes, ma'am."

♛

Dr. James spotted Lunch talking to Taran, but there was no sign of T-Bone. She spoke a hello and asked where her intern made off to.

"Taking a piss behind the bushes," Lunch said. "How goes the deliveries, Doc?"

"Good actually, but listen, before we break for lunch I have some more antibiotics to drop off at few apartments." She gave the package to Lunch. "Could you give these to Kirkland for me? I want to stop by and check on Taniesha and the baby. Maybe invite them over for Christmas."

"Cool," Lunch said.

Taran nodded. "It would probably do them some good to get out of the house."

"I appreciate it."

"No problem, Doc."

She turned and started off across the lawn towards Bank Roll and found herself halfway across the grass when Lunch called after her.

"Where's T-Bone?" he asked.

"I'll find him on the way."

By the time Dr. James made it to the building it dawned on her that she never had found T-Bone. But that didn't matter. A ceasefire had rocked Cabrini Green to sleep. All morning long, she saw the impossible. Kids were playing out in the yard. Some were jumping double-dutch. Some were taking advantage of last night's snowfall, making snow angels on the ground. Boys were playing on the baseball field. It was as if the cold of wintertime didn't even matter. They were just happy to be outside without the fear of bullets flying past them.

A swell of happiness filled her chest. Without doubt her efforts were making all the difference in the world. She spoke hello to the children as she passed them by. A little boy rode playful circles around her on his bike. She smiled at his giddiness and made for the breezeway to Anton's apartment.

When she raised her fist to knock on the door, it opened as if someone knew she was there. Before she could blink about it Zeno stood in the doorway. That bizarre prosthetic eye staring back at her. Today, the eye was solid gold. Dr. James supposed he wasn't in the mood for eagles on a Sunday. His dreads were oiled and neatly plaited back into two long braids that draped down his shoulders. Dressed in a crisp white T-shirt, dark denim and the whitest white sneakers, a thick gold rope chain dangled from his neck with a medallion the size of a dinner plate. A man appeared behind him, just as tall but with short trimmed dark hair and deep-set eyes.

Angelique mentally tried to muster courage for a detached hello, but her tongue was leaden. Out of nowhere, the eye dribbled bright red blood down his cheek. Without a word spoken, he reached into his back pocket, pulled out a handkerchief, dabbed the blood and reached for his coat.

She cut her eyes away to the ground and moved aside when he stepped past her into the breezeway. His ruffian cohort zipped the fly of his denim and grabbed his coat from the hall table—following Zeno out the door with a shameless, slack-jawed smirk on his face.

It suddenly registered what Taniesha had meant by her having 'appointments' the other day. But Dr. James had a job to do. She stepped inside the apartment and quietly closed the door behind her.

In the living room, little Amari sat playing with a plastic blue ball clutched in his hands. A quick glance around yielded no sign of Taniesha. Then she heard gagging coming from the back room.

Dr. James stepped towards the bedroom and slowly pushed the door open. Rumpled bed sheets were the first thing she saw. Then, her eyes fell to several opened condom packets on the nightstand. Next to the prophylactics was a burnt spoon, a wad of used, dirty cotton, a hypodermic needle, and a long tourniquet band.

Dr. James dared a step inside the room and froze when she saw the bathroom door barely cracked open. Taniesha was coughing unhealthily. Throwing up everything she had into the toilet. Whatever she'd shot up into her veins, clearly she'd done too much.

Angelique decided she'd seen enough. She turned and walked back out to the living room.

Anton was at the hospital visiting Ms. Ida and applying for a job opening. He probably wouldn't be back for hours. There was no one around to take care of Amari. Now it all made sense why Ms. Ida refused to go to the hospital. Leaving Taniesha to whore in her absence was not something grandma was willing to tolerate.

Taniesha was in no condition to take care of herself, let alone a baby. Angelique's disgust morphed into antipathy. *How could she do this with her kid in the living room?* If she wanted to get high every day that was her business. But procreating junkies were the worst kind.

Hurting herself was one thing. Flushing her child down the same shit toilet was beyond selfish. It was heartless.

Amari began to cry. Angelique went over to the playpen and picked him up. She soothed his soft hair with the palm of her hand. "Shhh, it's okay, little one. Shhh."

She tried bouncing him up and down. That didn't work. He just cried even louder. She tried rocking him from side to side. That didn't work. She grabbed his binky from the floor of the playpen and tried easing it into his mouth but he just slapped it away. It dawned on her that she knew nothing about babies. There was only one thing she could think of.

She picked up the phone from the coffee table, dialed Darrion's beeper number, and put in 911.

♛

Darrion flew down the last flight of stairs, cocked his Mossberg, and ran across the Head Quarters courtyard. He spotted T-Bone less than twenty paces away talking to a resident.

"Where's Angie?"

T-Bone spun around and blinked at him, shocked. "I thought she was with you?"

Darrion cursed and flipped up the face of his Movado. Bright red numbers flashed 99 kilometers on the display screen and 325.083 feet flashed just beneath it. That meant she was either in Hudson Mob or Bank Roll. Which one was anyone's guess.

Darrion took off towards Bank Roll. "Check Hudson Mob, I'll take Bank Roll! And call Lunch and Taran, now!"

T-Bone pulled out his brick phone and ran for Hudson Mob.

Darrion was at Bank Roll in a flash, shouting her name down every breezeway. By the time he made it to the fourth floor, Lunch and Taran were coming toward him. "Check every floor and if you don't see her, start kicking in doors!" He headed towards the fifth floor, ignoring the burning in his lungs. Every muscle in his legs began to tire but he didn't slow. All he could hear was his own heart pounding and the panicked sound of his own breath.

"Angie!" he shouted.

"I'm down here!" she finally called back.

Taran and Lunch caught up with Darrion and followed him down the breezeway to the wire mesh fencing.

Angelique was standing in the courtyard, holding Amari. Looking up at him. She wasn't bleeding. Her medical coat looked spot free. Her black slacks were untarnished. Every curl in her head was still in place and no one was anywhere near her.

All Darrion could do was stop in his tracks and let out a hard breath of relief to slow his pulse. His Mossberg slipped to the ground but he didn't even care. He threw a hand up to stop Lunch and Taran then took a few seconds to come down from the adrenaline.

Blood rushed through his ears as he made his was down the stairs. When he stepped onto the grass Angelique just stood there. Blinking brown eyes at him like a bewildered fawn.

Darrion DeGrate would never hit a woman, unless she came at him with a weapon. But in that moment, he knew he could shake the shit out of one.

"Is everything okay," Taran called down.

Darrion cracked his neck and waved it off. "She's fine. We're good down here." His heart was still drilling so hard he couldn't think. Then a wave of vertigo rushed to his skull. He rested shaky hands on his hips, looked at Angelique, and forced his voice as calm as he could. "What's wrong?"

"I just went up to Ant's place...To make sure Taniesha and the baby were okay."

Darrion looked up to the fourth floor. "Where's Ant?"

"He's at the hospital checking on Ms. Ida and putting in a job application. There's a position open in Environmental Services. He probably won't be back until dark."

"Is she alright?"

"She's sick. In the bathroom throwing her guts up. She spiking heroin. And when I was going in, Zeno and...some other guy were coming out. Looking well taken care of. I'm pretty sure she's whoring."

That was nothing new. Taniesha loved sex and not once in all the years he knew her did she make bones about keeping it a secret. Darrion let out a deep breath. "Yeah, that's Taniesha."

Angelique blinked up at him like she was shocked because he wasn't shocked. "In front of her baby?!"

He shrugged and lit a Newport. "She usually keeps him in the living room."

Her glare went from shocked to accusatory in a flash. "And how would you know?"

"The same way everybody else in Cabrini knows...And *you* are the last one *to* know."

"That's not an answer." She blinked away to the ground, suddenly aware that she was being intrusive. "That came out shitty, I know. But if you and her...with her habits...Darrion, I'm sorry I can't—"

"She has an older boy," he explained, "he's in foster care. She lost him not too long after he was born."

"I can sure as hell see why." Her voice was thick with disgust and loathing. "And if she doesn't watch it, she's going to lose this one." Darrion couldn't argue that one, so he kept his mouth shut. Angelique rubbed Amari's back and kissed his hair. "I know it's none of my business, but having her son around that shit...it's wrong."

Her eyes grew sad then. Darrion was reminded once more that he had not seen or spoken a hello to Taniesha on the telephone for more than a decade. Deep down he knew part of her ruin was his fault. That blame was not for Angelique to understand. But the least she could do was respect it. "It's medicine," he heard himself say. "Not magic."

Her eyes seemed to ease then. Darrion knew she understood.

He reached his arms out to Amari and scooped him up. "Come here, little man." The baby boy sneezed, making Darrion suddenly aware of his cigarette smoke.

"Bless you, little one." Angelique reached and hand up and ca-ressed his head.

"You hungry, little man, hmm?" Darrion asked. "You want a bottle?" He held out his hand to Angelique and nodded towards the stairs. "Come on."

Oddly enough, before he realized taking the hand of his brother's fiancé was inappropriate, she slid her hand in his as if without thought and let him lead the way.

ZANE

Zane hated meeting Alexander Van Zant.

Tonight, he had been summoned by the man as if he was on the Commander's payroll instead of the other way around. Every time they'd met it was in a different place. Motels. Basements of abandoned houses. Back alleyways. Under freeway overpasses. West side parks. Cemeteries on the southside. A week ago, he figured out the Irish bastard had family in Mount Greenwood. This time, he made sure they met there.

Of course, the Commander protested. Zane didn't care.

A man of his stature certainly had no problem meeting on the shit side of town. But to meet where the lawns were manicured and cars had no rust? Never. Until tonight.

Zane did do him the favor of choosing the Mount Greenwood Cemetery. At least they'd be meeting where no one alive would witness. That was the only mercy Van Zant was going to get. Zeno parked the old Cutlass and the instant the Disciples walked into the cemetery Van Zant's eyes were on them. Zane didn't dismiss his soldiers immediately. Even when he did decide to do so, he'd keep them no more than fifty paces away should the meeting turn to blood.

It was just past 7:00 at night and the sky was gray from the snowstorm, but it wasn't as dark out as Zane had hoped. He truly loved the dark.

As usual Van Zant's weighty frame was impeccably dressed in a long coat and dark suit. Thick salt and peppered hair lightly oiled and expertly trimmed. A scowl on his face as Zane and his men approached.

"Nice spot," he spat.

Zane gave a nod to his men. "We're good here." Three of his soldiers left them in privacy, but Zeno knew to stay. "What do you want, Van Zant. Why am I here on a Sunday? When I don't do business on Sundays?"

Commander Van Zant exhaled a cold puff of air. "Congratulations on your new accord. I'm sure you're looking forward to the more peaceful and much more profitable days that lie ahead. But I certainly hope you don't misremember this task force is not going away. And if you want to run your operation without interference from the law or Pope, you are going to need my help."

So the Commander was worried about the uprising against police coming back on his head. Zane shrugged. "My decision for a ceasefire had nothing to do with you. Like your Councilman's push to start up a task force had nothing to do with me. I need to eat. Porter needs votes. See, it's business, Van Zant. Never personal. So, you're telling me this because?"

"This alliance may be new to you and I'll put that on your age. But I've learned a thing or two in my sixty plus years and I've seen a truce before. Let me tell you something, Zane, a truce never lasts long. And in the end, neither side wins save the few who were clever enough to triumphantly fail. So instead of you thinking about sweet victory, I hope you're smart enough to think about the best way to lose."

Zane didn't respond for a long moment. A drawn out silence hovered over them colder than the graves at their feet. Then, he realized, Van Zant was trying to tell him something.

"What are trying to tell me, man?"

"I'm telling you that task force operations don't just pop up. Not without man-hours to back them. Not without intel to back that man-power. And not without a source feeding that intel."

It clicked.

Zane's eyes narrowed, but he wasn't surprised. It wasn't the first time he had a rat in his projects. It was, however, the first time an undercover plant brought one of the most aggressive law enforcement operations he'd ever seen. Zane had watched it on the news. It was to become a law vehicle—driving with all the power of federal, state, and local enforcement agencies, moving toward arrests and prosecution with multi-jurisdictional reach. "You're telling me I got one of yours in my projects?"

Van Zant's initial silence was his answer. "He's close. He's in deep. Deep enough that I knew about Pope's failed assassination attempt the same day you did."

Zane kept his cool, but he could feel his blood starting to rise.

"So now that you've kept your word and muscled out Pope," Van Zant went on, "I'm inclined to keep your affairs as clandestine as possible with your new connect. Coke is dead, so you say. Crack is the future, hmm? New product, new game, and new players in town to win it. I get it. But, Pope needs to be gone before he drops dime on me for spying for him and your ass gets greenlit for trying to take him out. You want to be king; it's the oldest rule in the art of war. No prince rises if the king still lives and let's get one thing clear, Zane, and hear me good. You want your rat, I'm going to need a little restraint from you and your hoods on my fellow officers. Just because you and I have a monetary agreement, doesn't mean I'll be looking the other way while you play widow maker to every cop that earned a badge."

"And let me be clear," Zane seethed, "if you don't find out who he is, I will lay down whatever poison I have to, to flush that rat out of my walls. I hope I'm crystal on that. And Pope is no longer your concern. I'll handle it." He knew by the Commander's silence they understood one another. "Now, tell me about this task force. What am I dealing with here?"

"I'll get back to you on all the details when I know more. For now, the task force will meet every Monday in Councilman Porter's office—which means I will be at those meetings and every detail will be facilitated by the Human Relations Commission." He exhaled. "Time for a little quid pro quo. You keep me informed on a few low-level dealers that you don't need anymore. Maybe a couple of Sampson's men sent down river will do to keep the Councilman satisfied, and I'll get you your rat."

Zane shook his head. "Turning rat, not my style. Besides, I need more than that. I need DeGrate and that nosey ass Doc out of my projects."

Van Zant's brow lifted. "Do I look like Derek Porter to you? You want to get rid of those unwanted eyes and ears, you need to find a way to bring them *my* way. DeGrate's got nothing but a juvie record that's been expunged and the Doc's a fucking saint. I can't just slap people in handcuffs because they piss you off or get on your nerves. You want them gone, give me something that'll stick. Use your head. Figure it out. You know how to reach me when you got something."

With that, Van Zant turned and started back the way he came. Zane and his men were left with all the silence of the graves.

ANGELIQUE

Dr. James spent her Monday morning drive on the phone.

Being briefed by Councilman Porter. Updated on his first task force meeting, which was to be conducted every Monday at 8:00 a.m. He kindly spared her all of the law enforcement details but spoke at length on the new Chicago Social Services program. Meant to be implemented to monitor the overall living standards of the parents and children in every occupied unit of the housing projects. Somehow, Angelique got the feeling that it wouldn't go as smooth as it sounded over the telephone.

By the time she made it to the hospital parking lot she was dreading it. The media frenzy had calmed at Cabrini because they found it less likely to dodge bullets for their footage at her place of practice.

She dodged the media swarm at the ER doors, blinking through camera flashes and shouted questions coming at her in a blur of chaos.

A few seconds of that madness turned making rounds with her clan of greenhorn interns into a cakewalk. She spent nearly a half hour assigning them low risk cases that were certain to yield no dead patients then she spent the rest of the morning watching over every step they made. It was no surprise that after nearly two weeks in Cabrini, Kirkland seemed the most confident.

By noon, she found time to walk down to the cafeteria for a bowl of cheese tortellini. Then she called Darrion and T-Bone and waited patiently for them to pick her up at the back entrance and sneak her out of the parking lot for the four-mile drive to the projects.

She had scheduled Muriel Harris' pre-op workup for Friday, three days after Christmas, so she could spend time with her grandsons. It shouldn't have mattered if that old woman saw her devil's spawns for the holidays or not. But it was a patient's request and like a good doctor, Angelique complied.

She stood there at Zane's door with her fist paused to the wood, suddenly realizing how far a Hippocratic oath could take someone. Darrion and T-Bone were in another meeting with the Disciple ruler. It was a good time to have a little chat with Cabrini's Queen Bee.

Q-Ball opened the door as exptected.

"Hello, Q-Ball," Dr. James said. "I've come to talk with Ms. Harris about her pre-op schedule. Is this a good time?"

"You can come in." He stepped aside and let her pass.

Muriel was in the same spot the doctor had seen her last, at the dining room table. Oxygen mask strapped to her face.

"Hello, Ms. Harris. How are you feeling today?"

"Like ten miles of bad road, if you really want to know the truth."

"Well we'll be doing something about that very soon, won't we? I've scheduled all of your pre-op work for the 28th, which is after Christmas. That's labs, an EKG, and a Chest X-ray, and I'm also going to need a urine sample. Then after that, you're free to go home and I'll be repairing your valve on the 4th of January, just a few days later."

Muriel gave a weak nod. "Uh huh, I see. You can't push it back no further than that?"

"I could, but that's not what's best for your heart. And it's the only opening I've got at Cook."

"Well ain't there some other hospital you can do it at?"

"I have privileges at Northbrook Heart, but I don't think that's a possibility for you."

Muriel's dark eyes grew darker. "Why not?"

"They don't have any openings until February. By then your heart could be too weak for the surgery to even be an option."

Ms. Harris gave a frustrated grunt.

"Is there a reason why you want to push the surgery back?"

"Family," the Queen Bee answerd. "My grandsons need me at home right now. Staying close is priority at the present."

Dr. James knew what that meant. Grandma was up to her dentures in the drug trade. Anyone who stood in that woman's presence for five minutes could feel the clout and influence seeping out of her pores.

"Of course," Dr. James said, nodding fake compassion. "But there are also other factors weighing in on the medical facility you're limited to."

"Like?"

"Like insurance...or...lack there of. Northbrook Heart only takes major medical insurance like Medicare, Blue Cross, Cigna...They don't take Medicaid and they won't even consider uninsured patients."

"Well you paying for it, ain't you?"

"I am, yes, ma'am. Which means I'm more concerned about your heart than whatever business you've got going on with your grandsons. So, since I'm paying for it, you'll be getting that valve repaired in January. Not after."

"Pushy little bitch, ain't you?"

Dr. James chose her next words very carefully. "When I need to be."

Muriel Harris stared at her for a long moment before she spoke again. "I knew your father."

Dr. James faded in an instant. Angelique was standing there in her place. Looking back at the embittered old fogey. So Muriel had done her homework.

Understandable. Now that her grandson had muscled out Pope, she was the first lady of the slums. Surely Zane kept her well informed. Using Angelique's father to pull a reaction out of her was a cheap shot. Once that card got pulled, she just shut off inside. "A lot of people knew my father. Or so I'm told."

"How is old Illinois James these days?"

"Fine," she said with a sigh. "Or so I'm told."

"Shame how he lost you." She coughed a harsh cough and sucked in a long, deep breath of rich O2. "Hunting accident. Wolves was it?"

Angelique was ready for this conversation to be over. "A wolf," she corrected.

"Tragic how parents lose their children. Even more tragic how children lose their parents. You should ask Viola about that sometime. She knows all about that."

Whatever the old bat was trying to drag her into, Angelique wasn't biting. But since they were on the subject of blatant child neglect, "speaking of Social Services, I was just briefed this morning on the minutes from the Councilman's meeting. In fact, every Monday there will be a task force meeting in his office. This meeting was in regard to CSS. Starting this week, every week a social worker will be stopping by to check on the living conditions. This family monitoring program will continue indefinitely. These visits will be unscheduled, they do not have to give prior notice before their arrival, and they will be here anytime between the hours of 9:00 a.m. and 5:00 p.m. Monday thru Friday. Today's Christmas Eve so I doubt they'll be stopping by today or tomorrow. But anytime after Tuesday they can stop by without warning."

Muriel did not look pleased. Her irritation was understandable. *Who wants a social worker walking in while mommy and daddy are smoking crack or have their face bent to a mirror sniffing lines?* This little family-monitoring program, Angelique knew, was going to become a serious, serious problem.

"Darrion is probably briefing Zane on that in their meeting as we speak." She paused intentionally, trying to think of something understanding to say. Anything to ease the dark daggers the old hag was staring at her. "I know this all is a disruption to the…" She froze. Not exactly knowing how to word being responsible for throwing a monkey wrench into a burgeoning drug operation. "…Normal flow of things," she recovered. "All I can do is warn you. I'm sure there's plenty of parents here who would appreciate the heads up." It was a dangerous thing, mustering up the gall to give a shit when it wasn't her turn to give a shit. "There's one mother in particular who would definitely appreciate the warning."

Muriel lifted an eyebrow. "And who would that be?"

Angelique's eyes widened. She knew she was pushing it.

"Taniesha Berry."

"Oh? Is that so?"

Muriel's eyes hardened to a glare that made Angelique remember she had a Colt strapped to her ribs with the serial filed off. "If there's any way Zane could arrange for her appointments to be managed elsewhere...other than her home, she would be dodging a lot of heat. From what I understand she already lost one son. I'm sure it would crush her to lose another."

Muriel's voice went flat. "Is that all?"

"Yes," Dr. James said. "Thank you." She politely said goodbye and turned to leave. She could barely keep from breathing a sigh of relief when she stepped past Q-Ball and out into the breezeway.

When Darrion's meeting was over, he drove her back to Scott Joplin. She split the rest of her day between proctering her tadpole interns and catching up in her office. Reviewing Muriel and little Shawna's medical files. By 8:00 p.m. Darrion drove her to his parent's home. She showered, fixed a peanut butter and jelly sandwich and settled on the couch in the den, thinking.

Tomorrow was Christmas and little Shawna Clark was soon to have two hearbeats instead of one.

ZANE

Zane didn't mind interrupting Taniesha and her john.

Even if they were already fucking.

Sometimes he liked to watch. Zane didn't buy magazines and he didn't buy tapes. Hugh Hefner could keep his Playboy Mansion. Live porn was always better. But today he had business to discuss and the old john bedding his whore was no show he wanted to see.

"Get out," he ordered.

The old man blinked up at him in wide-eyed shock. He pulled out of her, scrambled his thin bones off the bed, dressed in less than twenty seconds, and was out the door.

Taniesha closed her legs, sat up on the edge of the bed, and pulled her fix kit from the nightstand, then held out her arm. It had been almost twelve hours since he last shot her up. He had to control her dose. Back when she could handle her high, Zane could rely on her to pull more johns and make more money. But, just like any hype, eventually, the needle took over. As exceptions go the only difference was, she wasn't a stomp-down dope fiend yet and she still had all of her teeth. Back when she first started hooking for him, she was his number one money maker. Every john in the project wanted a taste of Taniesha Berry.

Now, her thick curves had gone thin. Most days she barely combed her hair and would oversleep. Pissed off Johns would come complaining that she never showed up to their apartments on time. She only had one thing on her mind these days. Her need. Even now just to look at her, Zane knew, she couldn't wait to see blood return in that syringe and escape reality. But the need would have to wait.

"I'm not here for that," he said with a scowl on his face. "Can't you wait until the end of the day anymore?"

"Yeah," she said weakly.

Zane folded his arms across his chest. "We got business to discuss. I'll straighten you out after."

Taniesha lowered her arm and pulled the sheets up to her chest.

"Social workers is coming through, so we have to set you up elsewhere. You'll get a call from the Queen about your new lay spot sometime tomorrow. Make sure you answer." He reached into the nightstand drawer and pulled out a small stack of folded up $20 bills. He quickly counted out eight Jacksons. "This is it?"

"It's been slow lately. Since that doctor's been coming around and the media and everything. Ain't nobody making no money, so…"

"I'm taking care of that. Money's gonna flow like it used to…and real soon." He pocketed six Jacksons and put the rest back in the nightstand. "So, how well do you know this Doc?"

She shrugged. "Not very. I really don't know her that well at all."

"Well get to know her. Everything about her. From her middle name to her worst fears to how many sugars she takes in her coffee. Everything."

"How I'm supposed to do that? We don't talk like that."

"Use your boy. I hear she got a soft spot for the little nigga. Slide in with her through him. That's your in. Ain't you supposed to be going to they house for Christmas dinner the day after tomorrow?"

She nodded. "They not doing dinner on Christmas because of some other stuff they got going on, so they doing dinner after."

"Good. Every time you meet up with her, report back to me."

If it was one thing Zane knew Taniesha learned, it was to never refuse him. Even if she hated his control over her. Even if she hated the control he had ever her family. She had to accept his orders and do as she was told. She stayed in line like his women were supposed to.

She nodded meekly. "Okay."

Zane looked the room over, satisfied that she obeyed. Then, his eyes gave a flicker of calculating interest. "You still cool with DeGrate? I know ya'll had a thing going on back in the day. You think you can still slide back in there with him?"

DeGrate's years away from Cabrini had changed things. Just one look at him the day he came back, and Zane knew. He wanted to take back the projects and make everything the way it was when his father, Duke ruled the Disciples.

DeGrate was a fucking fool. He would never take back the Green. Not while Zane was breathing. Whatever rallying power Pope had given him it was all for nothing.

Zane would trick him out like he did every other man he wanted to take down and he would use old, familiar pussy to do it. Taniesha had a need. He controlled access to that need. It was simple. Refusing him meant refusing her dose. So she'd reel DeGrate in if she wanted her fix. In the end, Zane would get what he wanted—DeGrate in the fucking ground.

Taniesha scratched at old puncture wounds on her arm. "I can see what's up with him and let you know."

Zane nodded. "Good. And go at him hard. Put a guilt trip on that nigga. Cut his conscience. That'll be enough to make him pull you close. And when he does, I'll let you know when it's time to put the thriller down. Send him to meet his dead homie."

With that, the Disciple king left Taniesha Berry alone in the dark room. Waiting for the phone to ring.

ANGELIQUE

Dr. James spent the rest of Monday at Duke and Viola's home. She made use of all the books she had on heterotopic heart transplant surgery.

Pouring over every page where she'd written notes in the margins. By midnight, she curled up on the couch and fell asleep.

Tuesday was easily one of the busiest Christmas Days Dr. James had ever seen. Since she started working at Cabrini, she spent sixteen hours at her trade. Eight hours were spent in Cabrini and another eight were spent with her interns at Scott Joplin Cook County. Today, her morning in the projects was fairly quiet. She made rounds with one of the new social workers and checked in on Taniesha and Amari to make sure they were still coming to Christmas dinner. By 2:00 p.m. she left for the hospital with Darrion, T-Bone, Lunch, and Taran.

They ate in the cafeteria. Afterwards Ant showed up at their table, dressed in his new gray environmental services uniform. He looked clean and well outfitted. To Dr. James, the new job seemed to make his youthful smooth skin look slightly more mature. Like a youngling ready to take on the responsibilities of society and leave the criminal life behind.

While the men fell into a conversation about old draft picks from the NFL, she stepped away and used Darrion's brick phone to page Kirkland to the ER nurse's station.

Then she interrupted their conversation long enough to let Darrion know where she would be and left to find Kirkland before Shawna's surgery.

Dr. James found the ER waiting room nearly packed. From the charge nurse's rant, there were no beds available on the floors for admitted patients, and the morgue was full. After about a minute of standing at the nurse's station, her intern called back. She told him to meet at the main hall elevators in five minutes then hung up.

♛

"You look nervous," Dr. James said.

Kirkland took another sip of his coffee and leaned his head back against the steel of the elevator. "I'm good."

She hmmphed, trying to hide her smirk. Of course he was nervous. In less than two hours he'd be in the OR, standing over a nine year old little girl, assisting in grafting a healthy heart onto a failing one. The double-ticker surgery that every intern and MD in the city had been buzzing about. Little Shawna Clark was nearly as publicized as Cabrini.

Right now, Kirkland couldn't have been more nervous if the donor heart was his own. Standing rigid, practically manacled to the wall of the elevator, still wearing the same scrubs from the night before. They had been nice scrubs sixteen hours ago. One insane stretch in the ER was all it took. Now they were crusted with stains and reeking of dried vomit. His eyes were bloodshot. His hair looked like a red mop. But always the brave face. Kirkland had been through a lot in the past few weeks. Jaliel's massacre. Shot at in Cabrini. Hurled into a world of drugs, prostitution, and gang violence. Valid reasons for an intern to carry that cautious air of an anxious professional.

No surgeon ever forgot the inundated hell of their internship and looking at him now vividly reminded her of her own jarring green days. Arriving in a crisp white coat certain to be fouled and contaminated by the end of the day. Pockets bulging with flashlights and reflex hammers. Note cards handy—crammed with every symptom and diagnosis. All of them already forgotten by the time she was presented with her first patient of the day. By the 36 hour mark with no rest, she was fantasizing about contracting some 24 hour bug so she could pass out, get strapped to a gurney with an IV drip, and get some sleep.

Scott Joplin Cook County Hospital was one of the best teaching facilities in the country. Of all the medical students accepted for the internship of '84 – '85, Dr. James was only charged with three crosses to bear. Kirkland Travis – born in Louisville, Kentucky. Taking aim for a career in cardiothoracics. Clarence Clark – born in Brooklyn, New York. Aspiring to become one of the best surgeons in plastics. Lastly, Izabelle Marsciano-LeTart – from Jacksonville, Tennessee – her sights firmly set on neurosurgery.

Thankfully not one of them had killed a patient. Yet. Right now they were all in that netherworld of wondering about their own sanity. Exposed to the dehumanizing aspects of medicine. Left questioning whether or not physical exhaustion and relentless accountability was a fair price to pay for joining the elite club of physicians.

Right now, Kirkland was in hell, but he was taking it like a soldier.

They got off on the fourth floor and walked the skyway from the main hospital to her office in the Chicago Specialty Medical Center building. Dr. James took a seat behind her desk and the instant Kirk sat down in the chair she handed him Shawna Clark's thick chart.

"This is for you to infuse your brain with in the next two hours," she said.

"What time is it?"

"No intern of mine will ever ask me that question."

Kirk turned and looked at the wall clock behind him. It was just past 3:00 p.m.

"Her heart should be arriving any minute and by 5:00 p.m., Shawna Clark will be receiving a second heart."

Kirkland opened the chart to the patient's recent history and progress notes.

"How many of these piggyback transplants have you done before, if you don't mind me asking?"

"Five," she answered. "With a team of nine. It'll be the same today. Can you name all of the specialists that'll be assisting?"

"One transplant cardiologist arriving from the Loyola Center of Transplantation, two pediatric cardiac transplant specialists arriving from Northbrook Heart. Leading the team is the director of the Heart/Lung Transplant Program. And he flew in all the way from UCLA. Three transplant nurses, two social workers, one medical psychiatrist...and a partridge in a pear tree."

Dr. James wasn't impressed. "Too easy." She went quiet for a moment. Thinking of how to trip him up. "The heterotopic heart transplant procedure from start to finish. And itemize well."

Kirkland looked far from dismayed. His eyes narrowed and when he spoke his voice was thick with arrogance. "After analgesia, sedation, and paralysis the patient is prepped and draped and the incision is made above the sternum, then you get out the saw. Some surgeons cut completely or partially down the middle...You cut all the way. Then you'll spread apart the sternum with a retractor and use electrocautery to seal the small blood vessels, maintain excessive bleeding, and cut through the pericardium. Next the patient's put on bypass, the heart is seized, and the donor heart is trimmed to fit the left atrium and fit snugly in the mediastinum on the right side of Shawna's own heart. After which the team of surgeons will work on attaching the left atria of both hearts to each other so blood flow from the lungs travels to both hearts. The aortas of both hearts are attached to transport blood from both hearts out to the body. Shawna's superior vena cava is attached to the piggyback's right atrium so blood from the body flows to both hearts. And finally, a graft from one of Shawna's blood vessels connects the pulmonary arteries of both hearts to send blood out to the lungs.

"Once the hearts are conjoined, Shawna will be taken off bypass, and her two hearts will beat as one. Once new and increased blood-flow is spread to all parts of the body, the team starts close and her sternum is put back together. Today, the old technique of using thick wire won't be used. You'll be trying a new technique of customized plates and screws to hold the sternum and the ribs in place as they heal. Total case time from start to finish should be no more than eight hours. From there, she'll be taken to the PICU and monitored for rejection. Worst case scenario, if her body rejects the piggyback heart, her old ticker will kick in, giving you ample time to treat the rejection before she drops dead from heart failure. Best case scenario, ten years from now, her weak heart is beating stronger than ever, her piggyback is removed, and all is well."

Damn. Somebody ate his Wheaties.

He was well studied up. But she wasn't done with him yet. "The first surgeon in U.S. history who invented and performed the piggyback heart and in what state?"

"Trick question," he said without a flinch. "It wasn't invented in the U.S. it was invented by a French surgeon who performed the double-ticker on a canine in 1905. And the first piggyback performed in America was ten years ago. The team was led by Dr. Christiaan Barnard. The first in Illinois was performed just last year. I do believe you held a ten blade in that case. And I do believe your grandmother, Dr. Eleanor Berkley, led that team of surgeons. Just before she retired."

Dr. James leaned back in her chair, pleased with his answer and the bold enthusiasm used to give it. But her face betrayed nothing. "Wow, you may be just as promising as you think that I know you're not."

Kirkland grinned right through her little insult. Blue eyes sparkling success.

Delores appeared in the doorway looking panicked and flustered. "I'm sorry, Dr. James, I don't mean to interrupt, but we may have a serious problem."

"What kind of problem?"

"Shawna's heart…it's stranded."

"What do you mean it's stranded?"

"The med-chopper had to make an emergency landing at Midway. They couldn't make it to our helipad. Some kind of engine problem. So they rented a car to transport by land, but there's a twenty car pile-up on I-90. I guess there was an ice storm last night and the roads are still slick."

Dr. James sat there in disbelief. "It's Christmas…What the hell is anybody doing on the road on Christmas?!"

"I know," Delores agreed.

"Are you telling me my heart is stuck on the Dan Ryan?"

Delores swallowed hard. "Yes, ma'am."

"What about the transplant team? Are they alright?"

"Dr. Maristani has a broken femur, Dr. Courdou has a few minor contusions but nothing serious, and the other two surgeons weren't with them…They arrived via commercial flight. Half of the injured are coming here, the rest are going to Memorial."

Dr. James stood from her desk, snatched up the telephone and started dialing.

"The ice for that heart is only good for a few hours!"

Delores threw her frustrated hands up. "I know! We're working on it, we're trying to get another chopper out there, but with the fire department, the ambulance crews, news vans everywhere and that's not including all of the wreckage. Highway patrol can't clear a landing!"

♛

Hello?"

"Are you and the boys still in the cafeteria?" Angelique asked.

"Until your shift is over," Darrion said. "Yes, ma'am, we are on duty."

"Meet me out by my car in five minutes."

She hung up, grabbed her purse, yanked Kirkland out of the chair, and ran out the door.

Five minutes later, her Firebird and T-Bone's blue safety hazard were weaving through downtown traffic, speeding towards the Eisenhower Expressway. By the time they hit the Dan Ryan, they fell in behind a congested long stream of break-lights. All fives lanes were barely inching forward at five miles per hour. Bumper to bumper. Then, as expected, all five lanes stalled to a halt. Nearly two miles ahead police lights, ambulances, and fire trucks were surrounded by the wreckage. Five news helicopters circled in the air around thick, dark billows of smoke blackening a stormy sky. Flames blazed out of crumpled cars every time the wind blew.

Angelique stirred nervously in the passenger seat. "We can't wait here like this." She looked out the rear windshield then from left to right at traffic. "Try to get over to the far right lane," she said to Darrion. "We're going to have to drive on the shoulder."

Ant leaned forward from the back seat and said, "Check the radio and see if they know what's going on up there."

Darrion pressed the radio buttons until he picked up AM 670. Seconds after the static cleared, breaking news came on the air. The story was nothing about the accident, but it was a catastrophe of equal proportions if not greater:

> *…this anonymous woman claims she and*
> *Councilman Porter had a brief affair while she*
> *was a dancer at the Rave night club two years*
> *ago. Furthermore, she claims he is the father*
> *of her child. This unnamed woman refuses to*
> *be interviewed at this time. Her publicist states*
> *she is willing to provide blood test results to*
> *prove that Derek Porter did in fact father a*
> *child with her, but those blood tests can only*
> *be released if and when the Councilman*
> *consents to give a blood sample for the test.*
> *Several attempts to reach the Councilman*
> *have been unsuccessful. Neither he nor*
> *anyone from his staff have been available for*
> *comment at this time. It is widely known that*
> *he is engaged to be married to Angelique James,*
> *the cardiothoracic specialist who has recently*
> *made a positive impact on the Cabrini Green*
> *housing projects through Scott Joplin Cook*
> *County Hospital's Gratis Faculty Program…*

Exactly what was happening to Angelique in that moment, she couldn't comprehend, but as she was listening to the news report, her mind froze. She stared at the radio. Thoughts blank. Stunned…Barely able to focus on the faceplate.

No one in the car made a sound for nearly a full minute.

They weren't talking about *the* Derek Porter. There were other Derek Porters in the city. They couldn't have been talking about *her* Councilman. She'd heard it wrong. *No way in hell are they talking about my fiancé bedding some stripper whore.* Derek Porter wasn't a father. This couldn't be happening. Except it was.

A loud explosion snapped her back to reality. A massive mushroom cloud of smoke and flames flared out, rolling up to the sky. For what seemed like an eternity, Angelique sat there paralyzed. Then she willed her fingers to shut off the radio. "Get over to the shoulder as fast as you can, Darrion!" She got out of the car and threw a hand up, blocking cars in the next lane over.

Darrion inched the Firebird onto the shoulder. Angelique motioned T-Bone's Buick though then got back in the car. "Floor it!"

Darrion sped up the shoulder until he reached a barricade of squad cars. Road flares blocked off the wreckage, keeping traffic back at more than 200 feet from the debris.

"You're gonna have to get out and tell the cop to let you through," Darrion said to Angelique. "I'm going with you. Ant, stay here."

They left Ant in the car and were approached by the first officer who had already spotted them. Tall and broad chested, he had brown skin and a clean shaved baldhead. He wasn't pleased. He waved them off before they even got near him. "You can't be here. Get back in your car!"

"I'm a surgeon from Scott Joplin," Dr. James said calmly. "There are two surgeons trapped in that wreckage with a fragile heart packed on ice that's probably thawing as we speak if it's anywhere near those flames! A nine-year-old little girl has been waiting for two years for that heart and she is going to die if we don't get it. I need that heart now!"

The officer blinked at her, shocked, and cursed. He ran over to the next squad car and spoke briefly to another officer, then came jogging back. "Alright, here's how it's going to go. We're going to walk you around the wreckage to the fire fighters. You need to give them a good description of what the cooler looks like. They'll retrieve it and hand it to you. We'll do our best to get the surgeons out of there."

Angelique jogged behind Darrion and followed him around to the firemen. The officer explained the situation and the firemen immediately took off towards the flames in search of Shawna's heart. Thunder clapped in the sky then. Within seconds the sun began to fade behind a thick wisp of dark storm clouds. Angelique hoped it wouldn't rain.

Less than five minutes later, two firemen emerged through the smoke. One of them carrying two medical duffle bags. The other carrying a large white organ transplant container marked: HUMAN ORGAN. It's edges were singed black from flame burns. Darrion grabbed the medical bags and Angelique took the organ cooler. One of the firemen explained both surgeons were being cut out of the rental car.

"We'll be using the jaws of life to get access inside the vehicle through the roof," he said. "One of the surgeons said he already called the hospital administrator and informed her of his condition and he knows his femur's busted up. He's in a hell of a lot of pain. But other than that, he says he's good."

Angelique nodded. "What about Dr. Courdou?"

"Who?"

"The other surgeon that's with him?" Kirk said.

"Oh, him! Yeah, he said that he's gonna stay with him and make sure he's stable. He'll ride with the other doctor in the ambulance. We'll have them out of here in the next thirty minutes."

Angelique thanked him and followed Darrion and the officer back to the Firebird. She unlocked the trunk to put the organ cooler inside and drew back. Not believing what she was seeing.

She was seeing it but it just wouldn't register.

Rectangular in shape, flat, and white. Each one had a blue scorpion stamped on it. She had seen Scarface once. What she stared at now looked very similar. Tony Montana would have been proud.

She didn't realize Kirkland was standing right behind her until she heard her intern gasp.

Darrion cursed.

"Is that what I think it is?" she asked.

"If it's what I think it is," Darrion said, "then it is."

"Is everything alright," the officer asked, walking towards car. "You guys have to get out of here. We'll clear you a way through, but you gotta go now."

Darrion ran back to the Buick and talked to T-Bone. Seconds later Taran and Lunch got out of the car and walked up to the trunk of the Firebird. Angelique sat the organ cooler on top of the trunk and forced a gentle smile at the officer.

"No problem, I just need to fit the cooler in the trunk."

"Do you need some help?"

"No officer I've got it, thank you." She sat the cooler down, lifted up the trunk, grabbed one of the medical bags and started loading up the kilos of coke. Her hands froze when she heard the familiar click of a pistol hammer. She looked up and spotted Taran holding his Beretta behind his back.

If things got bad, he was going to shoot the cop and anyone else who tried to stop them. Suddenly the sting of gastric juice rose in her throat. She buried the urge to vomit, swallowed it back down, and went back to loading up the coke. Twelve bricks in all. She was so mortified her brain couldn't function to do the math. But there had to be more than a quarter of a million dollars worth of blow in her car.

The cop gave more orders for them to load up and get off the freeway. Then, another metallic click. Lunch had reached in his suit coat for his weapon. With Darrion in front of them, the cop couldn't see their deadly intentions.

By the time Angelique loaded up the trunk and stood up, the cop was staring at Taran, Lunch, and Darrion with hard suspicious eyes. Kirkland had gone stiff as a pillar and twice as white.

"Is there a problem, gentlemen?" the officer asked, taking a step closer.

Darrion coolly shook his head. "No problem officer. Just waiting for the good doctor to load up the trunk."

She didn't know how she knew, but somehow she *knew* the cop was going to ask to take a look in the trunk. What came next, she couldn't believe. But she was doing the unthinkable. She pulled the bricks from the medical bag and lifted up the lid of the organ cooler.

"Well let me see what I can do to help speed you on your way," the cop said, taking another step towards the men.

"It's fine, really, we got it."

The cop's face turned serious. "Step aside."

Darrion didn't budge. Neither did Taran. Or Lunch.

Angelique put the last brick on top of the melting ice barely keeping Shawna's heart viable. Kirkland reached in and pressed down the lid. "Everything's fine officer," she said, standing up. "I just had to rearrange a few things in my trunk to make room for the cooler."

The cop kept his eyes on Darrion. "I can certainly take some of those things off your hands and put them in my trunk if it'll make things a little easier. Why don't I just take a look see at what I can load up in my squad car?"

Darrion glared back at him. No one moved.

"I said step aside, young man." The cop popped the clasp of his gun holster.

Darrion looked down at the gun then back up at the officer. Their face-off had gone on long enough.

"Darrion step aside," she heard herself say. "It's okay."

Darrion moved aside as did Taran. Kirkland was still a statue and Lunch didn't budge but he lowered his hand from the steel.

"You mind if I take a look inside your bags, ma'am," the officer asked.

Angelique shook her head. "No, officer, not at all."

He lifted up the medical bags and unzipped them. Then carefully sifted through the contents. He zipped them closed, sat them on the ground and motioned to the trunk. "The cooler please."

"I'm sorry?" Angelique said it like she didn't hear him right.

"The cooler," he repeated. "I need you to open it."

"I can't do that."

"You can and you will. Or I'll do it for you."

"I'm not trying to be uncooperative, officer, but this cooler is Celsius regulated," she lied. "If it drops below a certain temperature, the heart is no longer viable. The tissues start to die and it's no longer an organ capable of sustaining life. I won't be held responsible for contaminating and destroying a heart that a child has been waiting two years to receive. And trust me, officer, you don't want to be held responsible for that either."

"Is that so?"

"If she dies because this heart was contaminated, you could be charged with involuntary manslaughter," she said, embelishing the lie.

"If you got nothing to hide in this trunk, why do these men look like you do?"

Angelique let out a deep breath and held up her gun holster. "It's a Colt 1911. The serial's filed off."

The officer took her holster and held it up for inspection.

"I've never used it and the chamber's empty. I know it's illegal and I'm sorry. But these men are my bodyguards. They gave it to me because they're afraid for my life in Cabrini."

His brow lifted but he still looked cross. "I knew you looked familiar. You're that Doc on the news."

She nodded, swallowing more gastric juice.

The officer looked over at the other squad cars. None of the officers seemed to notice their roadside discussion. Angelique shot a quick glance to his nametag.

It read: Campbell.

He turned back to Angelique and held up the holster inches from her face. "I'm going to act like I didn't see this."

Consumed with relief, she closed her eyes and thanked him profusely.

"I should arrest you." Campbell pulled the Colt from the holster, inspecting the steel. "Let me give you a little piece of advice. If you're going to carry in Cabrini Green," he paused and chambered a round, "always keep a bullet in the chamber." He holstered the Colt and handed it back to her. "Load up and I'll give you an escort to the hospital."

Campbell turned back toward his squad car. As he passed Darrion and Taran, he gave them a look that made it clear he would never forget their faces.

♛

Darrion watched Angelique get behind the wheel.

She made her seatbelt click then stared murder at him. All he could say was the first thing that came to mind. "It's not mine."

"Then whose is it," she spat, "Zane's? You honestly expect me to believe that Zane's got you running coke for him now!"

She threw the Firebird in drive and slowly inched forward as an officer waved her through.

"Not knowingly," Darrion answered through gritted teeth. He cut his eyes away to the windshield, fuming. He hated being angry almost as much as he hated feeling nervous and he truly hated being both at the same time. She didn't believe him. Fine. Somehow those kilos wound up in her car. It didn't take much effort to jimmy a trunk latch. One of Zane's soldiers could have slipped the coke in her trunk at any time. Darrion was sticking so close to Angie the least of his concerns was the Firebird. There was ample opportunity to sneak out to her car and plant enough blow to have him buried under the prison for the rest of his life.

Now Darrion knew, one day, soon enough, he was going to blow Zane's fucking head off.

Kirkland cursed and put his seat belt on.

Anton leaned forward. "There's blow in the trunk?"

"Sit back and make your seat belt click, Ant." Darrion shook his head. "Just be cool and relax."

Angelique leaned forward, lifted up her medical white coat and pulled a kilo from the back of her jeans. "Hide it," she said to Darrion tossing it on his lap. "It wouldn't fit in the cooler."

Darrion handed it to Ant. "Slip it in your jacket and lean back in your seat. Keep your eyes forward."

Ant leaned back in his seat and zipped up the kilo. He watched Angelique fall in behind a fleet of squad cars and circle around the wreckage towards inbound traffic. Three Crown Vicks screeched to a halt on the freeway, wailing sirens. Stopping oncoming traffic as the motorcade took the freeway. Surrounded by police speeding down the Dan Ryan, Ant pulled the kilo closer to his chest and did the north-south-east-west thing with his free hand as he mumbled a silent prayer to God.

Darrion checked the side view mirror when another squad car passed them by. Nine made the motorcade. A glance at the speedometer and he watched the needle move past 90 mph. Then he looked at Angelique. She had a dark gaze in her eyes as familiar as his own ire. A look of total disconnect. Like she was operating on thoughtless vehemence. Adrenaline must have been pumping through her at warp speed.

Darrion never would have tought it possible. Flanked by police. Escorting enough blow to powder every nose in the city. Who wakes up on Christmas morning expecting that madness for a holiday?

She pressed the pedal to the floor.

A lurch of horsepower kicked in and the Firebird roared down the freeway. Just then a bolt of lightening split the darkened sky.

DEREK

We have a serious problem," Roth Garrett said.

"And that would be?" Derek asked.

"Turn to the news. Channel 9."

Derek switched the phone to his other ear and grabbed the remote control from his office desk. He sat there in stunned silence, listening to the news reporter ramble on about his sordid affair with an exotic dancer. A headline in bold red letters above the newscaster's head read:

Councilman Porter's Exotic Dancer Scandal!

"Call my mother!" Derek ordered.

"I did," Garrett said. "She's already on the way."

A hard knock came at the door then.

Derek put Garrett on hold and pressed the phone to his shirt. "Who is it?"

"It's me, son," Patricia Porter said. "Open the door."

♛

I'm sorry about this," Darrion said.

The last police car had just pulled out of the hospital parking lot. He watched the Crown Vick turn onto Damen Avenue and disappear into traffic.

"So it's Zane's," Angelique said, watching Turkell put the last brick of coke in the trunk of his Buick.

"I promise you we had nothing to do with this."

"He wants you gone that bad?"

Darrion nodded, watching Kirkland walk through the ER doors clutching the cooler. His face still that pale sickly white.

"Yeah, that he does." He lit a Newport. "Is Wonder Bread okay?"

"What?" Angelique followed Darrion's gaze to Kirkland. "Oh, he's good. He won't say anything."

"You sure? He looks a little shook up."

"With everything he's been through in Cabrini, I think he's well aware of the code of silence. If he wasn't I'm sure he would've sang like an oak tree full of birds by now."

"You trust him?"

"Yeah," she said. "I do."

Darrion took another long pull from his Newport and nodded.

"What are you going to do now?" she asked.

"Do you need me to stay?"

That was his polite way of saying he needed to leave.

As much as she wanted to say yes, she heard herself giving the selfless answer. "I'm fine. There's hospital security so, you've got business in the streets, I've got business in the OR."

"Okay. How long's the surgery?"

"About eight hours, give or take."

"I'll be back by midnight. Ant got off at 3:00, so I'll have him stay."

"I don't want him to uproot his plans on Christmas for me, Darrion."

"He needs to check on his grandmother anyway. If she's here, so is his Christmas. So he won't mind. He'll be by the house later with Taniesha."

Angelique nodded.

That was his polite way of saying she had no choice. It was already done and he probably already made arrangements with Anton anyway. Darrion and Taran pulled off in her Firebird. T-

Bone followed. She watched them turn onto Damon Avenue then walked back inside the hospital.

Twenty minutes later, Kirkland was in the men's locker room changing into clean scrubs. She had changed into scrubs as well and was standing in the doctor's lounge watching the news have their field day about Councilman Porter's Exotic Dancer Scandal. Without doubt 'the talk' was coming sooner or later. So she picked up the phone and got it out of the way.

Over the phone seemed easier.

If she saw him face to face, she'd probably slap him.

"Councilman Porter's office, Pamela speaking," a woman's voice said.

"Hi, Pam," Angelique said. "May I speak to my fiancé please?"

"Just one moment."

Derek picked up the phone less than a minute later. "Don't worry, my dove, it's being taken care of. This isn't going to hurt us."

"Who is this bitch, Derek?"

"It was a fling, it happened before you and I met."

"You couldn't be any more discreet than to bang a stripper whore? And you got her pregnant!"

"There's no proof that it's mine. Until she comes forward with a face to her accusations, then we worry. Until then she doesn't have a leg to stand on."

Angelique wondered about that. Why hadn't she come forward? Was she just grabbing for attention? Was she claiming her fifteen minutes of fame? Both? Or was she after something? Common sense and female logic told Angelique it was the latter.

"What's she after?" she finally asked him.

"I don't care," Derek spat back. "Whatever her angle is it's not going to—"

"Find out what the tramp wants and give it to her before she destroys everything we've worked for!"

"She's not going to do any damage to me or you or my campaign. I promise. My mother's working on it as we speak."

"You're mother?" Then it dawned on her what Patricia did for a living. According to her preceding reputation, Ms. Porter of Porter and Associates was the most widely respected and coveted crisis manager in Chicago. "Right," she said. "Crisis management." She let out a breath. "Is she really as good as everybody says she is?"

"She's the best," Derek assured her. "Trust me, babe, we want my mother on this. By the time Patricia Porter is done with this woman, she'll wish she never sent daggers my way."

"If you say she can make this go away, I'll believe you."

"She'll make this go away."

Angelique took in a deep breath. "I've got surgery. I have to go."

"Okay. I'll see you when you get home. I love you."

In spite of her anger, she said, "I love you." Then she slammed the phone down, cursed, and stormed out of the doctor's lounge.

♛

Patricia Porter walked into McCree's Pub and chose a seat at the bar next to Mark Wrath. She calmly sat her purse down and ordered a ginger ale. Wrath still looked the same. That affable face and those wry brown eyes. He still wore a suit well. But his age was starting to show in the grays at his temples.

He coolly sipped his glass of whatever brown liquor he'd ordered. Then came that conceited grin.

One day Patricia would slap it right off of his smug face.

"Okay, Mark," she said. "What does your client want?"

He looked at her and smiled. "A meeting with your son."

"Because you know he's, as of now, my client, you know that's not going to happen."

She never liked Mark and she took no pains to hide it.

Some publicists were respectable. Mark Wrath was top level on a regional scale. Most respected publicists remained that way because they would never be top level. Patricia knew there was nothing respectable about the way he earned his name.

"You still look good, Patricia," he said. "Eyes as green as envy. Those curls won't quit and I bet that pants suit costs more than the shop it was tailored in."

She saw through that flattery. So out it comes. Monies. "So that's what she's after. Money?"

"She is willing to be civil about this situation. In exchange for a fair compensation...for her silence of course."

The bartender sat her ale down. She ignored it. "Well...you can tell your *client* that my client is willing to be civil about this situation in exchange for her sanity, her solitude and her advantage of privacy. She's got 24 hours to recant her accusations. Or I will go to the first idiot with a camera, expose every john she's had for the past year—first, middle, and last name—discrediting any possibility that the child could be his, and smear her designation so deep in the mud, the only pole she'll be found swinging on is the one she hangs herself from."

"You could do that," Mark said. "But a dead stripper won't change the fact that your client's numbers in the polls are plummeting as we speak." He took another sip of his liquor. "The Councilman might be seen as an emancipator to the black community, but long after she's rotting in the ground, he'll be seen as nothing more than a playboy who got caught with his Ferragamos under the wrong bed to white voters. And his investors. And I can just see the Archbishop running so fast he can taste yesterday through the soles of his shoes before it even gets here."

Breaking a whore was the only card she had. For now. Mark had the advantage of political suicide. He'd won this round. But the fight was far from over. "I'll meet with your client," she said quietly. "But a meeting with the Councilman is out of the question. If she wants something from my son, she's going to have to deal with me. If she's got the brass for it. And if she makes one more statement to the press before this is settled, my client counters with defamation of character and that little coke snorting habit of hers goes public." She grabbed her purse and stood to leave the bar. "I would leave my card, but you know my number by heart I'm sure."

♕

Dr. James carefully applied polypropylene sutures to Shawna's superior vena cava. Outside, an evening thunderstorm had gathered but the atmosphere in the operating room was calm.

A strange menace to a milestone in the making. With any human organ, only a four hour window for a transplant was all any recipient had. With one surgeon in the ER being prepped for his own surgery, the OR team was one specialist shy of giving Shawna a new lease on life. Surprisingly enough, Kirkland listened well and learned fast.

Dr. James didn't let his gloved hands touch anything he wasn't ready for. But he held clamps well and he didn't miss a beat with the suction. Clark and LeTart watched through the observation room window. Their wide eyes reminded Dr. James of the first time she saw a beating heart in an open chest. "I was a resident before I saw my first beating heart," she said quietly to Kirk. "When you see it, it just grabs you. Lightening fast you're just caught. Like a trap door spider I saw once. There's nothing else like it."

"I was an intern when I saw my first beating heart," Dr. Courdou said. "For some reason I just wanted to reach in there and thump it. To see if I could throw it into V-fib."

"That is so sadistic," Dr. James said.

"Some of the greatest medical breakthroughs in history came from sadistic minds." He paused to get a better grip on Shawna's pulmonary artery. "Even the founder of modern medicine himself was batshit crazy. He was a 16th century Swiss doctor by the name of Paracelsus. Nowadays, it's nothing for people to pop a pill. But back then it was unheard of. He believed that being sick came from outside contaminants and that those threatening impurities could be cured with a mix of the right medication. While most people thought he was insane, his impulses paved the way for everything we use today. From penicillin to aspirin to the shady little morning after pill."

"Has that been approved yet?" the nurse asked.

Courdou shook his head. "Not in the U.S., but it got approved in the UK just last January."

"Wow, I hope that's not an excuse to promote promiscuity."

"There was a girl I went to med school with. Very smart woman. Spoke four languages and couldn't say no in one of them."

Everyone in the room burst into laugher. In light of recent events, Dr. James didn't find it one bit of funny.

"Pills don't promote promiscuity any more than they promote monogamy," he went on. "They just thin the population of illegitimate bastards being born because it wasn't there five years ago."

♛

Derek heard the key slide in the door just as he looked at his watch. He stood from the couch, watching Angelique walk in.

It was just past 1:00 in the morning. She paused briefly in the foyer when she spotted Patricia and Garrett in the living room. She spoke a hello, sat her brief case on the dining room table and gave Patricia a hug.

"We're going to work this out," Patricia said. "Don't worry."

Angelique gave her a probing look. "Have you met with her yet?"

"I will, first thing tomorrow. I just got off the phone with her publicist. He wants to set up a meeting in my office at 9:00 in the morning."

Angelique shook her head and turned to the living room window. "Some Christmas." She stared out over Lake Michigan for a long moment before she spoke again.

"If you spoke with her publicist, you already know what she's after. What does she want?"

Patricia let out a breath. "His money."

Derek could tell by her lack of surprise she saw that one coming. "Of course she wants his money. How much?"

"We haven't discussed a price. That's what we'll be meeting about tomorrow. But believe me, Angie, every red cent is going to come with a leash so tight she'll be miserable just thinking about the price of being rich from a Porter."

"I don't care about her being happy or miserable, I just want her gone."

Derek looked at his fiancé.

She was slender, beautiful, with imperious dark eyes. Her glare somehow reminded him of Viola's when she was angry. He came up behind her and put his arms around her waste. "She will be gone, baby." He kissed the slender curve of her neck. "Don't worry. Mom's already typed up a disclosure agreement.

She'll take the money and she'll vanish. We'll move on with our lives."

"And that agreement is going to come with a public renege," Garrett added. "This woman is going to get up in front of those cameras and publicly apologize for the false accusations made against the Councilman. In a year, no one will remember this."

Angelique kept her eyes on the water.

"What about this kid she claims you had?"

"She can't prove any of that," Derek said.

"She can if she has your blood."

"If I consent to it."

She turned and looked up at him. "Then consent to it."

Derek blinked at her and found himself reconsidering what had already been decided. Moments ago before she walked in, Garrett and Patricia had discussed at length whether or not to consent for testing. They decided not to appease Kimbella DeVoe. After all, she already broke the agreement that was set when they first met.

Derek carried on their casual tryst with three rules attached: He didn't want anyone knowing they were meeting, she agreed to come only when he called and she was not to stay the night. Ever. That was a year ago. Before he'd met Angelique. Now it was coming back to cut him where he'd bleed the most, his livelihood and his father's.

"No," Derek said. "If she wants testing, she's going to have to burn through a long list before she gets to me. When the other men are X-ed off that sheet then I'll consent. Until then, she can fish for a paternal obligation somewhere else."

"She's right," Patricia said. "You have to think about more than just your campaign, son. You have to think about the church, Derek. If the Archbishop finds out that you didn't even want to prove her wrong, he'll see deflection as an admittance of guilt and he'll pull away from your agreement with St. Victor. Then what?"

"But what if he is the father?" Garrett asked.

"I said he has to consent to the testing. I never said the results had to see the light of day. I've got a friend at the Paternity Center. I'll make a call."

🜲

Darrion saw the sirens flash in the rear view mirror. He pulled over to the curb and waited as the officer got out of his Crown Vic and approached the Firebird. When he leaned down to the driver's window, Darrion caught his nametag: Woodrow.

He rolled down his window.

"Did you realize that you've got a tail light out?"

Darrion cut his eyes away to the road straight ahead.

"No officer, I didn't."

"May I see your driver's license and registration?"

Darrion reached for his wallet and pulled out his license.

"This isn't my vehicle. It belongs to my charge."

"Your charge?"

"I'm private security for Executive Protection," Darrion answered. "This is my transportation for duty."

Woodrow gave a glance over the body paint. "Some transportation. Wait here please." He went back to his squad car, ran the license, and came back less than a minute later. "Sir, please step out of the vehicle."

Darrion looked up at him, stunned. He'd never gotten so much

as a parking ticket before. "What?"

"I said step out of the car."

Darrion got out.

"Place your hands on the hood."

Darrion did it.

"This car came up as suspect for narcotics. I'm going to search your person and if I find anything illegal, I will have to place you under arrest."

Fucking Zane.

Bet he wasn't planning on the dope already being gone before he called in his mole. Little bitch.

Darrion just shook his head and kept his mouth shut until the officer was done patting him down. Woodrow found the twin Colts strapped to his back. Darrion explained they were his, required for his occupation, and registered in his name for concealed carry.

Woodrow placed them on the hood. "Do you mind if I search your vehicle?"

Darrion motioned a whatever with his hand.

"Go right ahead, officer."

"Could you pop the trunk please?"

Darrion reached in the car and did it.

Less than a minute later, the officer came up empty handed. Darrion knew he had no choice but to let him go.

Woodrow pressed his shoulder radio. "Sir, this car is clean. I'm letting him go."

He handed Darrion his license and told him to get his tail light fixed. Then he got back in his squad car and drove off.

Darrion drove to the nearest pay phone and called T-Bone. He told him to call Taran and Lunch for a meeting in the main office of City Lights in a half hour. It was just past 1:30 in the morning.

♛

So he tried a stash and smash on you, huh?" T-Bone said, closing the office door.

"The officer's name was Woodrow," Darrion said. "I'm pretty sure he's moling for Zane. If he's not, whoever put him on me is."

"What'd he look like?"

Darrion waved off an accurate description. "All them crackers look the same to me. Blonde haired, blue eyed, and billy-clubbed up. I don't know."

"We're gonna have to have a little sit down with Zane before this shit gets out of hand."

"It's already out of hand," Taran said. "That stunt he pulled on the Dan Ryan could've gotten us all locked up. We set up his truce, he's back to making money, we are no longer necessary. He made that clear. I'm all for letting him know he's no longer necessary."

"He won't be missed." T-Bone said. "And we don't even have to get our hands dirty. We could hire one of them crazy ass Aryan brothers to do it. Anonymous retainer. They don't even have to know who we are."

"Why twelve bricks?" Lunch cut in.

"What?" Taran asked.

"Why twelve bricks?" he repeated. "Why not just one? If he wanted us gone, one key is all it would take."

"Exactly," Darrion agreed. "I've been doing a lot thinking since yesterday afternoon. That was whole lot of weight to drop in one trunk. And they all had a blue scorpion."

"Where are they now?" Lunch asked.

"In the vault with the diamonds," T-Bone said.

"Why don't we just sell 'em?"

"Because we're not drug dealers," Darrion cut in.

"Why can't we just get rid of 'em?"

"Because Zane just got rid of 'em," Darrion said. "New product, new distribution. That means he has a new supplier. I'm betting Pope's not feeling the white rock. Because dealing in keys racks up bigger profits. Zane disagrees. So, if he cut Pope out of Cabrini—"

"He can't use Xavier's supplier," Taran said, finishing his sentence.

"I'll bet every dime to my name, whoever those keys belong to is going to be looking for his bricks. Zane can't toss a quarter of a mil without consequences. And he's damned sure not going to say he lost them like a set of car keys. If I were as ruthless as him, I'd fix my mouth to say I got robbed. He'll be making enough money off of selling his new product to break even with what we supposedly ganked, but he's not giving that cash to Pope's supplier—which means Zane just made a quarter of a mil to have us all whacked. And that's exactly what his former kilo-man is going to do when he finds out we stole his dope."

"So what do we do?" T-Bone asked.

"We set a meeting with Pope. I think it's pretty obvious by now who tried to have him whacked in Stateville. Just out of sheer hatred and lust for revenge, he'll be more than willing to smooth things out with his supplier and send in his enforcers to kill Zane."

T-Bone's brow lifted. "I thought you wanted to do the honors?"

"I wouldn't mind being his sandman. For Amari, for Pope, and for everybody he spit on with no retribution, nothing would be sweeter then putting his ass to sleep. But killing him throws me into a drug war that I want no part of."

"Speaking of revenge, one of my snow bunnies came back with some info on ol' Bucky Kincaid. I know where he likes to kick it at. Some bar on Cicero in Mount Greenwood."

Now that was a death Darrion could do. He gave a nod and said, "Let me talk to Pope first and make sure that cracker has no Aryan ties in the prison that could blow back on us all."

ZANE

Patricia Porter sat quietly watching Mark Wrath enter her office. A gorgeous young woman followed close behind.

As much as Patricia hated to admit it, she looked like Derek's 'discrete' type. Large eyes. Perfectly coifed hair. Clear light brown skin. Full lips. Waist narrow. Lean firm curves swathed in a pure white pants suit.

She was stunning. So this was Kimbella DeVoe. Her stripper name: Diamond DeVoe. Patricia had a sense of dislocation from looking at her. As she quietly sat down before her, the exotic dancer seemed to vanish. A resolute woman took the table in her place.

Mark cleared his throat. "My client would like to start off by saying —"

Patricia threw a hand and kept her eyes on Kimbella. "If you're client would like to start off by saying, she's sitting not two feet from me, Mark. Let her say it."

Kimbella sat quiet. So Patricia gave her a push. "How much do you want from my son?"

"Twenty," she said boldly.

Patricia felt the word pass through her like a slow shockwave. "I know you mean thousand," she finally said.

Kimbella didn't blink. "Million. And I want a meeting with him."

"Five," Patricia countered. "And that's being generous. With a disclosure agreement, a public recant, and no meeting."

Kimbella looked at her publicist then back at Patricia. Surely she had to expect a counter much lower than her original amount. Perhaps this was her first time extorting a wealthy man, but it wasn't Patricia's first time thwarting a scheming vixen from gouging her client's bank account.

"Ms. DeVoe has a specific reason for wanting to speak in person with Mr. Porter."

Patricia looked at Mark. "Then perhaps she'd like to share that reason."

"It's a health matter of urgent importance."

Patricia looked at Kimbella. Suddenly she felt her heart squeeze in her chest. My God, she has AIDS. "Are you sick? An STD or—"

"No," Kimbella spat curtly. "My son."

Patricia felt her pulse drop out of the red zone. "I see. And what is the poor condition of his health?"

"That's for me to discuss with his father."

Patricia forced a smile. "No. That's for you to discuss with me—his crisis manager. And for me to discuss with him—my client. And whether or not you're aware, extorting my client for millions makes you very much a crisis. So he will not be meeting with you. Now, tell me, what is this health issue?"

Kimbella gave a quick, defeated glance to Mark. He nodded a go ahead. "His heart," she said. "There's a congenital defect. He's got three holes in his chamber walls. Derek told me his father had it. He said the men in his family have the flaw."

Patricia froze. Derek told her Duke was his father? He wouldn't do that. Her son would never confide the deepest family secret in a woman who was just...just...sex. Would he? Patricia had to be sure. She switched tact to see how much the woman knew. "I'm surprised he told you that," she fished. "He hasn't mentioned Marvin much since he died."

Kimbella blinked, confused. "Well, he only mentioned it briefly once, just in conversation."

The tension in Patricia's chest eased. This woman didn't know who Derek's father was. Only that he had one. "I'll mention it to my client and get back to you. Now, about the disclosure agreement, I—"

Mark held up a hand. "Ms. DeVoe won't be signing anything without the presence of a lawyer and furthermore, the price is still twenty million."

"Five and my client will consent to a blood test." Since she knew the baby was his without a doubt now, she wasn't giving up any leverage by offering that one.

"Five won't do," Kimbella spat. "I need more."

Patricia's brow lifted. "Whores always do."

"You can think whatever you want about me, but I've done the math. Der's surgery alone costs $50,000. That's not including his hospital bills since he was born, which is already $250,000. None of which I can pay because I can't work. I've been spending every free minute at the hospital. Even after his surgery, there's postoperative costs. And if his heart's not better by the time he starts school, he's going to have to be home-schooled. Then there's living expenses and college."

Okay. She was somewhat making sense. But in no rational thought did Patricia Porter believe it took twenty million dollars to raise one child. "Okay," she said. "From what you've just told me, *I've* just done the math. So, that's $300,000 total for the hospital bills. Home schooling costs from kindergarten until he's eighteen is roughly $5,000 annually. Times twelve years is $60,000. Even if he goes to Harvard for eight years instead of four, that's $320,000. For living expenses, add $100,000 annually to take care of you both until he has his degree. Grand total, that's 4.6 million. Give or take a few vacations in there — and if we add in your coke dealer — that's 5 million even. Unless you OD and drop dead first. So I'm failing to see what the extra $15 million is for."

Kimbella blinked at her, slighted and snubbed.

Mark leaned over and whispered something in her ear. Then, "Medical insurance, a vehicle for transportation, and a home for the both of us."

"I see," Patricia said calmly. "So medical coverage for your son, a car, and a three bedroom home is going to burn up $15 million dollars? Do I look that newborn to you?"

Kimbella said nothing.

"Whatever high end lifestyle you're used to, or think that you're entitled to just because the condom broke, isn't going to change my offer. What my client is offering is a lot of money to a lot of people."

Kimbella still said nothing. She nervously looked at Mark then swallowed and said, "Fifteen."

"Five."

"Five is barely enough for us to make it for the next eighteen to twenty years! What if he gets sick and needs another surgery?"

"Do what mother's have been doing to take care of their own for centuries. Get a job."

Kimbella shook her head. "I won't go lower than fifteen."

"Well my client isn't willing to go higher than five. So I guess we're at a bit of an impasse."

Mark leaned in Kimbella's ear again. She looked a Patricia, straightened up her posture in the chair and said, "Fifteen, or I confess my sins to the Archbishop."

Patricia just looked at her. It could have been a bluff. Then again, Derek wasn't in a position to call the bluff of a woman who could destroy him. There were other ways of making this go away. Of course that would mean making *her* go away. Permanently. For threatening her son, Patricia could do that. A black plastic bag, a bottle of lye, and a roll of tape was only a phone call way. But then what? Speculation alone of her sudden disappearance would bring more negative attention than Derek's campaign could bear. Taking her off the planet would bring too much noise. She needed to go away quietly. Giving her the money was the only way to do it without a mess.

Congratulations, Ms. DeVoe. You're a millionaire.

That didn't mean Patricia was going to make it easy for her to revel in it.

"Alright. Fifteen pending the following conditions. One, you will never meet with the Councilmen. Ever. That's five years from now. That's ten years from now or twenty. Never. Two, you will never hold a residence in the city of Chicago again." Mark scoffed at her and huffed a frustrated breath. She ignored him. "Three, you will sign a non-disclosure agreement. I don't care if you have to bring ten lawyers just to see it done. You will sign it. Four, no more press, no anonymous interviews, and my client will be providing private security around the clock to make sure that your whereabouts are well observed. And lastly, a public recant." She looked at Mark. "Do we have an agreement?"

His mouth twitched. "We still require a blood test."

"If my client will consent to a blood test and agree to the amount of $15 million, do we have an agreement?"

Kimbella looked at Mark and nodded.

"I'll speak with my client and get back to you after. Until then, you open that pretty little mouth of yours to one more reporter or set foot in that church, the deal's off and I will switch tact to make this little problem go away."

Mark rolled his eyes. "Oh stop with the empty threats, Patricia. We both know the child is his. You don't have a leg to stand on with this nor do you have another card to play. So just give it up already."

Patricia's eyes narrowed, but she kept her voice very calm. "I always have another card to play, Mark. But I work very hard at being good at what I do, so those cards stay up my sleeve. Because once they're out on the table, there's no going back. " She stood and held the door open for them to take their leave. "I'll be in touch."

VIOLA

Merry late Christmas!" Melody beamed.

She stepped through the door with a handful of presents.

"Merry Christmas to you," Viola said, stepping aside as Melody passed. Dutch closed the door then reached up a hand to her nose and gave a hard pull. Viola hollered in pain and punched him back as hard as she could. He didn't even feel it. Dutch just laughed, pulled off his coat and scarf, and followed Melody into the living room.

They were the last to show at nearly 7:00 in the evening on the day after Christmas. Everyone had come for the late celebration. Donald and Mary. Their twins were by the tree fussing over presents. Luna and Legend were by the sofa, fighting over a knotted rope.

Several guests from the church came. DaVita and Devin had early dinner the day before at a friend's house with Ronald. Much to Viola's dislike, Taniesha Berry was there along with Anton and the baby. She held no grudge against them personally, but just to see them Viola could feel Cabrini Green creeping back into her house again.

Darrion was in the kitchen with Duke working on the ham and the turkey. Taran was off somewhere making sure every gun in the house was loaded. Lunch was in the TV room talking with Derek. Angelique proved to be quite helpful with setting the table. Fang didn't celebrate Christmas. It went against his mighty Ainu principles. But just knowing he was with them in the house made her breathe a little easier. She couldn't keep the stalker off her mind. Since that incident, she had two nightmares about the wall in the Kozaks' place.

Fang had been a comfort to her. Leaving his dojo and his martial arts students, while she flew all over the city finalizing last minute shopping. Ever the quiet shadow, he always followed in silence. Because of him, somehow making Christmas happen this year seemed more soothing than any other year before. Viola assumed most of her even-temperedness was also because she set to keeping her mind off of Duke's heart surgery.

She joined the good doctor in the dining room to see if she needed anything.

"Are you doing okay in here?"

"Yeah, I'm fine."

Viola looked over the table with an approving nod. Plates. Saucers. Wine glasses. Water glasses. Dinner forks. Salad forks. Desert spoons. Soup spoons. Cloth napins. Three gravy boats. Two sauce servers. Everything seemed to be in place. "Good."

"Everybody seems so calm. Loud, but calm...in light of recent events. Nobody's running back and forth to the kitchen. I'm shocked."

"Waiting is a must in my kitchen," Viola said. "I have five rules for Thanksgiving and Christmas dinner at my house. Nobody asks twenty questions about the food or who made it; if you can't walk or serve yourself, sit your ass down until I get you a plate; if you have kids under the age of five and can't feed themselves; sit their little bad asses at the kiddy table until I get them a plate; There is only going to be one prayer before dinner and it won't go on until my blood sugar bottoms out; and last but not least, one plate at a time. My house is not a soup kitchen."

Angelique laughed.

Viola knew she needed to. Darrion said he and the boys had to sneak her and Derek out of the back door of buildings whenever they met for private meetings and they had to leave in two different cars just to escape without being followed by the press. That much pressure on a person could take the laughter out of the holidays in disparaging ways.

Viola walked into the living room, stood by the Christmas tree, and looked at the grandfather clock. It was just past 7:20. She summoned everyone in the dining room for dinner. Donald led the prayer and everyone sat down waiting to be served. The turkey was well baked and moist. Every bite of ham had the perfect glaze of honey. Mary's greens were tender and fresh. Everything Viola tasted was heaven and by the time her plate was empty, she was too stuffed to dare a slice of Melody's red velvet cake.

Dinner at the DeGrate house was over by 10:00. Darrion, T-Bone, Taran, and Lunch, were the first to say goodbye. They had to oversee a Christmas bash at City Lights. Viola hated that strip club. She had tried to convince Darrion to sell that sinkhole of a place. But every time she brought it up he would remind her that the club wasn't in his name, and as long as he employed a phantom proprietor to show his face every now and then, no one could tie the Family to it's earnings. If it wasn't a threat to the DeGrate public image then Duke couldn't use the church to make him get rid of it either. So Viola had to learn to look the other way.

Derek and Angelique were the next to leave. He and the doctor had 'meetings' he said. She imagined that had something to do with the recent scandal. But it wasn't her place to mention it. She walked them to the door and when they put their coats on, Taniesha came running out into the foyer.

"Amari's not breathing so good," she said. "I forgot his inhaler."

"At Cabrini?" Angelique asked.

Taniesha nodded

"Okay, I'll be in there to check on him in a minute."

Viola watched Taniesha walk back to the living room and sit by Amari. "She's awful quiet tonight," she said to Angelique.

"Yeah, I think she's worried about Ms. Ida. Amari's still not out of the woods with his asthma and all."

Viola turned and lowered her voice. "I don't think you should be going out there this time of night by yourself."

"I agree," Derek added. "It's out of the question."

"Oh I won't. I'm not that naive. I'll page Darrion."

Angelique put her scarf around her coat and looked at Derek. He seemed satisfied with her answer. Viola watched him nod and kiss her goodbye. Then he left.

"I'm gonna check on the baby," Angelique said. "I'll be right back."

Viola turned her attention to Taniesha. It had dawned on her that she barely touched her food. She looked healthy enough. But there was something about the way Taniesha had been all night. Quiet. Reserved. Like she felt out of place or in a room full of strangers. Viola turned to the window and watched Derek and his private security drive away.

Less than a minute later, Angelique came back into the foyer and grabbed her coat off of the coat rack. "I'm gonna head on over now, Amari's breathing is worse than I thought."

"Wait for Darrion," Viola warned.

"Oh I will," she said. "He had a phone installed in my car for Christmas." She smiled and buttoned up her coat. "He said it's a present. I say it's a mandatory communication device. Can I use your phone to call him? He said he'd be at the club."

"Use the one in the living room. Do you have my number?" Angelique shook her head.

Viola went into the kitchen and fished out a card from her purse and went back into the foyer. "Both my car phone and my brick phone are on that. Don't lose it."

Angelique nodded, slipped it in her pants pocket, and called Darrion. She left a message for him at City Lights and hung up. "I'll have him meet me at Cabrini. He'll call back in a minute. I told him to reach me in my car. I'll only be gone about an hour. Then I'll come back and help you clean up."

Viola waved off the offer. "Don't worry about the mess. I got it."

"That's not how I was raised by my grandmother. If you can help eat the food, you can help clean the pots that made it. I'll come back and help you."

"Okay." Viola opened the door. "Be careful."

♛

From Santa and his elves," Darrion said, handing the prison guard a thick envelope through his car window.

The Correction's Officer put the sedan in park, fanned through the cash, and looked at him, shocked. Darrion understood his confusion. He never paid to see Pope. Most did because it was customary. If you wanted an audience with the king of the Disciples, cold hard cash was expected and that didn't mean he would grant your request. But, out of respect for his former amity with Duke, he never expected Darrion to pay a dime to see him. Still, it was only hours past the one holiday when gifts were expected. So, it was rude to come empty handed.

"Since when do you pay to see the Pope?" the guard asked.

"It's Christmas."

"Christmas was yesterday."

"Yeah, I know."

"Drive up to the main gate. The guard'll let you in." The officer looked up and down the dark road, making sure no other cars were coming, then rolled up the window of his sedan and drove off.

Darrion drove the short distance to the main gate of Stateville prison and told the guard he was there to see Xavier Pope. He parked his Mercedes and five minutes later, he was patted down for contraband and ushered into a private visitation room.

Pope sat in imperial solitude.

His bulky frame swallowed the gilded chair in which he sat. He was at a table, dining on king crab legs and steak. Several of his soldiers stood back against the wall, silent and still. Darrion knew not to speak. Pope would talk when he was ready. He looked around the room and saw nothing to remind him of incarceration. The walls were adorned with portraits. A gold and white ceiling fan whirled silently over head. Tall vases stood in each corner. A thick Persian rug covered the hardwood flooring under the table. The Pope was living more like an emperor than a convict.

Pope dipped a thick chunk of crabmeat into his butter sauce, chewed silently then motioned for Darrion to take a seat across from him.

He did and waited quietly for Pope to speak first.

The Disciple lord pulled out a stack of money. "What's this?" He tossed it on the table. "You know you don't have to pay me."

Darrion shrugged. "It's the holiday."

"Christmas was yesterday."

"I know."

Pope nodded nonchalantly and started on his steak. "First things first, I reached out to the Aryans. One of the crackers Kincaid killed during the robbery was the cousin of a high-ranking member who's stationed in D House. He's hiding out at the Belleview Motel. On Cicero in Mount Greenwood. You take care of him and I'll be in a position to strike a truce on the yard and in the Roundhouse from A House to E House. The Black Mafia Gorillas, the Northern Aryans, the Los Lobos, and the Chinese Black Dragons. This last job you did at the bank put all of the gangs in monetary accord. All unpaid debts have been settled. All dues have been paid. Everyone has money on their books. My daughter is taken care of. Are you ready for the next gig?"

Darrion shook his head.

"Right now I can't risk anymore scores until after the new year. After the election."

"When you're ready let me know. I already have it lined up. And this time, the ex-cons I send your way will be less…ambitious then that crazy ass hillbilly was."

Darrion nodded.

"If you find Kincaid," Pope continued, "and give him his halo I'll be in a position to take back what's mine. Soon Cabrini will no longer be a problem and the streets will be just like they used to be." He took another bite of his steak. Chewed and savored. Then, "I thought it was Sampson all along at first. When one of your own breaks off and calls a mutiny, the actions fit the accusation. But it wasn't until you struck the truce that I knew it truly was Zane."

"Sampson is trying to eat," Darrion said. "Zane is trying to own every plate with a meal on it. And he'll be going after it at all costs, from ordering a hit on you to sending me down river for the rest of my natural born life. Taking back Cabrini won't be as easy as you think it will."

Pope took a sip of wine and cut another slice of meat. Then his fork paused. "How's that?"

"Twelve keys of dope wound up in the trunk of a car I was driving yesterday. All of it was marked with a blue scorpion. I'm guessing that's either the mark of your supplier, or which ever cartel they're buying from."

Pope just looked at him. Darrion spotted a hint of displeasure in his dark eyes.

"You two have a product dispute. He thinks rock is the future. You think dealing in bricks is more profitable. Because he disagrees, I'm guessing that's why he just gave your supplier the kiss off," Darrion continued. "And by now, I'm guessing that supplier's been informed I stole it." Pope ate another bite of his steak and the two men sat in silence before Darrion spoke again. "I'm not in your drug war. And what happens in Cabrini is none of my business when it comes to your product, but I'm telling you with Zane's new product, the devastation is swift. It's all over the city. Not just Cabrini. I've never seen fiends like this. There's nothing they won't do for their next hit. Off the boat, powder is still carrying power. But in the streets, powder is done. Even H is falling to the wayside. If you want to take back what's yours, you may have to take control of the powder Zane's using to monopolize on the rock he's selling. He's got a new supplier. You want Zane, go after his kilo-man."

"Who?"

"I don't know who. He's not talking to me. And lately, Cabrini's been quiet. Too quiet. All the breezeways are like ghost towns. Zane's found a new location to supply his hypes. Away from the media and Five-O. And somehow the fiends are getting from their apartments to the basement and back without being seen. I'm pretty sure those elevators aren't just stopping at ground level."

"How do you know that?"

"Street logic. If you can't supply above ground, go under."

"Basement? Cabrini Green doesn't have basements."

Darrion nodded. "I'm betting they do now. That's what I'd do. But that's just where he's serving. He's got to get his supply weekly. And with the news cameras everywhere, no street lieutenant is going to be seen anywhere near Cabrini with a re-up. So, if you want my guess, Zane's using tunnels. Somewhere, somehow, they connect to basements under the projects."

Darrion had no qualms with spilling every bit of Zane's org- anization. If the cocky slumlord hadn't tried to set him up to get pinched, there would be a bit more delicacy in his report to Pope. He already wanted him dead. But once Xavier got wind of how well Zane was doing with cutting him out of the profits, he would want him real fucking dead. Darrion wouldn't have to worry about pulling the trigger. The Pope would do it for him.

Any remains of Zane's fallen empire, the Disciples would mete out that power vacuum themselves.

Sometimes Darrion was so spot on it scared him. Seconds after he thought it, out it came.

"I want him dead," Pope commanded. "Him and that scar-faced, Cyclops brother of his!" He put his fork down and pointed a finger at him. "I don't give a shit about his supplier and I don't care how you do it. Deep six them both."

Darrion sat there, shocked. "Not once have I ever refused you. But this I cannot do. When he set me up yesterday, I wanted him dead. I wanted to blow his head off. But now that I've had time to think, I don't need another body on me, with the election coming up for Porter. My father is backing his campaign. I hit Zane, his soldiers will come after me and my family, and that's a faucet of blood I'll never shut off."

Pope gave him a look of such disapproval, Darrion wanted to melt into the wall. *And I thought only Duke could do that?*

"Nine years ago," the Disciple lord said, "you came to me asking for help. Turkell's people were being deported back to Haiti. You needed money to buy off immigrations. I set you up with a score to get you the money. I swore I would keep our arrangement from getting back to your father. A promise I agreed to keep so Turkell could feed his people in Florida and you could live the life you live without asking Duke for a fucking dime. Now my power is in jeopardy...I'm asking you to take down that threat, and you say no to me?"

Darrion's jaw clenched. He swallowed hard, but kept his face impassive. If refusing to kill Zane wasn't an option, *when* he would kill had to be open for discussion. "I can only do it if you're willing to wait for it. Let Zane play God for a little while longer. I can't make a move on him until after the election. If there's any way you can put the word out to every gang leader in the Roundhouse that his days are numbered, maybe that'll buy you some time until I can take him out."

"When is the election?"

"February."

"You have until March. And I want proof they're both dead."

"What kind of proof?"

"Bring me Zane's pinky ring. It's a black diamond. He never takes it off. For Zeno, bring me his eye. I heard he's got quite a few of 'em. I want the gold one. I hear that's his favorite."

DARRION

Darrion left Stateville prison with clenched teeth.

How was he supposed to kill Zane without suffering the repercussions? He knew Pope was right wanting him dead. But wanting him dead for power was one thing. Darrion wanted him dead for all the Antons and Tanieshas of Cabrini. Zane Harris was a disaster as regent. In a way, forcing Darrion's gun hand wasn't such a bad thing. After all, in killing one man, he knew he was saving more lives than he had ever taken, by far.

He wasn't more than a mile out from the prison when his pager went off. The same number appeared three times. He had left his pager in the Mercedes to avoid it being taken by the guards. They would have given it back after his visit with Pope, but he didn't like other people touching his belongings. He looked at the number.

Angelique's car phone.

He called her back and instead of heading to City Lights for the XXXmas bash, he escorted Angelique and Taniesha to Ant's apartment. For most of his time there, he was silent. While the women tended to little Amari's asthma, he spent the time mentally compartmentalizing how easy it was to kill and justify the reason for it. Vindication was as easy as breathing once he accepted who he was killing as opposed to whom he was allowing to live. He knew not one blink of sleep would be lost over deep sixing the Harris brothers. In fact, he had half of a notion to believe Cabrini might erect a neighborhood holiday for the day they got wiped off the map. But as consequences go, he knew the blow-back would be more than he could handle. Unless Darrion gave Zane's soldiers a reason to betray their king.

About a half hour later, Angelique was content with the baby's breathing. She gave Taniesha both her home and car phone numbers to reach her incase his breathing began to lapse and Darrion followed her back to Duke and Viola's.

♛

Darrion spent the next five days plotting the murders with Taran, T-Bone, and Lunch. Kincaid would die first. Then, they'd go after Zane and Zeno. They quickly figured out the only way to take Zeno's power and turn it against him was to offer every soldier in the projects something their slum-lord never would: Power.

That meant Pope would have to bend more than he cared to. But his offering of a few leadership positions would give Disciples, who had been working hard to climb the latter, a chance to not only rise in rank but also surpass Zane.

Darrion held another meeting with Pope and to his surprise, Xavier was more than agreeable to the idea. In fact, he expressed that several of Zane's men had earned their elevations long ago. He agreed to hand them down to a select few. Markelle "MG" Gordon, Anthony "Guesser" Wright, and Freddie "Machete" Barlow. He even agreed to send his second in command, Caesar Black, to initiate and welcome the men to their new positions. With that plot in motion, Darrion concentrated all of his energy on scheming to put Kincaid in the ground. The Northern Aryans had already put the word out on the street that no one was to harbor Kincaid or stand in Darrion's way.

Flushing that twist out from hiding would be child's play. All they had to do was wait for the word from the Aryans on the street. It was only a matter of time before the hillbilly showed his face.

♛

New Years Eve came at a whiplash pace, but even the Doc refused to take the day off, so it was the usual routine. Darrion drove his Mercedes to his parent's place, climbed in Angelique's Firebird, honked the horn and at 0745 in the morning. Fifteen minutes later he and the good doctor were at a diner eating breakfast. Then they met T-Bone at Cabrini. She made her routine check-ups and by noon they were at Scott Joplin.

Today was Ms. Ida's foot amputation. While Dr. James checked on her in the post anesthesia care unit. T-Bone left early to buy some new clothing and make sure the night club was ready for the New Years Eve/Truce party. Darrion found Ant with Punchy in the cafeteria during his lunch break. He bought a black coffee, sat at their table, and invited them to the club.

They talked for a while. Ant spoke on Ms. Ida being released to go home on New Years Day. Then he expressed his concerns on working for Zane.

"I just took the job at the hospital so I could step outside of Cabrini for a while," he said.

"How does your boss feel about that?" Darrion asked.

"He ain't said too much of nothing. As long as I keep bringing what I been bringing, he really don't care."

"How much are you bringing in?"

"About two, maybe three a day."

"Thousand?"

Ant nodded.

"How the hell are you pulling that much with you here five days a week mopping floors?"

Ant leaned forward over his French fries and lowered his voice, "Yo, I got mad clientele up in Cook. Nurses, a couple of patients, and a few doctors. They be blowing my pager up. I can walk in through them ER doors in the morning with three thousand dollars worth of rock and it be gone in probably twenty or thirty minutes."

"Yup," Punchy nodded in agreement. "All I gotta do is come with the re-up. Take the cash, make sure he got more rock to sell for the next day."

Darrion was in shock. He looked at the both of them, not believing what he was hearing. "Does Zane know about it?"

Punchy nodded.

"Hell yeah he know," Ant said. "Why you think he don't care that I ain't working the breezeways no more?"

Darrion folded his hands on the table. "And how much are you clearing off the weekly bank?"

"Enough," Ant sighed. "Just barely enough."

"Mmm-hmm," Punchy agreed. "Zane keeping us low-level right where he want us. Maybe at the end of the week, I'll have enough to help my sister with the rent. Ant might have enough for groceries and Pampers for his nephew. Maybe some sneakers. That's about it. And we gotta be back here the next day if we wanna keep making enough to eat. It's a on going grind, baby. It don't stop cause it can't stop."

"How much is he taxing?"

"I see why Sampson led a revolt," Ant said. "That's all I'mma say about that. Zane ain't no better than Pope when it comes to street tax."

"What's Sampson got to say about it?"

Ant shook his head. "Shit. And he don't have to. He still the leader of the Renegades. It's just free enterprise now so he don't have to answer to Zane or Pope. And I heard he ain't even taxing his soldiers."

Punchy nodded in agreement, took a bite out of his cheeseburger, and wiped his mouth with a napkin. "Yup, everything they make they take home. Every dime."

"All his peoples is eating. 'Til they fat, fat full." Ant stuffed a handful of French fries in his mouth.

Darrion took a sip of his coffee. "Why don't you bring it to Zane's attention?"

Ant paused mid-chew.

"What? And end up catching free flyer miles off his roof-top? Naw, I ain't feeling that."

"Me neither, man," Punchy said.

Darrion slid his coffee aside, reached in his pocket, and pulled out a money clip full of cash. He slid five Benjamins and a Cleveland to Anton and gave the same amount to Punchy. They both just sat there, staring at the crisp bills on the table like they had never been taught to count that high.

"Where'd you get a thousand dollar bill from?" Punchy asked him. "They don't make these."

"Apparently they do," Darrion said.

"What's this for?" Ant asked him.

"For the new year. Start off '85 on the rise. Buy yourself something fly for the truce party tonight."

"What you want for it?" Punchy asked.

Darrion's brow tented. God, it was that bad. They never got a dime without having to do slave for it? "What I want for it?" He looked up and spotted a nurse that caught his eye. Nice hips. Slender waist. Smooth skin and a wide firm mouth. "You know her, Ant?"

Ant turned around and spotted her.

"Yeah that's Tanya. She's a nurse on 3 West."

"You wanna put in some work to get paid?" Darrion asked Punchy. "Why don't you get her number for me."

Punchy looked down at the money. "Seven digits?"

Darrion nodded.

"For $1,500.00?"

Darrion nodded again.

"That's it?" Punchy cursed and got up from the table. "It's going down like two flat tires."

Ant chewed silently for a moment. Thinking. Then his eyes slightly squinted mischief. "Damn, that's some cappo de tutti type shit right there. If you ever had the notion to make that move." His pager went off. He checked it. "I'm up, KD. I'll see you tonight at the party."

By the time Darrion got a page from Angelique, it was nearly nighttime. It wasn't until they were halfway to her home that she informed him of the New Years Eve party at Walter Wheat's estate. She had to attend with Derek. She didn't sound enthused, but she did admit that schmoozing with the oil tycoon was necessary for his campaign.

Darrion dropped her off, parked the Firebird, then got in his Mercedes and drove home. He cooked pasta with meat sauce, ate quickly, then showered, and changed into a black shirt and black slacks. By 10:30 p.m. he drove to Lunch's house for a before-the-real-party-house-party. He had only planned to stay until the countdown, then go to City Lights for the stripper's contest. When midnight was near and the countdown came, every one was in the back yard, firing off their guns. It was an annual ritual in Chicago.

New York dropped a ball in Time's Square. Los Angeles toasted and boasted in all the hottest nightspots. But the Windy City emptied clips.

In the midst of the gunfire, an ear-piercing holler rang out. Darrion lowered his Colt, turned around and saw T-Bone down on the ground, bleeding like a homicide.

ANGELIQUE

Angelique hated these parties.

Though Wheat's estate was awe inspiring, she would have preferred to be at home, under the sheets with her fiancé. She'd shaken hands with so many people in the past two hours, she was surprised she didn't have warning signs of carpal tunnel. After the countdown, it was official.

1985 was here.

Angelique had the feeling it was going to be the most changing year of her life in more ways than one. She took another sip of her wine and found a quiet view by a window no one else occupied. Derek was off more than a hundred paces away. Charming every snake in the room. Cracking jokes with Walter Wheat and the blonde dame who looked young enough to be his daughter—though she clung to him like a pay-lay.

Just when her mind began to ponder Wheat's vast empire and the means he used to attain it, her pager went off in her purse. She checked it. Darrion's car phone number. She looked at her Movado. 12:15 a.m. She found a corner in the room that had a phone and called the number.

"Angie, it's Lunch," he said, panicked. "T-Bone's been shot in the shoulder!"

"How bad is he leaking?"

"It's pretty bad."

She looked around for the nearest exit then looked across the room at Derek. "Lay him on a flat surface and elevate his legs until they're higher than his head, and put pressure on the wound. Where are you?"

"At my house, in the basement."

"Give me the address. I'll page Kirkland, then I'm on the way."

Lunch gave her the address. She quickly hung up then looked for a pen and a pad before the street number left her head. She found a stationary on one of the end tables, scribbled it down and crossed the room to Derek.

He was as understanding as always, though she could tell by the slight derision on his face T-Bone being shot was no surprise to him. Mentally he was probably blaming Darrion for that one. But she didn't ask how it happened before she got off the phone with Lunch and in that moment of Derek's disfavor, she was glad to be uninformed.

She left the party, grateful for the excuse to leave the elitists, and sped back at the DeGrate's home. She ditched the red party dress and the painful high heels and snatched her knee high boots, white denim, and white long sleeved shirt out of the closet. Then it dawned on her that she hadn't worn her wolf's fur at all. Dutch was kind enough to have it delivered from Christian LeBarron and she didn't even given him the courtesy of wearing it to the Christmas dinner at Viola's.

She took it from the hanger and examined it for a few seconds. Thick and heavy, it bore outstretched paws and a wolf's head biting across the front towards the side, concealing the zipper. Held in place and flush with the fur by thick snap clamps.

She wondered what Darrion would think of it. But…why the hell was she worried about what he thought? It was cold out, she told herself. *I don't need a reason to wear my own damned coat.* She dressed quickly and paged Kirkland, then grabbed her medicine bag and flew out the door.

♛

Darrion and Lunch stood outside in the front yard by the gate and watched as Angelique pulled up next to several parked cars. Kirkland's beat up truck squeaked to a halt a few paces before the Firebird and the Doc was out of the car, running for his truck bed before he shut off his headlights. She jumped on his back tire and pulled a large black bag from the bed then the duo ran towards the back gate.

"Where is he?" she asked.

Darrion just blinked at her.

She was an attractive woman on most days. But tonight, she looked uncommonly beautiful. It was the first time he'd seen her wearing one of his uncle Dutch's furs. He could tell the gray pelt was well tailored for her. As of late he was beginning to see more than clear brown eyes and full lips. She had a brave soul and a giving heart. She ran out on Walter Wheat of all people just to help his best friend. Her whole being was shaped to stoke aspiration and —

"Darrion!" she said louder, throwing the wrought iron gate open. "Turkell...where is he?"

He mastered his bearings and motioned over his shoulder. "In the back. Down stairs."

She kept running and pointed towards the stairs by the side of the house. "Right here?"

"Yeah."

He led the way to the basement and told everybody to back away and give them some room. T-Bone was on an old oak long table, on his back. Legs propped up. Somehow his left shoulder was clamped down under a table vise.

Darrion cleared the crowd out of the basement. Taran and Lunch stayed.

Angelique looked surprised to see DaVita and Ronnie standing next to the table.

"How are you, DaVita?" She gave a nod to Ronnie.

"I'm good," she said, smiling. Then her smile faded and she shot a look at Angelique's two black bags. "If this is about to get even more bloody than it already is, I'm heading upstairs."

Kirkland nodded. "You might want to do that."

Ronnie led DaVita by the hand and told her he'd fix her a drink. Darrion shot him a look. He really didn't like how close Ronald Moss had become with his sister. "Make it a soda," he ordered. "For the both of you. I said keep an eye on her tonight not get her drunk, Ronnie."

Darrion's sister frowned at him. "Don't be such an asshole, Darrion." She pulled at Ronnie's hand. "Come on."

She led the way upstairs and Darrion felt a tinge of aversion coming to his face. DaVita made it clear she had quite the crush on Ronnie, but Darrion was going to keep watch on exactly how far it went. Gambler. Drinker. And now more in debt with his father than he could ever get out of. He looked at Lunch and asked him for a favor. "If you don't mind, could you go upstairs and keep an eye on the two of them? And make sure they stay in sight and don't disappear into any rooms."

Lunch nodded as if in a daze and pulled his eyes away from T-Bone's wound. He did that sometimes. Just stared at blood like it was the eighth wonder of the world. He made his way up the stairs and gave one last look at all the blood before it was out of sight.

"If you need a sink," Darrion said to Angelique, "there's one right behind you."

Angelique nodded, then slid off her coat, and unzipped the black bag. "Thanks." She put on a surgical mask and examined T-Bone's shoulder more carefully. "Whose idea was it to use the vise grip?"

Taran raised a hand. "Mine. It was leaking so fast, I couldn't put enough pressure on it to stop it in time. So..."

Kirkland nodded in approval. "Nice."

"That's probably the most innovative form of controlled bleeding I've ever seen." She went to the sink to wash her hands and Kirkland used another small table to set up a sterile field. "So what happened?"

"Ronnie slipped on a patch of ice while we were in the back yard shooting our guns off," Taran said. "That ass clown still had his finger on the trigger. Shot T-Bone dead in the shoulder."

Angelique walked over the sterile field her intern was setting up, hands dripping, and reached for a sterile towel. "Be glad he wasn't standing right behind you, Turkell, or we wouldn't be having this conversation. A few more inches to the right and a little higher and he would've shot you right in the head."

T-Bone scowled. "This shit hurts, man!"

"Are you allergic to anything?"

He shook his head.

"Are you taking anything? Street drugs, medication?"

"If we're talking Mary Jane, then yes. If we're not, no."

"Have you been drinking?"

He groaned in pain. "What kind of question is that? It's a house party full of alcohol."

Angelique smiled and slipped on a surgical gown.

While Kirkland checked the vise grip and examined the damage to T-Bone's shoulder, Darrion went over to the sterile table and looked over a mass of shiny instruments, needles, and knives he never wanted anywhere near his flesh. Angelique slipped on a pair of sterile gloves. "Thank you," he heard himself say.

"You don't have to thank me," she said. "You can always call me if you need my help."

Her words came with an honesty that almost physically hurt it was so foreign. No one he knew did anything for free or just because some one called and asked them to come. Yet there she was, keeping T-Bone from going to the hospital. She came without question. Without conditional demands. She didn't even ask why they didn't take him to a hospital. Her honesty deserved honesty in return. Darrion decided to tell her why.

"I won't forget this. I know it's not exactly on the books. You're saving him a lot of trouble. Turkell's...not exactly a legal citizen."

She gave him a searching look and her eyes were wide with as much surprise as he thought they'd be.

"Oh?" she said.

"He's Haitian. His family immigrated here when he was only five years old. That's why he speaks perfect French. But he's got no papers. If he goes to a hospital..."

Angelique nodded understanding. "Right. That would be very bad for him. As far as a lack of I.D. goes. But you know they can't call the police or immigrations, right? It violates a patient's rights." Her eyes narrowed with another smile. "I'm glad you told me though. And I won't tell anyone."

"I know."

"Excuse me," T-Bone interrupted. "I know it's all Gone With The Wind over there and shit, but would you mind plugging me up before I bleed the fuck out?"

Darrion and Angelique looked at Turkell then at each other.

Before Darrion could stop it, his face flamed. He wasn't aware that he was being so obvious. They both turned away from each other and walked over to the table. He could tell by the way she walked off she didn't like being ousted either.

"Wow," she said. "Somebody's grumpy."

"You take one in the shoulder," T-Bone said. "It won't be hugs across America for you either."

Darrion didn't like watching her work on his shoulder. He just made the bodies, he didn't need to see the patch work. He left Taran and Kirkland down stairs and went back to the party. More than hour went by before Angelique came upstairs with her wolf's fur in hand.

Turkell was given a slight dose of local anesthesia, antibiotics, an IV drip, and one unit of blood. He was still in the basement feeling prized and sedated. Kirkland was monitoring his breathing until he woke.

In the meantime, Darrion showed her around, introducing her to a few people. He eyed Ronald Moss across the room. DaVita was on his lap, sipping something in a plastic cup. Somehow Darrion knew it was liquor. Lunch was close by, so he was doing well to keep eyes to them.

Angelique sipped a cup full of wine and he could tell she got an instant heat flush. She fanned her face and asked him to take her outside for some fresh air. He led her to the back door and used a stopper to hold it open. She leaned against the doorway, tilted her head back, and closed her eyes. Letting the cold winter breeze cool the blush from her face.

"T-Bone's gonna live?" he asked.

She exhaled. Sending the sweet scent of wine wafting up to his nostrils. "I believe so."

"So what's for the rest of the night?"

"The party's probably still going on at Walter Wheat's estate. I should probably get going."

"So, it's back to caviar and Chateau O'Brien, huh?" Darrion qu-ipped.

Her eyes opened.

"Yeah, it's back to caviar and Chateau, smart ass."

Darrion arched an eyebrow at her. "Wanna go to a *real* party?"

"No," she said, smiling yes.

♛

Turkell woke twenty minutes later. Kirkland put his arm in a sling and monitored him for another thirty minutes, then they all piled into several cars and drove to City Lights. Darrion was surprised Kirkland came along. After days of non-stop flu patients, bums seeking pain meds, and gunshot victims, Angelique told him he deserved a break as long as he didn't tell anyone.

Every year City Lights hosted the Gentlemen's XXXmas party and a New Years Eve bash. From 2200 hours until 0500 on both holidays. Tonight, as it was a special occasion that came rarely, the club's owner, Curby LaShaw, held no cover charge. Free food, an open bar, and the city's hottest women — all competing in the Miss Candy Cane contest for a $10,000 cash prize.

Darrion recognized nearly every one of Zane's soldiers. Some of Sampson's were there as well. T-Bone was wide-awake and made no stops on his way to the dance floor. He grabbed a beautiful woman and started dancing like he didn't even have a hole in his shoulder. Taran and Lunch never danced. They made their way to the back wall near the dance floor and just stood there people watching.

Uncle Dutch and his wife, Melody, were there but they weren't dancing either. Melody was more involved with the strippers than her husband was. Leaned over the velvet rope barrier. Stuffing dollar bills in the G-string of a longhaired vixen. She slapped the stripper's firm rump and screamed for more.

Darrion told Kirkland to order whatever he wanted. Then, he led Angelique to the dance floor. He danced in the crowd with her for hours. Celebrating a New Year, a new truce, and a night of bliss as if he were on the very first holiday of his life.

DUKE

Duke didn't want to risk calling Patricia from the house.

On New Years day at 6:00 in the morning, even with entire city still asleep, Viola was wide awake.

His wife could hear the dust settle.

If he was on the phone, that woman would be able to tell just by looking at his face the person on the other end of the line was someone she didn't approve of. So he had to see Patricia in person. He waited until after Viola had left for the office, then he double checked the address for Porter and Associates and made the drive to Bellmont Heights.

Patricia Porter opened the door to her office and just stood there. Looking as beautiful and as surprised to see him as he expected.

Duke nodded in greeting. "Patricia."

"Duke," she said. "I didn't think you'd be up at this hour."

"I know I'm here unannounced. But it's important. It can't wait."

She nodded like she knew it was inevitable. "I suppose this meeting was coming." She stepped back from the doorway and let him in.

Duke looked around the cavernous ornate space. None of her employees were in sight. She crossed the room to the bar and offered him a drink.

"Sure," he said. "You wouldn't happen to have any uh...Ch—"

"Chivas Regal?" she said finishing his sentence. "I always keep a bottle of that lying around."

It felt wrong asking her to pour him a glass of that liquor. He'd only started drinking it when they began their affair three decades ago. She introduced him to it. It was the smoothest blend of Scotch whiskey he'd ever tasted. Every time he drank it, the smell, the taste reminded him of her. But his infidelities weren't why he was there.

"I thought I'd see your underlings scrambling about the office."

She reached into the liquor cabinet and poured him a drink. "My underlings are out scrambling about the city."

"That many clients are in crisis, hmm?"

She handed him the glass. "As of now, just one."

He didn't drink it. He just stared into the glass. Then his eyes turned serious. "Our son is in trouble, Patty."

"I know. We're working on it. I've got two private investigators, one hell of a defense attorney, and a very blood-thirsty reporter on my team. I'll save him, Duke. No one is going to hurt Derek. I promise. We will make this go away."

"Who is this woman? And what does she want?"

Patricia walked over to the conference table and grabbed a file. She handed it to him. Duke opened it to a candid photograph. She looked like his firstborn's type behind closed doors. Attractive and licentious. But her face wasn't ringing any bells. Then again, he couldn't keep up with half the women Darrion bedded. Let alone Derek.

"That is Kimbella DeVoe. Her stripper name, Diamond DeVoe... She sometime goes by Lady DeVoe."

Duke sat on the edge of the table and thumbed through the file. He read a few paragraphs. "Other than being a high school drop out," Patricia said, "a juvenile delinquent, and a self professed nympho with a coke habit, nothing about her strikes me as note-worthy."

"And the accusations?"

Patricia sighed. "True."

He looked up at her in surprise. "What?"

"I know. Shocked the hell out of me, too. But that baby is his."

"Blood test?"

"Not yet. But her kid's sick. He's at Northbrook Heart. Congenital. Same as you when you were a boy. We don't need DNA testing to prove what's obvious. But we're going to get one falsified just to shut her up. It'll read that it's his. But it won't come certified official. There will be no real paternity test that can be traced back to a valid Paternity Clinic. I've got a friend working on it. He owes me a favor. He'll falsify the results."

"And if she ever tries to claim that it's a fake?"

"Then I'll make sure the entire city agrees with her."

Duke nodded. "Did you double check at the hospital to make sure she's not lying?"

"I did. Kid's got a medical chart this thick." She mimed two inches with her fingers. "I even stopped by on Christmas to see him. I know a cardiologist there, used to be a client. He snuck me in. He's a cute little button."

"So what happens now?"

"I've already sent my reporter to block anything the woman's put out there."

"Who?"

"Riva. She's got a tie in with Fox 32 News. She was working at my son's newspaper. But he pissed her off and she quit. So I reeled her in to work for me. I had to keep her close to the Family somehow. Turns out she loves it. Right now, thanks to her sharp tongue, Ms. DeVoe is looking like a jezebel clawing at fifteen minutes of fame."

"And when her fifteen minutes are up, does she go away?"

"Yes, even if she's goes away a millionaire."

Duke cursed.

"She wants money, Duke. And lots of it."

"Give it to her."

"We're going to have to. But that cash comes with a drawback. She'll be so scrutinized every moment of her life, she'll wish she never met me."

"You're watching her?"

Patricia nodded.

"Derek's private security and I put one of my P.I.s' on her. Lately she's been sleazing around City Lights."

"What for?"

"Doing what nymphos do. Getting laid and paid for the pleasure I assume."

Duke sighed.

"Kivik is the best P.I. in this city. Every dirty little move she makes, he's got the camera clicks to prove it. My other P.I. is on her publicist, Mark Wrath. Right now, we know he's having an affair with his wife's sister. That'll be enough to make him drop Ms. DeVoe as a client. Then, we can back her into a corner and bargain to terms."

"How much is she asking for?"

"Fifteen."

"How much is Derek willing to give her?"

"I just got off the phone with him an hour ago. As long as she agrees to losing the luxury of free will, he'll give her every dime she asking for." She went quiet for a moment. Then laughed softly and shook her head. "I'm a grandmother. Dear God, I'm a grandparent, Duke."

He looked up into her green eyes.

"So am I, love. So am I."

♛

Angelique spent the entire morning, all afternoon and evening at home— in their own home—under the sheets with Derek.

By nightfall, they were still in bed. It felt good being lazy. Slothful and sexed. That was how every woman should spend New Years Day. It was nice to finally have him to herself for a change. Without the cameras and the scandal and strangers buzzing about him everywhere they went. Sex with him was always slow and unrushed. Strangely, from time to time, when Angelique came up for air, she found herself analyzing her feelings for Darrion.

Him showing up in her mind during sex with Derek was…she didn't know what kind of wrong to call it. She knew it was normal.

All women fantasize about other men. Some women fantasize about other women. Yet she found it strange, truly admitting to herself that there was an obvious attraction between the two of them. So obvious in fact T-Bone was half bled out before he was forced to call them on it. Her feelings toward him were expected. They had grown quite comfortable with each other over the past couple of months. She felt totally safe with him. Not one bullet went flying past her head in his company. At the same time, she felt careless and rash at the thought of being enticed by Darrion DeGrate. Most women were. He was nothing like Derek. He cursed like a sailor with Tourette's. Smoked like Bob Marley. His reputation in Cabrini was gangland ties and underworld dealings. Her attraction to him was childish. Selfish. Improbable moreover. She decided to block it out.

Lying peacefully with their legs entwined, and her breasts pressed against Derek's chest, she looked up at him.

"I almost forgot what sex with you was like," she cooed. "I miss it."

Derek smiled and slid down to her chest. She slid a hand over his head when he kissed her breasts. Then the phone rang.

"Don't answer it," Derek said, trailing kisses down her ribs.

It kept ringing.

When they hung up and called right back, she knew it was urgent. She cursed and rolled onto her back.

"Whoa," Derek said. "What's with the mouth? Since when do you curse like that?"

She ignored his scrutiny. "Somebody had better be half dead."

He sighed and stared up at the ceiling. "When they call you, they usually are."

"I'm sorry," she said, reaching for the phone. "Hello?"

"It's Taniesha." Her voice was tight and squeezed. She sounded frightened to pieces. "It's Amari. His breathing is really bad this time. I gave him the medication but it's not helping and I don't know what to do."

"Call an ambulance and I'll meet you at the hospital."

"I'm not at home. I'm at a pay phone in Durso Park. And I don't have no more change."

That didn't sound right.

Why would she be at Durso Park of all places at night? Unless it was to score H from a dealer. Then again, couldn't she have walked home and used her house phone to call? Unless it was cut off. Durso Park was no place for anyone to be, especially a baby. They called it Hell's Back Yard for a reason. But, she didn't have time to question Taniesha's logic.

"Okay…where are you?"

"I'm near the drug store. Can you please come? I don't know what to do if he stops breathing."

"I'm on the way."

She hung up and just like that, Angelique—the sexed fiancé—vanished. Dr. James pulled herself out of bed and started dressing.

Derek sat up. "Well, are you going to at least tell me where you're going this time of night?"

"It's Taniesha," she said. "The baby's sick."

Derek let out a sigh and lay back down.

"Taniesha…again," he said. "You know, that woman relies on you so much to take care of that kid, he's probably ill because he's more used to your breast milk than hers."

She rolled her eyes. "Stop it."

"Make sure you page Darrion. And wait for him before you go anywhere near Cabrini."

She grabbed her coat from the closet, then went to the bed and kissed him. "Hold on to that for me. I'll be back before your lips are dry."

He pulled her into him and kissed her again. "You be back before your lips are dry. Both sets."

♛

Dr. James paged Darrion then drove to Durso Park. She spotted Taniesha and Amari outside of Nickle's Drug Store on the corner of Oak and Larrabee. She pulled out her prescription pad, then went to the pharmacy and purchased Ventolin and a children's aero-chamber inhaler.

For more than five minutes she sat in the back seat with Amari, making sure his breathing improved after the medication had been given. Taniesha sat in the front seat, quietly looking out the window. When Angelique was satisfied his respiration had returned to normal she sat behind the wheel and tried Darrion's number again via car phone. It went to the nightclub's answering machine.

She'd paged him twice earlier.

He still hadn't called back.

Where the hell was he?

"If his breathing gets worse, we'll take him to the hospital," Angelique said to Taniesha. "Until then the medicine I just gave him should help for a little while."

Taniesha nodded nervously and turned her gaze to the window. She looked afraid. But, somehow Angelique knew it wasn't a mother's fear. It was a different kind of fear. An outside fear someone has when they have no control over their surroundings. She couldn't blame her. Day and night soldiers prowled the highrises. Looking for a life to snatch.

"He's going to call," she reassured her. "Don't worry."

♛

Darrion was in the vault for nearly an hour. Sorting through everything they had in cash, coke, and diamonds. Keeping the vault in City Lights was the easiest way to keep an eye on any viable resources yet to be filtered for laundering or stored in a safe deposit box. So far it totaled just over six million. He sat his pager and brick phone on a table in the vault and went to his office for a quick meeting with Zane and Zeno.

Moving through the mass of people, it never ceased to astound. How hundreds of men in the city had no children and weren't married. Or they were husbands and fathers but tonight had no qualms pretending they weren't. Good advertising always yielded maximum turnout.

Tonight all twelve penthouses in the club were available for private encounters. Whenever City Light's hosted a party, the club was full so far beyond capacity he was certain the city's fire code was beyond violated.

Darrion went upstairs to the main office. Curby LaShaw, the club's owner was waiting for him on the couch. Darrion shut the door. Blocking any noise from the loud speakers on the main floor.

Darrion and Turkell hired LaShaw because the man had a talent for publicizing and promotion, a Bachelor's degree in business, and he was a good front man, a face to present to the IRS and the Bureau of Fire Protection. He covered the money laundering with a tailored suit and tie. No one questioned his presence. Everyone knew him as the sole proprietor. Employing him seemed a good investment. Until now.

"I'm expecting a couple of people in here for a meeting, so we're going to have to make this quick, Curby."

"They're at the bar. I'll send them up when we're done."

"So you're screening my meetings now?"

"I just wanted to bend your ear for a minute is all."

Curby looked his best as he always did. His hair was freshly trimmed and he had selected one of his finest black suits. Even with the thickness of his gut, he made the age of forty-nine look worthy and right.

Every bit the entrepreneur, he interrupted Darrion's meeting to discuss expanding his trade beyond the legitimate world. For nearly ten minutes, Darrion listened to his grand larceny ambitions, knowing full well T-Bone already told him no. Now Curby sat there on the couch. His proposal reformed. Determined to wheedle approval out of Darrion instead.

He never liked Curby. He was too ambitious and sometimes overly pushy. There was very little LaShaw discounted in the club. But liking the profits he rendered was another matter completely. Because of constant high revenues, his hardened motivations were forgiven.

Darrion leaned against the desk and folded his arms across his chest. "I don't understand what your skin profits have to do with expanding on our business. Are you bored or something? You're making more than enough money to keep your mouth wet. You ain't eating? I know cats all over this city who would cut their hands off if they had yours."

Curby rested a thick hand on the arm of the sofa. "What I was trying to tell T-Bone and what I'm trying to tell you is, I get cats in here all the time bragging about what they got. Houses, diamonds in the safe the wifey don't know about. HH bonds. I mean these cats come in here, man, and they get a little liquor in 'em and they start bragging about every thing they got and everything they gon' get. So what I'm saying is, I can set it up. Get work for your retainer. Who ever they are. And I know they get their percentage after you do the take. But you can pull your next take from me. Some of the shit I could put you on to…you wouldn't believe."

Darrion was unimpressed. "What we do has an earned excl-usivity. Our retainer ain't going to just outsource to an unknown just because you're ready to smash and grab. It don't work like that. And I thought T-Bone already had this discussion with you?"

A disapproving scowl set in on Curby's face.

"All I'm saying is you all get a percentage from me and my girls. If we do business together other than the club, I wouldn't even need to take a percentage from the girls. You could take your cut straight from them. Which would give you more at the end of each week. And whatever I would make percentage-wise as a finder's fee would even us out."

Darrion just looked at him with the same expression of faint distaste he had worn since the day he met him. After his meeting with Pope, he was in no mood. "Curby," he said as calmly as he could, "you're not hearing me. We've had this arrangement for the past nine years...We take scores...You run the club. You're a pimp. Fine. Turkell and I, we don't pimp. We pimp the pimps. But we don't want to take over your business. Why you're trying to switch shit up now, I don't understand. We are in a business arrangement for obvious mutual benefits. You are the name on the papers. You're the front man. You are the face they see when the State Department asks to speak to the owner. You are the reason why the money we filter through here is never in question. Your ass is in the chair with the accountant when they audit this establishment. It's been that way for damn near a decade. And we ain't trying to change it.

"And even if I wanted to, you're too loud with it. But you earned the right to be loud with it. So the three houses you own, the fleet of cars you drive, nobody questions it. You start living the life I live, that'll change. And I can't have it. So, the answer is no. Run the club, stick to what you do best."

Curby looked pissed. But he didn't say a word. Darrion waved him off, ending the discussion. "That's it."

Curby huffed at his answer and walked out of the office. As he was leaving, T-Bone came in. He knocked on the doorway and smiled a mouth full of gold. "I got another Christmas present for you."

Darrion's brow lifted. "Oh yeah?"

He nodded. "The jade penthouse. Hit that after the meeting. I already tried her. That dame is right."

A few moments later, Zane and Zeno walked in. Both said nothing. Darrion offered them a seat on the couch and closed the door. T-Bone stood by the desk. Zane plopped down like he owned the place. Darrion couldn't help but to notice the pinky ring on his left hand. If things went according to plan, that diamond would soon belong to Xavier Pope. Zeno went to the window and stared down at the crowd on the main floor.

"I don't want to keep you," Darrion began. "So, I'll make this brief. I had a meeting with Pope a few days ago. As you can imagine, he's none too happy with being cut out of Cabrini. Since war is not an option, he's only got one card to play. Out of respect for the restraint you've shown with the good doctor, I'm giving you fair warning on Pope's next move."

Zeno turned from the window, staring that false eye at him. Today it was metallic red. Darrion wondered exactly how many jeweled eyes he actually owned.

"He's planning on chopping off the head to your body. He's going after your supplier."

"Is that so?" Zane spat.

"Oh yes, that's so."

"How about this, message boy, you go back and you tell Pope that his threats mean less than shit to me. If he goes after my connect, I go after his daughter. I know right where that bitch stay at. And I don't issue empty threats. He tries me, DeGrate, I'll gut her like trout. His days are done, his time is over. He needs to get over it and be glad he's lived long enough to see his golden years."

Darrion hmmphed. "You failing to end those golden years wasn't from a lack of trying. Now was it?"

Zane's face went dark and his eyes flashed fury.

"He knows you tried to kill him, Zane. For my interest in keeping the truce, I'm letting you know he ain't letting it ride. Pope is not just gonna turn the other cheek while the one you slapped is still red and flaming. He's still got reach on the streets. Just because that reach is diminished, doesn't mean it's dead. You want my advice, maybe you should cut him back in. Make your peace. This ceasefire means everything to this city. I'm asking you to consider that before you start another war."

"Actually I don't want your advice and cutting him out was your suggestion, DeGrate. Does Pope know that?"

"No. Just like he doesn't know that your street tax is just as bad as his was if not worse. Now that he's figured out you tried to kill him retaliation is the only thing on his mind. And if you want to dodge that bullet, make your peace. Because cutting him out to be better than him is one thing. But cutting him out because you want to be just like him? I never thought monkey see monkey do was your style, Zane."

"And I never thought stepping and fetching was your style, but Pope always has his gophers."

Darrion said nothing. So Zane kept on, "Pope needs to consider what's best for this city before *he* starts another war. I slaved for that nigga for damn near two decades. All I was to him was a regent. He never thought I was worthy of an elevation and he was looking the wrong way when the pawn took his king. I'm not backing down. Cabrini is mine. It's curtains for the Pope. He can take a bow or take a bullet. End of talk."

Zane stood abruptly and walked out.

Zeno, ever silent and faithful, followed without saying a word.

T-Bone shut the door with his good arm. "Predictable as always."

Darrion nodded and a devious grin came to his face. "I couldn't have planned it better."

"So, Zane is going to warn his connect."

Another nod.

"And all we have to do is wait and watch him when he gets his next re-up. Then we follow him to the tunnels under Cabrini?"

"If we can find out how Zane's getting his product in, just like he tried to set us up on the Dan Ryan, payback's a bitch. And that bitch is gonna be lovely. One phone call and the Councilman is going to have the best day of his life."

♛

Darrion walked into the jade penthouse and locked eyes on a stunning vixen lying on the bed. Her dark hair was a cascade of curls. Long-lashed, large eyes. Clear, light brown skin. Narrow waist. Red lace swathed her bra and panties, figure-hugging full breasts and lean, firm hips. More than a few erotic positions flashed in his mind. But, first things first. He pulled off his twin Colts then laid them on the nightstand and took a seat in the leather chair next to the bed.

"You're new here?"

She nodded.

"I only ask two questions when it comes to females. First question. Are you here because you want to be or because you have to be?"

She smiled at him. "I'm never anywhere I don't wanna be."

Someone taught her well. But he wasn't buying it. "Why are you here?"

She gave him a quizzical look. "What do you mean?"

"Don't get elliptical with me. Why are you here? You don't look like you're starving to me. Are you here to make money, snatch up a benefactor to get ahead personally, or because you like to fuck? Which one is it?"

She seemed stunned by his question. It was obvious by the look on her face. This vixen wasn't used to being grilled. But his inquiry was necessary. When it came to Curby's women Darrion never felt that he checked their background thoroughly enough. If she belonged to another pimp, it was going to be a problem. If she had a boyfriend, it was going to be a problem unless he didn't mind her sleeping with strange men for hours on end. Either way, he knew her answer wouldn't be just for the fuck of it. No girl working for Curby did anything just because. If she gave him that answer, he'd throw her out.

"Money," she finally said. "And I don't mind having sex to get it. Some women work johns because they have to. I wouldn't be here if it was *have to*. I love sex and there's no shame in what or who I do. Some people can handle that. Some can't. Does that answer satisfy you? Or do I need to call the Pentangon and pull my file for you first?"

"Smart mouth," he reponded. "You're going to be a problem here. I can see that already."

She let out a breath. Through with being insulted. "And question number two?"

"You know who I am?"

She nodded. "I've been told."

"Good. Then you know not to put me in a twist."

"Why would I do that?"

Zane wanted him dead. Zosa didn't think too highly of him drawing breath. Kincaid was sure to strike sometime soon. Sending a female to set him up seemed like a low down stunt they would pull.

"Same reason most women on a pay-lay do," he said. "For your man, for your pimp. Maybe both. I don't know what your motives are, but if you try me, know now, I'll break your neck just like I'll break your nigga's neck." There was no getting any more crystal clear than that. But, just to make sure, "Are we crystal?"

"Yes."

"Come here."

She climbed off the bed and walked over to him.

"Take off your clothes."

She was naked in less than ten seconds. He stood there for a moment and drank in all of her. From head to toe, she was flawless. A perfect picture of wanton desire. No commitments. No promises. Just lust.

They had furious sex for nearly two hours.

When he woke and checked his watch it was almost midnight. He dressed quietly, grabbed his Colts and headed for the door. She was awake. He could tell by her breathing. He heard the ruffle of sheets behind him.

Darrion stopped at the door. "What's your name?"

"Diamond."

♛

Darrion still hadn't called back and they'd been sitting in the car for more than two hours. Angelique checked her Movado again. It was almost midnight. On instinct her eyes flicked to her side view mirror. A wave of horror went through her body. Several hooded men were crouched low. Shotguns in hand, moving up along a row of parked cars in her direction. Before she could reach for the keys to start the car and speed off, they were already on her. In a flash of speed, the butt of a shotgun slammed through the driver's window. Glass exploded and Angelique screamed.

Everything that happened next came like a nightmare.

A hand gripped her head and slammed her forehead to the steering wheel. She was snatched out of the car so fast she lost her balance. When her head hit the cement, the world flashed white then darkness took her.

Where she was didn't register when her eyes opened again. She was in a room. She was looking up at the ceiling. When her eyes scanned around, nearly all of the windows were busted out. A rat scurried past her head and disappeared into a hole in the wall.

A hooded man with a ski mask was grunting over her. Then she heard the sound of a zipper. At first she did not understand what was happening; then she realized both of her arms were outstretched and her hands were cuffed to metal looped spikes in the floor. A hard pressure between her legs forced her to scream out loud. He grabbed her hair and put a hand to her mouth. In that fleeting moment, she saw a small tattoo on his neck. The letter K, a crown and the letter D. Then she felt excruciating pain as he forced himself inside her.

She tried to shout aloud for help, but pressure from his hand over her mouth stifled her calls to muffled wails. He was rutting on top of her with so much force all she could do her eyes tight and scream through the pain.

When he was finished, he pulled out of her, and pressed a knife to her cheek. She felt the blade digging into the lower lid of her eye. Then the most foul breath she had ever smelled assaulted her nostrils.

"If you don't tell your prince to pull out of Cabrini," the hood breathed, "we have this conversation again, Doc. And next time there'll be blood on my knife instead of my dick."

He grabbed her by the throat, snatched her up off the ground, and punched her in the face so hard she flew back to the concrete. Darkness came even more swiftly than before.

♛

Angelique didn't know what time it was when her lids parted. All she could see was darkness all around her. And voices. A child screaming for someone to help the lady. Then more than one voice was drifting closer. Closer. Closer. Until she could feel breath on her ear. It was a he. She screamed and tried to thrash and kick, but her limbs were still cuffed to the spikes.

"You're going to be okay," he said. "Don't worry." He turned and shouted out so loudly her ears hurt. "Get some fucking help!"

"No," she grumbled. "No...Pl...please." She forced her eyes to focus in the dark. When his face came into view, she breathed relief.

It was Anton.

"We got to get you to a hospital." He pulled off his coat and threw it over her. It wasn't until he covered her that she realized how badly her clothes had been ripped off. She was so cold her toes were numb and she couldn't feel her fingers. She heard a groan to her left. Punchy was pulling the spike out of the flooring. The instant she felt the spike release she rolled over onto her side and curled into a ball.

"Get some bolt cutters, Punch," Anton said.

She reached a shaky hand up to her head and felt something wet and sticky. It was blood. She was too afraid to touch her face and inspect for further damage. Suddenly the panic set in followed by shocking vivid clarity. She had just been raped. If Ant called an ambulance, her attack would be all over the news and Derek would pull her out of Cabrini. If she called Patricia, Derek would definitely know and he would pull her out of Cabrini. Then Zane won. He won, she lost. Every innocent person hoping for a better life, praying for the downfall of a tyrant, lost along with her. She decided right then she would rather be dead than just take what was done to her and quit. She'd get her revenge. And she'd do it her way. She forced her mouth to move. "No help."

"Dr. J, we have to take you to the hospital." He rushed to her right side and pulled out the other spike. "You're head's bleeding all over the place."

"It's old blood," she muttered. "I can feel it. It's sticky. Not new." It dawned on her that she kept Viola's number. She'd switched it from the pants she wore to her coat so she wouldn't lose it. "There's a number in my coat pocket," she groaned. "Call it. Ask to speak to Viola."

VIOLA

Viola pulled into the parking lot of Nickle's Drug Store.

It was 3:00 in the morning. T-Bone and Lunch jumped out of her Cherokee and drew their guns. She jogged around the corner to the front entrance where Ant said he would be waiting and paused in horror at the sight of the doctor's car. Someone gave it a good work over with a bat. Both taillights were busted. All the windows were smashed and someone keyed both sides from front bumper to the back.

"Mrs. V," Ant whispered. He motioned her inside the store.

"Lunch, Turkell," she said, motioning them to follow.

Ant led them towards the back. A Punjabi man she assumed was the owner motioned them to a doorway. "The lady needs help. Please come! Quickly!"

"She's back in the storage room," Ant said. "I had to get her out of there. She wouldn't let me take her to a hospital."

Viola's heart stopped when she saw her.

Curled up on a small cot in the corner Angelique laid unmoving. One eye was blood red, slightly cut, and starting to welt. Her scalp was crusted with dried blood. Her upper lip was swollen and both wrists looked red and bruised. That was just the damage she could see. The rest of her was wrapped up in a thick quilt.

"Lunch, help me pick her up. Be careful!"

He picked her up as lightly as a kitten and carried her out to the car. T-Bone helped lay her in the back seat. Viola's first instinct was to get behind the wheel and get the hell out of there. But, her suspicion set in. How did Anton know where she was and Darrion didn't?

"How did you find her?"

Ant blinked out of his shock. "What?"

"How did you know where she was?"

"Uh, Capricia's little boy. Sammy. He don't always go home like he's supposed to. He likes to ride his bike through the low-rises. He found her in one of the abandoned apartments. Then he came running for me."

"Thank you for that. Your help won't be forgotten. Any idea who did that to her car?"

Anton shook his head.

"I'll call you when we get her taken care of." Viola got behind the wheel, slammed the door, and looked over at Turkell. "Where the fuck was my son!"

She sped off and left Anton on the sidewalk.

"Let's get her to Cook," T-Bone said.

"No!" Angelique called out from the back seat. "I'll give you Kirkland's pager number, Viola. He's my intern. Tell him to meet you in the back of the hospital with exactly what I tell you to get. Then we'll take care of my wounds somewhere else."

"We can go back to my house," Lunch offered.

"No," Viola said. "We'll go back to my place. Duke's sound asleep. He doesn't even know I left."

Viola met Kirkland at the back of the hospital. It had to be him from Angelique's description. A tall, lanky white boy with freckles. Red hair. She couldn't miss that in a crowd. He wasn't from Chicago for a start. He had everything she'd asked for: a suture kit, two IV bags, and two rape kits.

She told him Dr. James needed it for someone in Cabrini who got assaulted. Technically it wasn't a lie. She got back in her Jeep and drove home.

♛

What part of the house is this room in?" Angelique asked.

"This is my private study," Viola answered. "Duke never comes in here." She looked at all of the medical supplies.

Everything was open and laid out on the desk as Angelique instructed. She was on the table. Lying on her back with her legs open. A sheet covered her from the shoulders down to her knees. Viola slid on her bifocals and pulled up closer to the table in her chair. She let out a nervous breath. "Okay, you're going to have to talk me through this." At first Angelique didn't reply. She was staring blankly up at the ceiling. "Angie," Viola said softly.

She blinked out of her daze. "Open the rape kit."

"It's already open."

"Okay, good. The first thing you want to do is…check for anything that was left behind. Cloth. Semen. His hair. There should be a comb. You have to pass it through the pubic hairs a few times, then put it in the plastic bag and seal it."

Viola took the comb and ran it through lightly. Then placed it in a bag.

"Next, there should be several long swabs. You want to scrape the labia, vaginal walls, and the cervix. Semen has DNA, so…After wards place them in a plastic bag and seal them."

Viola did so carefully. Trying to work through Angelique's groans of pain was awful, but she did it. There was some bleeding still.

"You're bleeding a little."

"I know. It'll stop on it's own."

She talked Viola through the rest of the instructions until she was finished.

"Now, take the second rape kit and do the same thing again."

"Don't you only need one?"

"One's for whoever did it. The other one is for when the first one goes missing from the police department."

Half of the cops in the city were on Cabrini's payroll. Smart girl. "You learn quick," Viola said.

The phone rang on the desk.

"Hello?"

"It's Lunch, ma'am. Darrion's at the club."

"Did you tell him what happened?"

"Not yet, I only talked to Curby. He said he's in the office right now."

"Don't tell him anything. I'm on the way." Viola hung up and tried to calm her nerves before she had a cursing fit.

"Don't tell him I was raped," Angelique said. "Promise me?"

"Why? Angie he will find the bastards who did this and he'll put them in the ground."

"Then the truce will be over. He kills them, Zane comes after him, Pope will back Darrion. Then Cabrini will be at war. I can't risk it. Just tell him I got mugged and they damaged my car to scare me off."

As much as Viola wanted to argue, all she saw staring back at her was the anguish on her battered face.

"Please."

"Alright," she caved. "I promise."

Viola got a call from Derek asking where his fiancé was. She had to tell him what happened. But she left out the rape. He immediately wanted to speak with Angelique but she was already asleep. As expected he demanded to speak to Darrion. Viola told him she would pass on the message then hung up. She went upstairs to the guest room, woke Angelique and insisted she stay in bed until the wounds healed and the stitches on her scalp were less red and swollen. She fixed her some tea and told her to drink it slow. With the cut under her lip the hot tea stung like mad. Once she had her tucked into the guest bedroom, she got in her Jeep and drove to City Lights.

Viola found Darrion coming down the main spiral stairs by the bar. Just when she walked towards him, a tall, slim woman brushed passed her and headed out he door. She was gorgeous. Viola stopped in her tracks and watched the woman sashay out the door.

"Morning, mom," Darrion kissed her on the cheek. "You never come here. Is everything okay?"

She looked up at him. "No, everything's not okay. Angie got attacked at Cabrini last night." She had to stop and mentally force herself to spill the lie. "Somebody robbed her. Then trashed her car! And where the fuck were you! How could you let this happen?"

"Where is she?" He pulled his keys from his pocket and ushered her out the door.

"Resting at my house. You can see her later. Derek wants to see you. And you'd better have a damn good excuse for your father.

DARRION

Darrion cursed.

The only thing worse than fucking up was fucking up in front of Derek.

At ten past 0700 in the morning Darrion was on the Dan Ryan, putting a call into Anton. He asked him for a favor and hung up. His car phone rang seconds later. It was Derek.

Weaving through rush hour traffic made it easier for the Councilmans' explitives to go floating through one ear and out the other.

"Angie told me that she paged you for an hour! Not one answer! Your job was simple, Darrion. Just keep her out of trouble. That's it."

"Let's keep in mind that I didn't ask for this task, your fucking highness. And the next time you talk to her, maybe you can ask her why she took her ass down there without me when she knew better!"

"I don't think we should continue this conversation over the phone," Derek said. "I don't trust cellular devices. Neither should you. My Near North office is being remodeled. I'm at my secondary office in City Hall. We'll finish this conversation when you get here."

He hung up.

Twenty minutes later, Darrion was sitting in the back of Derek's sedan, having a file tossed in his lap.

He opened it and his breath caught. It was the vixen he bedded just hours ago. Every candid photo was of him in bed with her. In several erogenous positions, on the chair, the couch. Up against the wall.

His face flamed.

"Look familiar?" Derek seethed. "Recognize the two psychos smashing all over the penthouse of your little strip club? If not, why don't you grab a mirror and turn on the news."

Darrion closed the file and looked up at him. The news? What did this have to do with the press?

"Yes, genius," Derek went on. "The one you just got through bedding is the woman who's responsible for the scandal. Her name's Kimbella DeVoe, her cum-belcher name is Diamond." His voice gradually raised to a scream. "And you just got played at the cost of my fiancé damn near losing her life!"

He'd figured out why his pager didn't go off. He never got a signal in the vault. That's where he left his beeper and the brick. "I didn't know who she was," Darrion said as calmly as he could. It was the best he could do for an excuse. The sad thing was, it was an honest excuse. It was a paltry excuse. But that didn't make it a reason. Derek's dark glare was proof enough of that.

"Do you have any idea what this woman is threatening to do to me? I've got P.I.'s on her day and night and my mother brings me this." He pointed to the file in Darrion's lap. "She's a lunatic. I knew that when I met her. Never planned on it going any further than a suck and a swallow, so I couldn't care less about you bedding her. You can keep laying the pipe to her if it suits you, but there is a time and a place for getting laid. And it's not while Angelique is getting beaten to a pulp."

"I will find out who was responsible for the attack and I will take care of it."

Derek exhaled harshly. "I want her out of Cabrini. But she threw a fit. Says she owes too many people. Out of respect for the hard work she's put in there, I'll show some restraint. For now. You've got until the election to find out who did it and put them in the ground. You don't, I send in the task force to take care of it myself and every gangbanging, drug dealing thug you keep company with, you'll be on their permanent shit side. Including Pope." He paused, then, "Duke wants to see you. I suggest you come up with a damn good lie about your whereabouts last night. I told my mother to keep the photos of your little tryst from getting back to him. It'd break his heart to know you were buried in pussy while the doctor who's supposed to fix his heart was getting attacked by the same hoods you were charged to keep her from." The Councilman went back to reading his newspaper. "Leave the file on my seat. Get out of my car."

Without another word spoken between them Darrion stepped out of the car. He was standing out in the January cold, fuming with anger, watching Derek's black sedan pull away from the curb. Then his brick phone rang.

"What?" He spat more harshly than intended.

"It's Ant. Me, Punch, and Old Man Freeman set up that building across the street like you asked."

"I'm on the way."

Darrion drove to Cabrini and pulled into the empty lot of an old unused building. It was a vacant day care center no one used.

He walked through the door and took in the cavernous space. Examining its unfinished floors. Its bare stained walls. Old Cassius Freeman walked out of the back room, hobbling on his bad knees with a cane.

"Darrion DeGrate," he said. "Didn't think I'd be seeing you here. Planning on buying the place from me, huh?"

"It's a favor for a friend."

"Anton told me. He's in the back with Calvin."

Mr. Freeman looked much older than Darrion remembered. A well known veteran in Cabrini and everyone knew him. All the years showed on every line of his face. His hair had grayed. Dark moles speckled his dark skin, and he looked more thinned than he used to. Age was not kind to him.

"How long before you can have it fully furnished and up and running?"

"I ain't never made no clinic before," Freeman said.

"I called in a favor. A guy named Kirkland is going to be stopping by soon. He'll tell you everything you need to set the place up."

"Okay, give me about a month or so, we should be good."

"Good." Darrion's pager went off then. He checked the number. His mother. "I have to go. My realtor will be by to finalize the paperwork."

"Very good then. You watch yourself out there young man," Old Man Freeman nodded. "Nothing but goons and goblins out there for you, son. Goons and goblins."

♛

Darrion was in the guestroom with Angelique for a long time. When he came downstairs to the living room, his face was solemn. Viola didn't press the issue of Angelique's condition. He felt grateful for that. Another round of harping would have been counter-productive at this point.

"Where are you going?" Viola spat.

"I got business to take care of."

"Duke wants to see you. He in his library, waiting."

Darrion knew that was coming. Dealing with his father, answering for what happened to Angelique, would have to go on the back burner. A scolding from Derek was enough. "He'll have to wait a little longer. I'll be back to check on Angie. I promise."

She gave him a disapproving look. That Viola glare always made him inwardly cringe. But Darrion wasn't in the mood for a fight and he didn't have time to verbally defend himself. Though even if he made time, he'd just end up fighting with her by default. So, instead of saying another word, he leaned down, kissed her cheek then threw on his coat and was out the door before his mother could object.

ZANE

T-Bone called the meeting with Zane in a public place.

Darrion told him to set the time between 1030 and 1300. Somewhere with a lot of people. A place Zane wouldn't dare make a ruckus. Turkell called back in less than half an hour. He'd set up their meet at Murphy's Café across the street from the Chicago police department. At first Zane objected. But Darrion told him if he didn't, there were other options of getting his ear.

None of them would be to his liking and all of them involved not being able to stop the Councilman from raiding Cabrini. That put Zane's ass in the café booth less than an hour later. It took every ounce of restraint Darrion possessed not to snatch him across the table and put a fork through his eye.

Taran gave the owner a Benjamin to keep the CLOSED sign flipped. Lunch stood by the front window and waved off a couple who tried to open the doors.

T-Bone sat across from Darrion and Zane's table at the bar. He politely asked the owner to give them a few minutes of privacy.

"DeGrate," Zane said in a curt greeting.

"You were supposed to keep a leash on your guard dogs. That attack on Angie…unacceptable. And if you don't find out who was responsible, your truce goes out the window. So does Muriel's fixed ticker. I'll pull the doctor out of Cabrini and those projects can go right back to the shit hole it was before. Only this time there'll be one less Harris with a boot on their necks."

Zane looked calm for a man whose life had just been threatened. All the more admission of fault in Darrion's opinion.

"I don't know who was responsible for the attack on her, but I can assure you it was none of my men. I wonder if you've had this little sit-down with Sampson's men?"

"Why would I when a kid found her beaten and bloody in the half of the lowrises that's your turf. Unless the two of you swapped real estate in the last 24 hours, you're still running the lower half. Are you not? So why would I think the Renegades are responsible for an offense that happened on your territory?"

"Because her presence threatens their operation and Sampson wants her dead, so he made it look like a King was sent to do it. Why would I harm the surgeon set to save my grandmother's life? If she dies, so does my grandmother. Does that make any sense to you?"

"Here's what does make sense to me. I had a talk with Dr. James this morning. She had quite a few interesting things to tell me. Like how Taniesha called her out at night to Durso Park because her son was sick. And how she was nowhere in sight when the doctor was getting attacked. Sounds like some calculated shit to me. Wouldn't you agree?"

Zane said nothing.

"If I find out you were behind this Zane—"

"I just told you it was none of my men. But I'll tell you what, I'm gonna dismiss that you just threatened me. You all up in your feelings about the Doc. I get it. You need some time to cool off. I understand. I'll set up a meet with Sampson, we'll make a joint effort to look into it. But I guarantee you, it was none of my soldiers."

Zane stood and cut Lunch a terse look when he neared the doors. Casper didn't move to let him by.

"I'm watching you motherfucker," Lunch spat.

Zane threw up both middle fingers and said, "Good watch these."

"Let him go, Lunch," Darrion said.

Lunch stepped aside and let him leave.

Darrion went to the door and watched Zane get into his Mercedes. Zeno was behind the wheel. They drove off like they owned the block, without a care in the world.

"He's fucking dead," Darrion said. "I don't care what the repercussions are. He's a corpse."

♛

When Angelique woke and could actually will herself out of bed. It had been days since the attack and it was just past 10:00 in the morning on the 4th of January. The day of Muriel's valve repair surgery. She dressed quietly and examined herself in the mirror. Her face wasn't as bad as she thought. Slight bruising to the eye. A small cut by her lower lid. Her lip wasn't as swollen as it felt. That partially had to do with the cut being under her lip and not on top of it. Her wrists weren't tender anymore but they were still slightly bruised. Her hips were sore and it burned like hell to urinate, but she could walk.

She was certain Muriel had probably assumed her surgery wasn't happening in light of recent circumstances. Darrion had insisted it was Zane's men. But she didn't mind playing their game. Muriel was already on the OR schedule. Dr. James refused to cancel it. Stubborn rage alone made her grab her purse, call a cab, then quietly leave Viola and Duke's home for her office.

She sat behind her desk staring at Muriel's medical records. Then the phone.

Then her records. The phone. The records. She went back and forth in her mind about it for a long time. Then mustered up the courage and dialed Muriel's number. The old crow answered on the first ring.

"Hello?"

Angelique faked cordiality. "Hi, Muriel. It's Dr. James. I'd like to make sure you're ready for your surgery today."

Muriel was quiet for a long moment. Then, "Of course."

"Good. You're surgery is set for 5:00 this evening. I trust you've been fasting and you'll be here."

"Wouldn't miss it."

Dr. James could detect an unpleasant undertone to her voice. *Don't worry, bitch, I won't be getting careless with the scalpel. I won't be killing you on my table. You're not worth my license. I want you to live for a long, long time.*

"I need you here no later than 3:00 p.m."

"Can my grandsons come as well?"

Angelique shut her eyes tight. "Of course. See you then," she said. Then hung up.

She sat thinking in silence for a moment. Then picked up the phone and called Derek.

"Hello?"

"It's me," she said. "You want to have lunch with me in my office? I need to talk to you."

"I'll be right there, little dove."

Derek arrived with her favorite by 11:00.

Two butter croissants and a steaming latte. He brought one large tin container of lasagna for himself. They both ate in silence for a while. She didn't come up for air until only one bite remained on her napkin.

"How are you feeling, babe?" he asked her.

She sipped her latte. "I'm okay. Still sore in the face, but I'll live."

He wiped his mouth with a napkin. "I see you found your purse."

"What?"

"You got mugged," Derek reminded her. "I guess they didn't take your purse."

She looked at the Louis Vuitton on her sofa. She'd forgotten all about those little details. "Oh, it was dark," she recovered. "They probably didn't realize it was a Louis...or they didn't want to stick around for anything but the money they took. Or it wasn't about the money at all."

Her answer seemed to satisfy him. "What did you want to talk to me about?"

"Cabrini."

"Okay. I'm listening."

"I really want you to consider taking a few weeks off. For me."

"I would, if I could. But that's not possible. I have surgeries lined up for quite a few sick tenants. They're relying on me, Derek. Their surgery is already paid for."

He slid the lasagna away and went quiet. "Okay. But if anything else happens, it's over. I mean it, Angie."

She nodded. "Okay."

"When are you going back?"

"Today's Friday. So probably on Monday. I'll take the weekend off. Let my face clear up some more."

"Okay. I want you to take some extra men from my private security. It's not up for debate. They go with you from now on."

She nodded. "Speaking of security, Darrion seemed pretty pissed when I talked to him the other day."

Derek gave her an impassive look. "Okay."

"Could you talk to him for me? Calm him down before he does anything stupid?"

"Angie—"

"I know he feels guilty, but it wasn't his fault. He didn't ask to be there and he can't be everywhere at once."

Derek sighed, then pulled out a manila envelope, and handed it to her. "That's where he was that night."

Angelique opened the folder and froze. It was like looking at stills from a pornography shoot. Darrion's face was as plain as day, but the woman he was ravaging she didn't recognize. She tore her eyes away and tried to close the folder, but her fingers were shaky and the damned photos wouldn't go back in the envelope fast enough. Frustrated, she slapped the photos on top of the envelope and pushed it aside.

She wasn't shocked that he was having sex. He was a man after all. But it rang out all too loudly that he chose to ignore his pager. He chose to get laid over his obligation. She found it hard to absorb that fact with emotional detachment. "Guess I know why he didn't answer his pager."

"I'm showing you this because you're going to find out who she is anyway," Derek said. "The last thing I want is for you to find out on the news or from someone else. If you're going to be my wife, you deserve to know the truth. I'm not going to start off our marriage on lies and secrets."

Her brow arched.

Angelique didn't like where this was going. "Who is she?"

"Her name is Kimbella. She's the woman trying to extort me. And her son is mine."

"Oh my God," she heard herself stammer as she drew back in shock.

"This woman is a psycho, Angie. She doesn't care who she hurts."

Suddenly his words began to slur in her ears, her vision blurred, her stomach lurched, and those flaky croissants and that smooth roasted coffee set to a queasy boil. She got up from the desk, ran into the bathroom, and threw up.

Derek insisted she go home for the day, but she refused. Throwing up didn't mean she was dying. She would eat later when her stomach settled. They talked for a little while longer about his plans to put an end to Kimbella's wrath and by the time Angelique looked up at the clock, it was nearly 3:00.

She convinced him that she would be well enough to handle her surgery case. He left only on the condition that she'd call as soon as she got out of the operating room. She reached into her closet and changed into scrubs. Just as she neared the door, her phone rang.

"Dr. James."

"It's me," Viola said. "How are you?"

"I'm fine," she lied.

"I didn't hear you leave. I was worried."

"Oh, I didn't want to bother anybody. I have a surgery case today, so…"

"I know. I'd be the perfect opportunity to let a 10-blade slip. Muriel Harris. I'll set off fireworks at Wrigley field the day that bitch drops dead."

How the hell did she know?

"Who told you I'm operating on Muriel today?"

"Cabrini's a small world, sweetheart. It used to be very much my world, remember?"

Anton, Angelique guessed. It had to be him.

Viola was as intimidating as ever.

She knew he worked at the hospital. And she knew he cleaned the OR on occasion. A little pressure from Viola DeGrate and he'd have folded.

"Yeah, well, my Hippocratic oath."

"Yeah, I'm sure," Viola said. "Well, gotta go. I'll talk to you later. Let me know if you need anything."

"Okay, I will."

"And one more thing."

"Yeah?"

"Cut my son some slack. He carries guilt like you wouldn't believe. He feels bad enough already."

"Sure...I mean of course," Angelique said. She hung up, grabbed Muriel's chart, and crossed the skyway to the hospital. *Time to face off with the Queen Bee.*

Dr. James went to the Ambulatory Unit on 4 West, stopped at room 425 and slid back the curtain. Muriel was sitting up in bed. Gowned and waiting.

"I see you're ready for your surgery."

Muriel glanced over her bruised face. She didn't speak right away. Then, "I am."

"Good. Michelle will be your nurse and Dr. Vanderbilt will be your anesthesiologist. Do you have any questions for me?"

"I would keep on with the pleasantries, but it's not my style. I know you blame my grandson for what happened to you. And I thank you for keeping your word to me about the surgery. But, just so it was said, if I should suffer some unforeseen complication during the surgery, let's just say I got contingencies in order."

That was more big words than Dr. James thought possible coming from Muriel. She swallowed down the threat and kept her composure.

"You're set to be prepped for surgery now. Transportation's on the way. You'll be taken to the holding room until it's time to operate. Staffing has approved my request so your grandsons will be allowed to change into scrubs and observe the surgery with the interns in the viewing room."

She pulled the curtain closed so fast it may as well have been a door slamming in the old biddy's face.

Less than thirty minutes later, Muriel Harris was intubated, an arterial line was placed to monitor her blood pressure during the surgery, and she was on the OR table.

Her procedure was on a large television screen for everyone watching. Dr. James couldn't help but notice her interns standing clear on the other side of the view room. Away from Zane and Zeno—who stood close to the entrance door, watching the television. Though the Harris brothers were masked and capped and in scrubs, they still looked as menacing as ever.

Dr. James went to work. Muriel's valve repair went smoothly.

Two hours after the case had begun, it was time to close up Muriel's chest. Dr. James had never felt so glad to be out of the OR.

DARRION

Darrion spent the next few weeks in a blur of guilt. Self-resentment and blame trailed close behind.

Duke was not pleased with him for what happened to Angie. But he was glad to know that his meeting with Pope went well during her attack.

It was a lie Darrion could live with. Derek being pissed off at him was one thing. He could live with that. Viola's wrath, he'd been drinking a little more than usual trying to get back into her good graces, but he could tolerate that. She even went along with the lie about meeting with Pope, just to keep her husband's heart protected from the stress. But his father losing faith in him — that look of disappointment from a father to a failed son, Darrion could not take.

It wasn't as if Duke would call Stateville to find out if it was true. So sweeping that little falsehood under the rug was easy. As long as it stayed under the rug.

While he worked on waiting to ensnare Kincaid at his motel in Mount Greenwood, he also checked in on the progress of Angelique's new clinic. It was the least he could do to keep her out of harm's way. It would be that much harder to hurt her if Zane's thugs had to come where Darrion's brothers were waiting on him. Knowing that helped him breathe a little easier. No more traveling the breezeways of the highrises. Her patients would have to walk the short distance from their buildings to her clinic. No exceptions.

♛

By January 20th, the new Cabrini Green Health Clinic was nearly finished. Cassius Freeman was very polite and kind to her. In spite of his arthritic knees, he showed up every morning for nearly a week, helping Dr. James set up. She grew fond of him quickly. He was quite the helper. Painting the walls with Kirk, Ant, and Punchy. Polishing the furniture. Organizing all of her patient charts and he even took the time to bring her croissants in the morning.

Kirkland seemed to get along with him better than she did and they often fell off into strange conversations. Mr. Freeman laughed at him for being well into soul music and Kirkland laughed at Mr. Freeman for having a love for marijuana in his old age.

As much as she didn't want to break up their odd, blossoming friendship, she had to send Kirk back to the hospital. Clark and LeTart needed to get used to the clinic as well. She had to be fair and rotate all three of her interns.

No sooner than Kirland left, Mr. Freeman arrived with a surprise. He came from the back room, and hobbled into her office, carrying a massive portrait. "For your wall behind the desk, there," he said.

Angelique held it and waited while he used a chair to boost himself high enough. He put a huge hook-nail in the wall. Once he'd stepped back down, she used the chair to hang the portrait, while he leaned against her desk and gabbed.

"Everybody was talking, you know. After you got mugged. 'She too scared to come back. She leaving.' I got worried there for a little while. Things been real peaceful-like for me since you been here. I mean, there's been some riff-raff here and there. But I ain't never seen so many kids running outside to play after school. In the snow! You hardly hear any more gunshots. Everybody walks on by without worrying about if somebody's gonna take they life for looking at 'em the wrong way. Everything's changed. I got a little worried, that if you left, things would get right back to the way they were. So, me and a few folks around here, we got together and decided to give you a reason to stick around a little while longer."

Angelique tried to balance the portrait on the nail.

It slid crooked. She adjusted it. "Ant told me this used to be a daycare center. Your daughter used to run the place."

Mr. Freeman nodded.

"Where is she?"

"Dead," he said bluntly. "You remind me of my baby girl. If you don't mind me saying so. Before the drugs took her. I…I suppose, I liked you from the start. I'm glad you decided to stay."

Angelique looked down at him and smiled. "Thanks."

"No, Doc, thank you."

She stepped down from the portrait and stepped back. Admiring it. Suddenly she realized who she was looking at. "Oh my God…is that—"

"Mmm-hmm." Cassius Freeman nodded. "You mentioned once that you wanted to know about the history of Cabrini. I thought this painting might help."

She couldn't believe it. "Is that…Duke?"

"Mmm-hmm. You're looking at the Five Founding Fathers. The Original Gangsters of the King's Disciples. There's Duke, in the middle there. Pastor Troy on the far right. Xavier Pope is next to him. And on Duke's right there's Zane and Zeno's father, Zander Harris. On his right is Lunch's father, Casper Phoenix, Sr."

Duke looked so much like Darrion it was scary. They had that same wide smile of flawless teeth. "Wow. Look at that smile."

"Oh, Duke DeGrate was quite the ladies man. Superfly. That's what they called him. Back then, they had plenty to smile about."

"Like what?"

"From the 1st of September, 1939 until the 2nd of September 1945, was World War II. Factories owned this city. And the jobs were the world over. You couldn't step outside your front door without somebody trying to hire you. Most black men had to turn down work they had so much overtime. Then, the inevitable happened."

"What?"

"No war lasts forever. When the world struck peace, it was the poor who suffered most. By 1950, six years and a day of war was long over, so were the factory jobs and most families were on public assistance just to survive. And by 1960, this city was in sheer turmoil. It was a time of high racial tension. Segregation was still very much enforced as the law. Back then, if you was black, Hispanic, or anything else that didn't look white, you got hassled."

Angelique listened quietly while Mr. Freeman talked about the riots of 1968, following Dr. Martin Luther King, Jr.'s assassination. He talked about Duke and Zander. How they came together and kept the neighborhood of Cabrini from suffering the devastation of the riots. When his story had ended, he said, "Things always get ten times worse before they get better."

Angelique heard the office door behind her. They both turned. Zane and several of his soldiers walked in. Zeno followed behind the soldiers. As if announcing himself wasn't even necessary.

"Old Man Freeman," Zane said in greeting. He plopped down in a chair in front of Dr. James' desk, "up bright and early this morning. So I hear." He looked up at her. "Where's your man, Mr. Was-Back-When?"

She exhaled. "What can I do for you, Zane?"

"You can answer my question, Doc. Where is DeGrate and who the fuck are they?"

She glanced to Derek's private security team just outside the door. "They're private security. In light of recent events, I think it's warranted."

"And I *think*, you didn't clear it through me."

"My appointment protocol has changed...I'll no longer be traveling the breezeways to apartments and all visits scheduled will have my patients coming from the towers to me. My security team will remain with me at this clinic. They won't be roaming the halls or traveling from building to building. You don't have to worry about them interfering with your business."

"If they set foot in Cabrini without my sanction, they're interfering with my business. If you need security, I'll send a few of my soldiers to post up outside your door."

"These men, they don't want anything to do with your enterprise. They're here to safeguard the medications I have stored here and to make sure that I'm safe during office hours."

Zane looked her up and down. "You bleeding anywhere?"

"What?"

"I said did you get shot on the way here this morning?"

"No."

"Your safety in Cabrini is on my say so. I'm the only reason you'll be walking out of here alive tonight. My restraint with my men is the only reason why they aren't busting down this door to slit your throat for bringing outsiders into my project. That can change with one phone call, bitch. Get rid of them."

Angelique was so tense and nervous she wanted to throw up. Then, out of nowhere, something took hold. She was tired of being scared. Tired of worrying when they would come for her again. Sick of wondering if she would live to see her 36th birthday.

She snapped.

"My restraint with the Councilman and the chief of police is the only reason why 500 cops aren't storming this shit hole to shut you down! That can change with one phone call. Bitch. They stay. And if memory serves, none of you gentlemen have an appointment with me today, so get the hell out."

Zane looked at her for a long moment. Then his face changed to a smile. It was a quiet rage. A controlled rage. So much like Zeno's a shiver raced up her spine.

He stood from the chair, coolly walked to the door, and looked at Mr. Freeman. "See you around, Old Man."

She let out a breath of relief the instant the door closed, then sat in her chair and put her head in her hand. Mr. Freeman hobbled over to a stack of books and set to placing them on the bookshelf.

"Get ready for the worse, Doc," he warned. "'Cause the better is a distant second around here."

♛

When her office door opened again, it was almost thirty minutes later. She jumped up hoping it wasn't Zane.

It was Darrion.

Her heart sank. She did not want to see him. Mr. Freeman took his leave without saying more than a hello to Darrion. He nodded back and watched the old man leave.

"How have you been?" he asked.

"Fine," she lied.

"Is he keeping you company?"

"Yeah, he's good. He's been really helpful and sweet."

"I know you're angry with me," he said. "I get it. And I'm sorry about what happened to you. But hating me is not going to—"

"I don't hate you, Darrion," she said abruptly. "That's not it."

"Then what is?"

"I've been well informed, lately. By Patricia. She's working the DeVoe case for Derek. Lately you have been…not yourself. You've been spending a lot of time at the club. Cabrini is a problem for you. So is Zane. And I'm not your mother. You're not obligated to me. You're a grown man. You don't have to do what Derek tells you to do. Do what you want. Sleep with who you want. But, until you get…focused, I don't want you protecting me in Cabrini anymore." She went silent and it took all of her will to look up into his eyes. "I don't trust you with my life anymore."

She walked out of the office and left him standing there.

♕

By Saturday, January 25th her clinic was just two days from its grand opening. Darrion planned on stopping by whether she wanted him there or not, yet another problem seemed to arise that Darrion did not expect. He noticed as of late, Angie was still avoiding his phone calls. She still allowed T-Bone and occasionally Taran and Lunch to escort her to Cabrini. But she was clearly still angry with him.

Which meant she had not forgiven his failing to be there when she needed him.

It was true. He was spending more time at City Lights and there were a few women here and there. Diamond was a fucking mistake. But that was a mistake that wouldn't be happening twice. He threw back a few more drinks than usual, but it was nothing he couldn't handle. Still, Angie was holding it against him. There was a way around that.

He just put Ant up to keeping tabs on her at the hospital. Then put Mr. Freeman up to keeping tabs on her at the clinic.

He told himself that he would respected her request for space, until he got the phone call that made him confront her.

Anton gave him a warning that Zane planned to snipe two of the men keeping protection with the doctor and Kirkland. When Darrion asked which men Zane was after, Anton said, "I don't know, some white boys in suits with ear wigs...T-Bone and Taran and Lunch, them he don't mind. But them white boys, you better get them out of the projects, man. Zane ain't playing. He flat out don't want 'em here."

Darrion drove the Mercedes to Scott Joplin and parked in the 'Patients Only' lot of the connecting medical building. He looked up and caught a glimps of the good doctor walking the skyway overhead. He waited, watching her ride the clear glass elevators to the ground level floor. Darrion glanced at his watch. It was just past 1200 hours.

He walked up to her and several of Derek's men got out of their sedans and walked near him. It was a subtle warning.

Darrion ignored it. He stepped in front of the doctor, blocking her path, and before she could even register that he was standing there he lit into her.

"You don't want to me around anymore? You don't trust me? That's fine. But having these caspers in Cabrini, it's coming to a halt. You're gonna get them killed and the last thing we need is a bunch of white boys dead on the news. You're not keeping company with unfamiliars. After today, they're fired. It's not up for debate. And if Derek's got a problem with it he knows my number."

Angelique flinched at the bite of his words and her lip quivered. She opened her mouth to say something, but before she could utter a word he walked off.

Now he really felt like a dick. But what he'd said to her needed to be said. She still didn't have a clue as to how ruthless Zane could be.

His brick phone went off.

"What?"

"It's me," T-Bone said. "It's hillbilly time, playboy. You ready for some REDRUM?"

♛

When T-Bone finally got intel from one his girls, that one of her Aryan pay-lays had spotted Kincaid, the men waited until sundown. Then rode in T-Bone's lemon to the Bellemont Motel. Taran walked into the lobby. Five minutes later he came back to the car, slid in the back seat, and shut the door.

"I got a spare key to Kincaid's room."

Darrion eyed the Belleview Motel entrance and looked at Taran. "The guy at the desk just gave it to you?"

He shook his head. "No, the woman did. I walked in and she was just smiling at me so I told her that I was in room 309 and I locked myself out. So she gave me another key, no questions asked."

Darrion hmmphed. "Did you spot any cameras?"

"Not a one."

"Okay. Lunch, you stay in the car and keep watch in case Kincaid has some unexpected visitors other than us that we don't know about. Taran, you take the lead, me and T-Bone will back you up. We're on silencers for this one."

T-Bone pulled out his Beretta and screwed on his silencer. Darrion and Taran did the same. Then the three men got out of the Buick, ran up to the back of the building and up the back staircase to the third floor.

Taran stopped at 309, opened the motel room door, and with shocking speed walked in aiming his Beretta. The room was dark. The room was empty. White sheets were rumpled on the bed and spotted with blood. It looked like someone was asleep under them. Taran dared a step closer, threw back the sheets and stepped back at the sight of a bloodied corpse. Her exposed breasts were slashed open to the flesh. A huge swastika was carved into her abdomen. Her legs were still sprawled open as if sex was the last act she'd committed before death. Long dark braids were wildly spread on the pillows. Without doubt it was a black woman. But her face was so badly beat in it was hard to tell what she looked like. Kincaid was nowhere in sight.

Taran lowered his gun and stood there, trying not to throw up. Darrion and T-Bone flowed in behind him, aiming their weapons. Then both men froze just as he did.

"What the hell?" Darrion whispered.

He'd made plenty of corpses before. But he was no butcher. Kincaid was worse than a white trash piece of shit.

He was a carver.

"Is that one of Curby's girls from the club?" Taran asked.

T-Bone shook his head. "Can't be. I put snow bunnies on Kincaid. It must be a pro working the boulevard nearby."

Taran nearly jumped when his brick phone rang.

"What?!"

Anton's voice came blaring through the phone so loudly all the men heard him. "It's Ant!" Anton huffed. "I need to talk to Darrion. It's an emergency!"

Taran walked over to Darrion. "KD," he handed him the phone. "It's for you."

Darrion lowered his Colt and took the phone. "Hello?"

"It's Ant. The Doc's been kidnapped. Zane holding her hostage at Cabrini! The task force is here. They threatening to send in the National Guard! Where the fuck are you at, man?!"

Darrion stood there in that bloody motel room, blinking shock as his entire world froze.